第二十世紀中國文學概論

EARLY TO MID-TWENTIETH CENTURY CHINESE LITERATURE

AN INTRODUCTION

for

INTERMEDIATE LEVEL CHINESE LANGUAGE STUDENTS

prepared by
John Francis Kinsella
VINCENNES BOOKS

cover photo by author
A salon on the first floor of the residence of former British Consul General in Shanghai, this masterpiece of Roman architecture dates from Victorian times. It was first built in 1882.

Acknowledgements

This modest book could not exist without the works of the great writers quoted herein, namely: Lu Xun, Mao Dun, Zhou Erfu and Ba Jin. In addition are their translators and publishers, to which must be added many learned commentators, academics, linguists and historians.

The multiple sources are too numerous to list, but a special mention must be given to the Foreign Languages Press of Beijing. In addition are the many Wikipedia references and specialised Internet sites, sources without which, if it was admitted, many of us would be lost today.

This book, as is often the case with such books, is essentially a work of research, selection and transcription. The errors and oversights found on these pages will, regretfully, be many, but it is hoped readers will be indulgent considering the progress I must make in this vast subject. Any reader input will be greatly appreciated.

A special thanks goes to the Institute Confucius at Université Paris Diderot, for the perseverance in their endeavours to inspire abstruse students such as myself.

Lastly, I hope I will be forgiven for my inordinate lack of modesty in attempting to tackle this vast and complex subject, a work which was inspired by the extraordinary history of twentieth century China .

John Francis Kinsella

Preface

The goal of this book is to offer intermediate level students of the Chinese language a brief and simple introduction to the reading of early to mid-twentieth century Chinese classics.

Many students are confronted with the difficulty of reading Chinese novels and questions relating to their translation. This small collection of texts is drawn from well-known modern classroom standards written in the vernacular, as opposed to the classical style that persisted until the Revolution of 1911.

With the appearance of writers such as Lu Xun, Ba Jin, Mao Dun and later Zhou Erfu, pioneers in this new style, Chinese literature became accessible to all.

This book presents short extracts from their popular novels that have been translated into English. These are presented in their original Chinese text with traditional or simplified characters, together with an English translation, a synthesis of the individual characters and their pinyin phonetics, accompanied by English dictionary equivalents.

These translations, essentially drawn from those published by Chinese institutions, may appear somewhat guileless to many present day readers. This has prompted the author of the present book to suggest, in certain cases, alternative versions that are perhaps more in keeping with current literary styles. This said, it is necessary to take into consideration the style and way of thinking that prevailed at the time the novels were written and at the time of their translations.

The efforts of past translators are to be admired given their limited resources, that is before the advent of the personal computer and Internet, which have greatly facilitated such work.

The primary goal here is neither grammar, nor literal translation, it is simply to offer a lifeline to intermediate readers in understanding the Chinese language in one of its stylistic forms.

John Francis Kinsella 2014

'When I use a word,' Humpty Dumpty said in a rather scornful tone, 'it means just what I choose it to mean - neither more nor less.'
Lewis Carroll
Alice in Wonderland

Selected Works

The four novels chosen are amongst the best known classroom standards in China today, and equally used by a growing numbers of foreign students of the Chinese language. They are: *A Madman's Diary*, *Morning in Shanghai*, *Midnight*, and *Family*. These four books, or parts of them, have been translated many times into English and employed by teachers and students in many different full and abridged versions.

The stories cover the tumultuous period in Chinese history, from 1911 to 1951, during which the Middle Kingdom was transformed from an imperial feudal society into Mao's revolutionary communist People's Republic of China.

A Madman's Diary was published in 1918 by Lu Xun, one of the iconic figures of twentieth-century Chinese literature. This short story, which became a corner stone of the *New Culture Movement*, is one of the first and most influential modern works written in vernacular Chinese. It is considered to be China's first modern short story.

In *Family*, first published in 1931, Ba Jin describes the world into which he was born, in 1904, and grew up in. Part of the trilogy entitled *Torrents*, it is an autobiographical novel describing the transformation of a wealthy traditional Chinese family throughout this dramatic period in his country's history.

Midnight, published in 1933, written by Shen Yanbing under the pen name of Mao Dun, is situated in Shanghai in the early nineteen-thirties. It was a time when hard driving businessmen and industrialists exploited factory workers against the background of a long and bitter conflict, during the struggle for power between the Nationalist government and Communist revolutionaries.

Morning in Shanghai, written by Zhou Erfu, was published in 1955, and also set in Shanghai shortly after the Communist victory in 1949 (The War of Liberation (1945-1949). During a brief period, between Mao's declaration of the People's Republic and the early part of 1952, capitalism continued to cohabit with communism in an uneasy peace. The story recounts the transition of a rich family of industrialists to communism.

These authors, influenced in their styles by Western literature, were to become cultural icons in the Chinese communist pantheon, and their works transformed into models and integrated into Maoist post-revolutionary thought.

One wonders how these writers would react to present day Shanghai and its billionaires; tycoons such as Dalian Wanda's Wang Jianlin and Alibaba's Jack Ma, or to the conditions of Foxconn workers in Shenzhen.

It is equally evident, however, that life in modern China, in spite of the country's shortcomings, is an immeasurably improvement, for the vast majority of Chinese, on the social conditions that endured prior to and during the early period of the Republic.

Translations

The linguistic and cultural differences between Chinese and English are great, in addition the distance between today's society and that of China's in the early part of the twentieth century is immense.

The world of Ba Jin's youth is so far removed from twenty-first century Western society and ideas, it makes it almost impossible for present day readers to grasp the meaning of its traditions and existence. When the changes came to China, with the collapse of the Qing Dynasty in 1911, they were described by Western journalists as 'dumbfounding'.

To understand the difficulty of translation it is worth referring to Eugene Nida (1914-2011), one of the pioneers in translation theory and linguistics, who explained: 'Since no two languages are identical, either in the meanings given to corresponding symbols or in the ways in which such symbols are arranged in phrases and sentences, it stands to reason that there can be no absolute correspondence between languages. Hence there can be no fully exact translations. The total impact of a translation may be reasonably close to the original, but there can be no identity in detail.

'Since "there are, properly speaking, no such things as identical equivalents" (Belloc 1931 and 1931), one must in translating seek to find the closest possible equivalent. However, there are fundamentally two different types of equivalence: one which may be called formal and another which is primarily dynamic.

'Formal equivalence focuses attention on the message itself, in both form and content. In such a translation one is concerned with such correspondences as poetry to poetry, sentence to sentence, and concept to concept.

'In contrast, ...a translation of dynamic equivalence aims at complete naturalness of expression, and tries to relate the receptor to modes of behaviour relevant within the context of his own culture; it does not insist that he understand the cultural patterns of the source-language context in order to comprehend the message.

'In any discussion of equivalences, whether structural or dynamic, one must always bear in mind...different types of relatedness, as determined by the linguistic and cultural distance between the codes used to convey the messages.'

'Procházka defines a good translation in terms of certain requirements which must be made of the translator, namely: (1) He must understand the original word thematically and stylistically; (2) he must overcome the differences between the two linguistic structures; and (3) he must reconstruct the stylistic structures of the original work in his translation.'

All this is easier said than done for the non-specialist.

Historical Background

The first half of the twentieth century was a very tumultuous period in Chinese history. It commenced under the greatly debilitated Qing Dynasty that had caused China to suffer an unending series of humiliations at the hands of imperial powers. The downfall of the Qings and the establishment of the Republic of China in October 1911 sparked new hope.

A century has now passed since Lu Xun published his short story *A Madman's Diary*, an event which marked a turning point in the history of Chinese literature, breaking some two thousand five hundred years of classical literary tradition, with his use of the vernacular; the language of the common people.

In this spirit of reform and renaissance a group of intellectuals, led by Hu Shi, proposed a major new direction for Chinese literature and language in 1917. Up to that time, all serious literature was written in classical Chinese, a stylized language far removed from the everyday spoken language of the people, an evident hindrance to widespread literacy.

Hu Shi, one of the leading and influential intellectual figures in the *May Fourth Movement,* and later the *New Culture Movement*, was the prime advocate of the literary revolution, which aimed at replacing classical Chinese by the vernacular, thus cultivating and stimulating new forms of literature.

As such Hu Shi laid down the rules that all Chinese

writers should follow:

Write with substance. By this, Hu meant that literature should contain factual feeling and human thought. This was intended to be a contrast to the traditional evocations that Hu saw as being vacuous.

Not imitate the ancients. Literature should not be written in the styles of the long-gone writers, but rather in that of the present.

Respect grammar. Hu Shi did not elaborate on this point, but simply stated recent literary forms had neglected proper grammar.

Reject melancholy. Recent young authors often chose grave pen names, and wrote on such topics as death. Hu rejected this way of thinking as being unproductive in solving modern problems.

Eliminate old proverbs and idioms. The Chinese language has always had numerous four-character sayings and phrases used to describe events. Hu Shi pleaded with writers to use their own words in descriptions.

Not use allusions. Hu Shi was referring to the practice of comparing present events with historical parallels even when there was no meaningful analogy.

Not use couplets or parallelism. Though these forms had been pursued by earlier writers, Hu Shi believed that modern writers should learn the basics of substance and quality, before returning to these matters of subtlety and elegance.

Accept popular expressions or popular forms of characters. This rule, perhaps the most well-known, directly linked to Hu's belief that modern literature should be written in the vernacular, rather than in classical Chinese. He believed that this practice had historical precedents, and led to greater understanding of important texts.

In 1918, Hu simplified the original eight points into just four:

Speak only when you have something to say.

Speak what you want to say and say it in the way you want to say it.

Speak what is your own and not that of someone else.

Speak in the language of your own times.

The new movement, which called for using the vernacular language (*baihua*) as the written language, was rapidly accepted by Chinese writers. Lu Xun, now considered the father of modern Chinese literature, wrote the first short story written in the vernacular: *A Madman's Diary*.

Many literary works of the period were modelled after those of Western writers, especially Russians, including Gogol and his novel *Diary of a Madman* written in 1835, and certain parallels were drawn between *Midnight* and Zola's novel *L'Argent*, though Mao Dun refuted this.

It was in 1919, the vernacular language of Beijing was adopted as the national language (*guoyu*). Then, after violent student riots in Beijing in the same year, following the failure of the Chinese representatives at the Versailles Peace Conference to negotiate the return of the former German concessions of Shandong (attributed to Japan), writers became increasingly more active in politics, with many producing critical realist works having strong social undertones.

Critical realism continued to dominate modern Chinese fiction until the late nineteen-forties, when it was replaced by proletarian works, in line with the communist directive, following the establishment of the People's Republic.

The reformist movement, known as the *May Fourth Movement*, was defined by its rejection of Confucian tradition and the adoption of Western concepts. Certain of the movement's left wing intellectuals, inspired by the Russian Revolution of 1917, went on to form the Chinese Communist Party.

In the nineteen-twenties and thirties the situation in China worsened as the government struggled to unite the nation; by then disintegrated into self-declared fiefdoms controlled by belligerent warlords. At the same time, as the Nationalists fought Communist revolutionaries and then Japanese invaders, many writers turned to the left, forming the *League of Leftist Writers*, led by Lu Xun.

Shanghai had become a new cultural centre, a hive of literary activity and production, a meeting point between East and West. By 1937, 'an overwhelming 86% of books published in China appeared under a Shanghai imprint'*.

The major literary works that rose from the chaos, despair, and desire for change during this determining period of China's history have since become reading classics for all students, both in China and abroad.

Chiang Kai-shek and Mao Zedong in Chongqing (1945)

* 'Mediasphere Shanghai' Alexander Des Forges 2007

Lu Xun

A MADMAN'S DIARY

狂人日記

A Madman's Diary

狂人日記

Today, Lu Xun (1881-1936) is considered the father of modern Chinese literature. He has been described as the greatest writer Asia produced in the twentieth century. Lu Xun's importance to modern Chinese literature lies in the fact that he contributed significantly to almost every modern literary medium during his lifetime. His works note the starting point of modern Chinese vernacular literature and have become established classics.

Lu Xun

Lu Xun’s classic short story *A Madman’s Diary* was first published in 1918, and has since been translated many times, notably by Wang Chichen, Yang Xianyi and Gladys Yang in 2002, and William A. Lyell in 1990.

Lu Xun was born Chou Shuren in Shaoxing in 1881. He moved to Shanghai in the late 1920s and lived near to Duolun Lu, in the Hongkou district, north of the Suzhou River, as did many other early twentieth century literary figures, including Mao Dun. It was there the *League of the Left-Wing Writers* was formed in 1930, at the instigation of the Chinese Communist Party under the influence of the Lu Xun, though he himself never joined the party. In February 1931, five members of the League were executed by the order of the Kuomintang Nationalist government (中國國民黨 Zhōngguó Guómíndǎng).

Lu Xun died of tuberculosis in 1936.

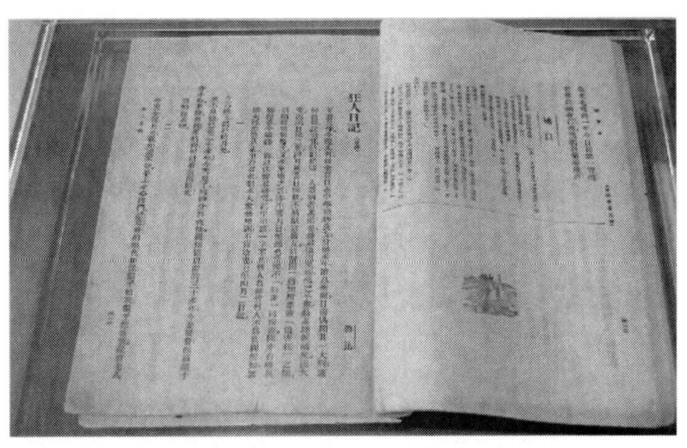

1918 printed edition of A Madman's Diary

The paranoid diarist in *A Madman’s Diary* lives in the home of his traditional Chinese family. He clearly suffers from serious psychological problems. In the story the diary is prefaced by a narrator who claims to have obtained it from the madman's brother. The narrator's preface offers an explanation as to the origins of the diary. (The original Chinese preface is not included here.)

The diarist is obsessed by cannibalism, a recurring theme in China's long history, recently examined by Yang Jisheng in his book *Tombstone* (墓碑 Mùbēi), published in Hongkong in 2008, which investigates the Great Famine of 1958-1962. Yang estimates 36 million souls died of starvation and associated causes in this short period of time. In his story, Lu Xun uses the theme of cannibalism as an allegory to oppression.

The Chinese text is reproduced here in traditional characters, annotated by simplified characters in the syntheses. This presentation forms a useful exercise for those students used only to simplified forms.

A man in a yoke (cangue), 打枷 dǎjiā, in Shanghai, circa 1870 (see p.30)

Narrator's Preface

Two brothers, whose names I need not mention here, were both good friends of mine in high school; but after a separation of many years we gradually lost touch. Some time ago I happened to hear that one of them was seriously ill, and since I was going back to my old home I broke my journey to call on them, I saw only one, however, who told me that the invalid was his younger brother.

'I appreciate your coming such a long way to see us,' he said, 'but my brother recovered some time ago and has gone elsewhere to take up an official post.' Then, laughing, he produced two volumes of his brother's diary, saying that from these the nature of his past illness could be seen, and that there was no harm in showing them to an old friend. I took the diary away, read it through, and found that he had suffered from a form of persecution complex.

'The writing was most confused and incoherent, and he had made many wild statements; moreover he had omitted to give any dates, so that only by the colour of the ink and the differences in the writing could one tell that it was not written at one time. Certain sections, however, were not altogether disconnected, and I have copied out a part to serve as a subject for medical research. I have not altered a single illogicality in the diary and have changed only the names, even though the people referred to are all country folk, unknown to the world and of no consequence. As for the title, it was chosen by the diarist himself after his recovery, and I did not change it.

衙役 yáyi – petty official in the Yamen's office,
衙门 yámen – imperial office, official or bureaucrat (see p.37)

The term yamen continues to be used in colloquial Chinese to refer to government offices. It can carry a negative connotation, meaning an arrogant or inefficient bureaucracy.

<u>Note</u>

In the following translation, as is the case for other translations in this book, the reader will note the use of both Wade-Giles and pinyin romanizations. At the time the original translations were made, the Wade-Giles system was in common usage. The pinyin system was developed in the 1950s based from pre-existing forms of romanization. It was finally approved and adopted by the Chinese government in 1958; a number of revision have since been made to the system.

Diary

Chapter I

今天晚上，很好的月光。

我不見他，已是三十多年；今天見了，精神分外爽快。才知道以前的三十多年， 全是發昏；然而須十分小心。不然，那趙家的狗，何以看我兩眼呢？

我怕得有理。

Translation 1.

Tonight the moon is very bright.

I have not seen it for over thirty years, so today when I saw it I felt in unusually high spirits. I begin to realize that during the past thirty-odd years I have been in the dark; but now I must be extremely careful. Otherwise why should that dog at the Zhao house have looked at me twice?

I have reason for my fear.

Translation 2.

This evening, the moon is very bright.

I have not seen it in more than thirty years; after seeing it now, my spirits are unusually reinvigorated. Only now do I realize that for the past thirty years, I have been very bewildered, however, I must be extremely cautious. Otherwise, why would the Zhao family's dog have looked at me twice?

I have reason to be afraid.

Synthesis

今天	晚上,	很	好	的	月光。	我
jīntiān	wǎnshang	hěn	hào	de	yuèguāng	Wǒ
Today	evening	very	good	part.*	moonlight	I

不見	他,	已	是	三十	多年;	今天
不见 bùjiàn	tā	yǐ	shì	sānshí	duōnián	jīntiān
not see	him (it)	already	is	30	many years	today

見	了,	精神	分外	爽快。	才	知道
见 jiàn	le	jīngshen	fènwài	shuǎngkuai	Cái	zhīdào
to see	part.	vitality	unusally	refreshed	Just how	to know

以前	的	三十	多年,	全	是	發昏;
yǐqián	de	sānshí	duōnián	quán	shì	fāhūn
before	part.*	30	many years	all	is	confused

然而	須	十分小心。	不然,	那	趙家	的	狗,
ránér	xū	shífēnxiǎoxīn	Bùrán	nà	赵 Zhào jiā	de	gǒu
but	must	be careful	If not	that	Zhao family	part.*	dog

何以	看	我	兩	眼	呢?	我	怕
héyǐ	kàn	wǒ	liǎng	yǎn	ne	Wǒ	pà
why	look	me	twice	eye	part.	I	fear

得	有	理。
de	yǒu	lǐ
part.	have	reason

* 的 Particle

Chapter II extract 1

今天全沒月光，我知道不妙。早上小心出門，趙貴翁的眼色便怪：似乎怕我，似乎想害我。還有七八個人，交頭接耳的議論我，又怕我看見。一路上的人，都是如此。其中最兇的一個人，張着嘴，對我笑了一笑；我便從頭直冷到腳跟，曉得他們布置，都已妥當了。

我可不怕，仍舊走我的路。前面一夥小孩子，也在那裡議論我；眼色也同趙貴翁一樣，臉色也鐵青。我想我同小孩子有什麼仇，他也這樣。忍不住大聲說，“你告訴我！”他們可就跑了。

Translation 1.

Tonight there is no moon at all, I know that this bodes ill. This morning when I went out cautiously, Mr Chao had a strange look in his eyes, as if he were afraid of me, as if he wanted to murder me. There were seven or eight others, who discussed me in a whisper. And they were afraid of my seeing them. All the people I passed were like that. The fiercest among them grinned at me; whereupon I shivered from head to foot, knowing that their preparations were complete.

I was not afraid, however, but continued on my way. A group of children in front were also discussing me, and the look in their eyes was just like that in Mr Chao's while their faces too were ghastly pale. I wondered what grudge these children could have against me to make them behave like this. I could not help calling out: 'Tell me!' But then they ran away.

Translation 2.

Tonight, there is no moonlight at all. I know that cannot be good. I was careful when I went out this morning. Zhao Guiweng gave me a strange look, as though he was afraid of me but at the same time wanted to kill me. There was also seven or eight people talking about me in hushed tones, hoping that I would not see them. Everybody that I encountered along the street was like this. The most intimidating among them was one who smiled at me with an open mouth; it sent a chill from my head down to my toes. I then knew their plans for me were ready.

I could not show them I was afraid, so I continued along the street. Ahead was a group of children also talking about me. They gave me the same look Zhao Guiweng had given me. Their faces were ashen. I tried to think what possible animosity these children could have towards me to behave in such a way. I could not help shouting out, 'What do you want!' But they simply ran off.

Synthesis

今天	全	沒	月光,	我	知道	不妙。
Jīntiān	quán	méi	yuèguāng	Wǒ	zhīdào	bùmiào
today	all	have not	moonlight	I	know	not encouraging

早上	小心	出門,	趙貴翁	的	眼色
Zǎoshang	xiǎoxīn	chūmén	赵贵翁 Zhào Guiwēng	de	yǎnsè
Morning	be careful	go out	person's name	part.	look

便	怪:	似乎	怕	我,	似乎	想	害
biàn	guài	sìhū	pà	wǒ	sìhū	xiǎng	hài
then	strange	apparently	afraid	me	apparently	wish	to harm

我。	還有	七八	個	人,	交頭接耳
wǒ	还 Háiyǒu	qī bā	个 gè	rén	交头接耳 jiāotóu-jiē'ěr
me	In addition	seven or eight	class.*	people	to whisper in one another's ear

的	議論	我,	又	怕	我	看見。	一路上
de	议论 yìlùn	wǒ	yòu	pà	wǒ	kànjiàn	Yīlùshàng
part.	to discuss	me	also	fear	me	see	On the street

的	人,	都	是	如此。	其中	最	凶
de	rén	dōu	shì	rúcǐ	Qízhōng	zuì	xiōng
part.	people	all	are	this way	Among	most	terrible

的	一个人,	張	著	嘴,	對	我
de	yīgèrén	张 zhāng	着 zhe	zuǐ	对 duì	wǒ
part.	one person	open up	part.*	mouth	towards	me

笑了一笑;	我	便	從頭	直	冷	到
xiàoleyīxiào	wǒ	biàn	从头 cóngtóu	zhí	lěng	dào
smiled	I	then	again	vertical	cold	to

脚根,	曉得	他們	佈置,	都	已	妥當
jiǎogēn	晓得 xiǎode	tāmen	bùzhì	dōu	yǐ	妥当 tuǒdàng
heel	know	they	preparation	all	already	ready

了。	我	可	不怕,	仍舊	走	我	的
le	wǒ	kě	bùpà	réngjiù	zǒu	wǒ	de
part.	I	can	fearless	still	walk	my	part.

路。	前面	一	夥	小	孩子,	也	在
lù	Qiánmiàn	yī	huǒ 伙	xiǎo	háize	yě	zài
road	Ahead	a	class. groups	small	children	also	at

那裡	議論	我;	眼色	也	同	趙貴翁
nàli	yìlùn	wǒ	yǎnsè	yě	tóng	Zhào Guìwēng
there	discuss	me	look	also	same	person's name

一樣,	臉色	也	鐵青。	我想我	同	小
一样 yīyàng	脸色 liǎnsè	yě	铁青 tiě qīng	Wǒxiǎngwǒ	tóng	xiǎo
same	complexion	also	ashen	I suppose	same	small

孩子	有	什麼	仇,	他	也	這樣。
háize	yǒu	什么 shénme	chóu	tā	yě	这样 zhèyàng
children	have	some	animosity	he (they)	also	like this

忍不住	大聲	説,	你	告訴	我!	他們
Rěnbuzhù	大声 dàshēng	説 shuō	Nǐ	告诉 gàosu	wǒ	Tāmen
Cannot help	loudly	say	You	tell	me	They

* 個 (个), 伙 classifiers

可就	跑	了。
kějiù	pǎo	le
then	run	part.

Chapter II extract 2

我想：我同趙貴翁有什麼仇，同路上的人又有什麼仇；只有廿年以前，把古久先生的陳年流水簿子，踹了一腳，古久先生很不高興。趙貴翁雖然不認識他，一定也聽到風聲，代抱不平；約定路上的人，同我作冤對。但是小孩子呢？那時候，他們還沒有出世，何以今天也睜著怪眼睛，似乎怕我，似乎想害我。這真教我怕，教我納罕而且傷心。

我明白了。這是他們娘老子教的！

Translation 1.

I wonder what grudge Mr Chao can have against me, what grudge the people on the road can have against me. I can think of nothing except that twenty years ago I trod on Mr Ku Chiu's account sheets for many years past, and Mr Ku was very displeased. Although Mr Chao does not know him, he must have heard talk of this and decided to avenge him, so he is conspiring against me with the people on the road. But then what of the children? At that time they were not yet born, so why should they eye me so strangely today, as if they were afraid of me, as if they wanted to murder me? This really frightens me, it is so bewildering and upsetting.

I know. They must have learned this from their parents!

Translation 2.

I tried to think what possible grudge Zhao Guiweng or the others on the street could have against me. The only thing that comes to mind is that I trod on Mr Gu Jiu's old accounting papers twenty years ago. Mr Gu Jiu was not happy when I did that. Even though Zhao Guiweng does not know him, he certainly must have heard something. Perhaps that is why he is against me; has turned the others on the street against me. But what about the children? They were not even born when that happened. Why would they give me such strange looks, as if they both feared me and wanted to kill me. This made me feel truly afraid. It also set me back and hurt my feelings. I understand. Their parents are making them behave like this!

Synthesis

我	想:	我	同	趙貴翁	有	什麼
Wǒ	xiǎng	wǒ	tóng	Zhào Guìwēng	yǒu	什么 shénme
I	think	I	same	person's name	have	some

仇,	同	路	上	的	人	又	有	什麼
chóu	tóng	lù	shàng	de	rén	yòu	yǒu	什么 shénme
animosity	same	street	on	part.	people	also	have	some

仇;	只有	廿	年	以前,	把	古久先生
chóu	zhǐyǒu	niàn	nián	yǐqián	bǎ	Gǔ Jiǔ xiānsheng
animosity	only	twenty	year	before	part.	Mr Gu Jiu

的	陳年	流水簿子,	踹	了	一	腳,
de	陈年 chénnián	liúshuǐ bùzǐ	chuài	le	yī	jiǎo
part.	old	account books (ledgers)	trample	part.	one	foot

古久先生	很	不高興。	趙貴翁	雖然
Gǔ Jiǔ xiānsheng	hěn	不高兴 bùgāoxìng	Zhào Guìwēng	虽然 suīrán
Mr Gu Jiu	very	unhappy	person's name	although

不	認識	他，	一定	也	聽到	風聲，
bù	认识 rènshi	tā	yīdìng	yě	听到 tīngdào	风声 fēngshēng
not	know	him	certainly	also	hear	talk of

代	抱不平；	約定	路上	的	人，	同
dài	bàobùpíng	yuēdìng	lùshang	de	rén	tóng
take place	injustice	decide	on the street	part.	people	together

我	作	冤	對。	但是	小孩子	呢？
wǒ	zuò	yuān	对 duì	Dànshì	xiǎoháizi	ne
me	make	hatred	in reply	But	small children	part.*

那時候，	他們	還沒有	出世，	何以	今天
nàshíhou	tāmen	还没有 hái méiyǒu	chūshì	héyǐ	jīntiān
at that time	they	not yet	born	whence	today

也	睜	著	怪	眼睛，	似乎	怕	我，
yě	zhēng	着 zhe	guài	yǎnjing	sìhū	pà	wǒ
also	open eyes	part.*	strange	eyes	apparently	afraid	me

似乎	想	害	我。	這	真	教	我	怕，
sìhū	xiǎng	hài	wǒ	这 Zhè	zhēn	jiāo	wǒ	pà
apparently	think	harm	me	This	really	teach	me	fear

教	我	納罕	而且	傷心。	我	明白	了。
jiāo	wǒ	纳罕 nàhǎn	érqiě	shāngxīn	Wǒ	míngbai	le
teach	me	bewilderment	but also	hurt	I	understand	part.

這	是	他們	娘	老子	教	的！
这 zhè	shì	他们 tāmen	niáng	lǎozi	jiāo	de
this	is	they	mother	father	teach	part.

* 呢, 着 particles

Chapter III extract 1

晚上總是睡不著。凡事須得研究，才會明白。

他們——也有給知縣打枷過的，也有給紳士掌過嘴的，也有衙役佔了他妻子的， 也有老子娘被債主逼死的；他們那時候的臉色，全沒有昨天這麼怕，也沒有這麼凶。

最奇怪的是昨天街上的那個女人，打他兒子，嘴裡說道，“老子呀！我要咬你幾口才出氣！”他眼睛卻看著我。我出了一驚，遮掩不住；那青面獠牙的一夥人，便都哄笑起來。陳老五趕上前，硬把我拖回家中了。

Translation 1.

I can't sleep at night. Everything requires careful consideration if one is to understand it.

Those people, some of whom have been pilloried by the magistrate, slapped in the face by the local gentry, had their wives taken away by bailiffs, or their parents driven to suicide by creditors, never looked as frightened and as fierce then as they did yesterday.

The most extraordinary thing was that woman on the street yesterday who spanked her son and said, 'Little devil! I'd like to bite several mouthfuls out of you to work off my feelings!' Yet all the time she looked at me. I gave a start, unable to control myself; then all those green-faced, long-toothed people began to laugh derisively. Old Chen hurried forward and dragged me home.

Translation 2.

I cannot sleep at night. I must think over everything very carefully, only then can I attempt to understand it.

These people; some of whom had been forced to wear a yoke by the local magistrate; others who had been beaten by members of the local gentry; certain had had their wives taken away by petty officials, or their parents hounded to death by creditors, none of their faces had ever shown the kind of fear and ferociousness that they had shown yesterday.

The strangest was a woman on the street yesterday. She was hitting her son. I clearly heard her say, 'Young man! I'd like to take a few bites out of you just to vent my anger!' Yet, her eyes were fixed on me. It gave me such a start, I could not help flinching. That terrifying gang of bystanders burst out laughing. Chen ran over and dragged me home.

Synthesis

晚上	總是	睡不著。	凡事	須	得	研究，
Wǎnshang	总是 zǒngshì	shuìbùzháo	Fánshì	须 xū	de	yánjiū
Night	always	unable to sleep	Everything	must	part.	consideration

才	會	明白。	他們	也	有	給	知縣
cái	会 huì	míngbai	他们 Tāmen	yě	yǒu	给 gěi	知县 zhīxiàn
only then	can	understand	They	also	have	given	magistrate

打枷	過	的，	也	有	給	紳士	掌
dǎjiā	过 guò	de	yě	yǒu	给 gěi	shēnshì	zhǎng
yoke	asp. part.	part.	also	have	given	gentleman	slap

過	嘴	的，	也	有	衙役	佔	了	他
过 guò	zuǐ	de	yě	yǒu	yáyì	占 zhàn	le	tā
asp. part.*	mouth	part.	also	have	officials	taken away	part.*	his

妻子	的,	也	有	老子	娘	被	債主
qīzi	de	yě	yǒu	lǎozi	niáng	bèi	zhàizhǔ
wife	part.	also	have	father	mother	by	creditor

逼死	的;	他們	那时候	的	臉色,	全
bī sǐ	de	他们 tāmen	nàshíhou	de	脸色 liǎnsè	quán
hound to death	part.	they	at that time	part.	look	all

沒有	昨天	這麼	怕,	也	沒有	這麼
méiyǒu	zuótiān	这么 zhème	pà	yě	méiyǒu	这么 zhème
never	yesterday	as	afraid	also	never	as

凶。	最	奇怪	的	是	昨天	街上	的
xiōng	Zuì	qíguài	de	shì	zuótiān	jiēshang	de
fierce	Most	strange	part.	is	yesterday	on the street	part.

那個	女人,	打	他	兒子,	嘴裡	說道,
那个 nàge	nǚrén	dǎ	tā	érzi	嘴里 zuǐlǐ	说 shuōdào
that	woman	beat	her	son	mouth	said

老子呀!	我	要	咬	你	幾	口	才
Lǎoziya!	Wǒ	yāo	yǎo	nǐ	几 jǐ	kǒu	cái
exclam. (impolite)	I	want	to bite	you	a few	mouthfuls	just

出氣!	他	眼睛	卻	看	著	我。	我出了
chūqì	Tā	yǎnjing	què	kàn	zhe	wǒ	Wǒ chū le
vent anger	Her	eyes	however	look	part.	me	I

一	驚,	遮掩	不住;	那	青面獠牙	的
yī	惊 jīng	zhēyǎn	búzhù	nà	qīngmiànliáoyá	de
a	started	conceal	no longer	those	ferocious-looking	part.

一夥人,	便都	哄笑起來。	陳老五
yīhuǒrén	biàndōu	hōngxiàoqǐlai	陈老五 Chén Lǎowǔ
crowd, gang	all	roar out laughing	Mr Chén Laowu

趕上前,	硬	把	我	拖	回家	中了。
gǎnshàngqián	yìng	bǎ	wǒ	tuō	huíjiā	zhōngle
hurried forward	firmly	took	me	drag	back home	in

* 過 aspect particle, 了 particle

Chapter III cxtract 2

拖我回家，家裡的人都裝作不認識我；他們的臉色，也全同別人一樣。進了書房，便反扣上門，宛然是關了一隻雞鴨。這一件事，越教我猜不出底細。
前幾天，狼子村的佃戶來告荒，對我大哥說，他們村裡的一個大惡人，給大家打死了；幾個人便挖出他的心肝來，用油煎炒了吃，可以壯壯膽子。我插了一句嘴，佃戶和大哥便都看我幾眼。今天才曉得他們的眼光，全同外面的那夥人一模一樣。

Translation 1.

He dragged me home. The folk at home all pretended not to know me; they had the same look in their eyes as all the others. When I went into the study, they locked the door outside as if cooping up a chicken or a duck. This incident left me even more bewildered.

A few days ago a tenant of ours from Wolf Cub Village came to report the failure of the crops, and told my elder brother that a notorious character in their village had been beaten to death; then some people had taken out his heart and liver, fried them in oil and eaten them, as a means of increasing their courage. When I interrupted, the tenant and my brother both stared at me. Only today have I realized that they had exactly the same look in their eyes as those people outside.

Translation 2.

After dragging me home, they all acted as if they didn't know me. They looked like complete strangers to me. I went into the study, and they locked me in, as if sticking a chicken or a duck in a cage. This episode made it even harder for me to figure all this out.

A few days ago, a tenant farmer from Wolf Cub Village came to tell my elder brother that the crops had failed. He then recounted how a notorious character in his village had been beaten to death by the crowd. Some of the villagers then cut out his heart and liver, fried them in oil, and ate them. This was supposed to increase their courage. I made a remark to the tenant farmer and my elder brother, but they just stared at me. It was only today that I realized that their eyes had exactly the same look as those of the crowd outside.

Synthesis

拖	我	回家,	家裡的人	都	裝作	不
Tuō	wǒ	huíjiā	jiālǐ	dōu	zhuāngzuò	bù
Drag	me	return home	people at home	all	pretend	neg.pref.

認識	我;	他們	的	臉色,	也	全同
认识 rènshi	wǒ	tāmen	de	脸色 liǎnsè	yě	quántóng
know	me	their	part.	look	also	identical

別人	一樣。	進	了	書房,	便	反	扣上
biérén	yīyàng	进 Jìn	le	书房 shūfáng	biàn	fǎn	kòushàng
others	same	Go in	part.	study	then	return	lock up

門,	宛然	是	關	一	隻	雞	鴨。	這
门 mén	wǎnrán	shì	关 guān	yī	只 zhī	鸡 jī	yā	这 Zhè
gate	as if	is	close	a	class.*	chicken	duck	This

一	件事,	越	教	我	猜不出	底細。
yī	jiànshì	yuè	jiào	wǒ	cāibùchū	dǐxì
a	matter	even more	cause	me	suspect	details

前幾天,	狼子村	的	佃戶	來	告
前几天 Qián jǐ tiān	Lángzǐcūn	de	diànhù	来 lái	gào
A few days before	Wolf Cub Village	part.	tenant farmer	came	to tell

荒,	對	我	大哥	説,	他們	村裡的
huāng	对 duì	wǒ	dàgē	说 shuō	tāmen	cūnlǐde
crop failure	to	my	eldest brother	said	their	in village

一	個	大	惡人,	給	大家	打死	了;
yī	gè	dà	èrén	gěi	dàjiā	dǎsǐ	le
a	class.	big	evil person	by	everyone	kill	part.

幾個人	便	挖出	他	的	心	肝	來,
几个人 jǐgerén	biàn	wāchū	tā	de	xīn	gān	lái
a few people	then	cut out	his	part.	heart	liver	happen

用	油	煎炒	了	吃,	可以	壯壯	膽子。
yòng	yóu	jiānchǎo	le	chī	kěyǐ	zhuàngzhuàng	胆子 dǎnzi
use	oil	fry	part.	eat	can	reinforce	courage

我	插	了	一	句嘴	佃戶	和	大哥
Wǒ	chā	le	yī	jùzuǐ	diànhù	hé	dàgē
I	add	part.	a	remark	tenant farmer	and	eldest brother

便	都	看	我	幾眼。	今天	才	曉得
biàn	dōu	kàn	wǒ	几眼 jǐyǎn	Jīntiān	cái	晓得 xiǎode
then	both	look	me	looks	Today	now	know

他們	眼光,	全同	外面	的	那	夥人
tāmen	yǎnguāng	quántóng	wàimian	de	nà	yīhuǒrén
their	regard	identical	outside	part.	that	crowd

一模一樣。
yīmúyīyàng
exactly the same (idiom)

Chapter III extract 3

想起來，我從頂上直冷到腳跟。

他們會吃人，就未必不會吃我。

你看那女人“咬你幾口”的話，和一夥青面獠牙人的笑，和前天佃戶的話，明明是暗號。我看出他話中全是毒，笑中全是刀。他們的牙齒，全是白厲厲的排著，這就是吃人的傢夥。

照我自己想，雖然不是惡人，自從踹了古家的簿子，可就難說了。他們似乎別有心思，我全猜不出。況且他們一翻臉，便說人是惡人。我還記得大哥教我做論，無論怎樣好人，翻他幾句，他便打上幾個圈；原諒壞人幾句，他便說“翻天妙手，與眾不同”。我那裡猜得到他們的心思，究竟怎樣；況且是要吃的時候。

Translation 1.

Just to think of it sets me shivering from the crown of my head to the soles of my feet.

They eat human beings, so they may eat me.

I see that woman's words 'bite several mouthfuls out of you,' thc laughter of those green-faced, long-toothed people and the tenant's story the other day are obviously secret signs. I realize all the poison in their speech, all the daggers in their laughter. Their teeth are white and glistening: they are all man-eaters.

It seems to me, although I am not a bad man, ever since I trod on Mr Ku's accounts it has been touch-and-go. They seem to have secrets which I cannot guess, and once they are angry they will call anyone a bad character. I remember when my elder brother taught me to write compositions, no matter how good a man was, if I produced arguments to the contrary he would mark that passage to show his approval; while if I excused evil-doers, he would say: 'Good for you, that shows originality.' How can I possibly guess their secret thoughts, especially when they are ready to eat people?

<u>*Translation 2.*</u>

I remembered something that sent shivers from the top of my head down to the tips of my toes.

If they're capable of eating people, there's nothing to say they won't eat me.

I heard that woman say, 'I'd like to take a few bites out of you,' and the laughs of the ferocious crowd of bystanders, the tenant farmer's words were obviously secret signals. I can now see the venom in their words and the daggers behind their smiles, the rows of white, sharp, teeth. These people are evidently of the kind that eat men.

If I think about it, even though I am not a bad person, ever since I trod on the Gu family's account books it's been hard to decipher things. It seems like they have something in mind, but I can't guess what it is. In any case, once they turn on someone, they will vilify him. I still remember when my elder brother taught me how to write essays. No matter how good a person was, if I included a few petty remarks, he would circle that part in approval. If I included a few words of excuse for a bad person, he would say, 'You have real talent. Exceptional.' How could I ever guess what they are really thinking, especially if they are about to eat me.

Synthesis

想起來,	我	從	頭上	直冷	到	腳根。
xiǎngqilai	wǒ	cóng	tóu	zhílěng	dào	jiǎogēn
remember	I	from	head	cold	to	heel

他們	會	吃	人,	就	未必不	會	吃	我。
他们 Tāmen	会 huì	chī	rén	jiù	wèibì	会 huì	chī	wǒ
They	can	eat	people	then	maybe	can	eat	me

你	看	那	女人	咬	你	幾	口
你 Nǐ	kàn	nà	nǚrén	yǎo	nǐ	几 jǐ	kǒu
You	see	that	woman	bite	you	a few	mouthfuls

的話,	和	一夥	青面獠牙	人	的	笑,
dehuà	hé	yīhuǒ	qīngmiànliáoyá	rén	de	xiào
words	and	crowd	ferocious-looking	people	part.	laugh

和	前天	佃戶	的話,	明明	是	暗號。
hé	qiántiān	diànhù	dehuà	míngmíng	shì	暗号 ànhào
and	before yesterday	tenant farmer	words	obviously	are	secret sign

我	看出	他	話	中全	是	毒,	笑	中全
Wǒ	kànchū	tā	huà	zhòngquán	shì	dú	xiào	zhòngquán
I	see	he	speech	full	is	poison	laugh	full

是	刀。	他們	的	牙齒,	全	是	白	厲厲
shì	dāo	他们 Tāmen	de	牙齿 yáchǐ	quán	shì	bái	厉厉 lìlì
is	knife	They	part.	teeth	all	are	white	sharp

的	排著,	這就	是	吃人	的	傢夥。
de	pái	zhèjiù	shì	chīrén	de	jiāhuǒ
part.	rows	these	are	cannibals	part.	people

照	我	自己	想,	雖然	不是	惡人,
Zhào	wǒ	zìjǐ	xiǎng	虽然 suīrán	bùshì	èrén
According to	me	one's self	think	even if	not	bad person

踹	了	古家	的	簿子,	可就	難	說	了。
chuài	le	Gǔ jiā	de	bùzǐ	kějiù	难 nán	shuō	le
trample	part.	Gu family	part.	accounts	can	difficult	say	part.

他們	似乎	别有心思,	我	全猜	不出。
他们 Tāmen	sìhū	biéyǒu xīnsi	wǒ	quán cāi	bùchū
They	apparently	don't mind	I	guess	cannot

況且	他們	一	翻臉,	便	說	人	是
Kuàngqiě	他们 tāmen	yī	翻脸 fānliǎn	biàn	shuō	rén	shì
besides	they	a	to fall out	then	say	people	are

惡人。	我	還	記得	大哥	教	我	做
èrén	Wǒ	还 hái	jìde	dàgē	jiāo	wǒ	zuò
bad person	I	still	remember	eldest brother	to teach	me	to do

論,	無論	怎樣	好	人,	翻	他
论 lún	无论 wúlùn	怎样 zěnyàng	hǎo	rén	fān	tā
essays	no matter	how	good	man	overturn	his

幾句,	他	便	打上	幾	個	圈;	原諒
几 jǐjù	tā	biàn	dǎshàng	几 jǐ	个 ge	quān	yuánliàng
comment	he	then	make	few	class.	circle	to excuse

壞人	幾句,	他	便	說:	“翻天妙手,
坏人 huàirén	几 jǐjù	tā	biàn	shuō	fāntiān miàoshǒu
evil-doer	comment	he	then	said	exceptional

與眾不同”。	我	那裡	猜	得	到
与众不同 yǔzhòngbùtóng	Wǒ	nàli	cāi	de	dào
out of the ordinary (idiom)	I	there	guess	part.	to

他們	的	心思,	究竟	怎樣;	況且	是
他们 tāmen	de	xīnsi	jiūjìng	怎样 zěnyàng	kuàngqiě	shì
they	part.	thoughts	after all	how	moreover	is

要	吃	的	時候。
yāo	chī	de	shíhou
want	eat	part.	time

Notes

論 lún – essays, commentaries, arguments

Chapter III extract 4

凡事總須研究，才會明白。古來時常吃人，我也還記得，可是不甚清楚。我翻開歷史一查，這歷史沒有年代，歪歪斜斜的每頁上都寫著“仁義道德”幾個字。我橫豎睡不著，仔細看了半夜，才從字縫裡看出字來，滿本都寫著兩個字是“吃人”！

書上寫著這字許多，佃戶說了這許多話，卻都笑吟吟的睜著怪眼看我。

我也是人，他們想要吃我了！

Translation 1.

Everything requires careful consideration if one is to understand it. In ancient times, as I recollect, people often ate human beings, but I am rather hazy about it. I tried to look this up, but my history has no chronology, and scrawled all over each page are the words: ‘Virtue and Morality.’ Since I could not sleep anyway, I read intently half the night, until I began to see words between the lines, the whole book being filled with the two words: ‘Eat people.’

All these words written in the book, all the words spoken by our tenant, gaze at me strangely with an enigmatic smile.

I too am a man, and they want to eat me!

Translation 2.

Whatever the question, one must study it in order to understand it. In ancient times, people were often eaten. I can vaguely recall reading that somewhere. I looked up a few history books. Regardless of the period, the pages were filled with words like, 'virtue and morality.' In any case, I could not sleep, so I spent half the night concentrated on reading, it was then I started to see words written between the lines. The books were filled with the words: 'Eat people!'

A lot of words had been written in these books. The tenant farmer had spoken a lot of words. Yet, he gave me that peculiar look and that strange smile.

I am also a man, and they want to eat me!

Synthesis

凡事	總	須	研究,	才	會	明白。
Fánshì	总 zǒng	须 xū	yánjiū	cái	会 huì	míngbai
everything	alway	need	study	only then	can	clear

古來	時常	吃	人,	我	也	還	記得,
Gǔlái	shícháng	chī	rén	wǒ	yě	还 hái	jìde
In old times	often	eat	people	I	also	still	remember

可是	不	甚	清楚。	我	翻開	歷史
kěshì	bù	shèn	qīngchu	Wǒ	fānkāi	历史 lìshǐ
but	not	very	clear	I	look up	history

一	查,	這	歷史	沒有	年代,	歪歪斜斜
yī	chá	这 zhè	历史 lìshǐ	méiyǒu	niándài	wāiwāixiéxié
a	search	this	history	has no	age	tremulous

的	每	頁	上	都	寫著	"仁義道德"
de	měi	页 yè	shàng	dōu	写著 xiězhù	仁义道德 rényìdàodé
part.	each	page	on	all	to write	idiom: humanity, justice

幾個	字。	我	橫豎	睡不著,	仔細
几个 jǐge	zì	Wǒ	横竖 héngshu	shuìbùzháo	仔细 zǐxì
few	words	I	anyway	could not sleep	attentive

看	了	半夜,	才	從	字缝裡	看出字來,
kàn	le	bànyè	cái	从 cóng	zìfènglǐ	kànchū zì lái
read	part.	half night	until	through	word spaces	start to see words

滿	本	都	寫著	兩	個	字	是	“吃人”！
mǎn	běn	dōu	写着 xiězhe	liǎng	个 gè	zì	shì	chī rén
filled	class.	all	writing	both	class.	letters	are	eat people

書	上	寫著	這	許多	字,	佃戶	説
书 Shū	shàng	写着 xiězhe	这 zhè	许多 xǔduō	zì	diànhù	说 shuō
book	on	writing	these	many	words	tenant farmer	to say

了	這	許多	話,	卻	都	笑吟吟	的
le	这 zhè	许多 xǔduō	话 huà	却 què	dōu	xiàoyínyín	de
part.	these	many	words	but	all	laugh	part.

睜著	怪	眼看	我。	我	也	是	人,
睁着 zhēngzhe	guài	yǎnkàn	wǒ	Wǒ	yě	shì	rén
open(eyes)	strange	looks	me	I	also	am	man

他們	想要	吃	我	了！
他们 tāmen	xiǎngyào	chī	wǒ	le
they	to want to	eat	me	part.

Notes

仁义道德 rényìdàodé – compassion, duty, propriety and integrity (idiom)

Chapter IV extract 1

早上，我靜坐了一會兒。陳老五送進飯來，一碗菜，一碗蒸魚；這魚的眼睛，白而且硬，張著嘴，同那一夥想吃人的人一樣。吃了幾筷，滑溜溜的不知是魚是人，便把他兜肚連腸的吐出。

我説“老五，對大哥説，我悶得慌，想到園裡走走。”老五不答應，走了；停一 會，可就來開了門。

我也不動，研究他們如何擺佈我；知道他們一定不肯放鬆。果然！我大哥引了一個老頭子，慢慢走來；他滿眼凶光，怕我看出，只是低頭向著地，從眼鏡橫邊暗暗看我。

Translation 1.

In the morning I sat quietly for some time. Old Chen brought lunch in: one bowl of vegetables, one bowl of steamed fish. The eyes of the fish were white and hard, and its mouth was open just like those people who want to eat human beings. After a few mouthfuls I could not tell whether the slippery morsels were fish or human flesh, so I brought it all up.

I said, 'Old Chen, tell my brother that I feel quite suffocated, and want to have a stroll in the garden.' Old Chen said nothing but went out, and presently he came back and opened the gate.

I did not move, but watched to see how they would treat me, feeling certain that they would not let me go. Sure enough! My elder brother came slowly out, leading an old man. There was a murderous gleam in his eyes, and fearing that I would see it he lowered his head, stealing glances at me from the side of his spectacles.

Translation 2.

This morning, I sat quietly for a while. Chen Laowu sent me some food; a bowl of vegetables and a bowl of steamed fish. The fish's eyes were white and hard. Its mouth wide open, just like that crowd who eat people. I took a few mouthfuls with my chopsticks, but it was so slimy that I could not tell whether it was a fish or a person. I ended up vomiting the whole lot.

I said, 'Chen, tell my elder brother that I am feeling claustrophobic and I'd like to take a walk in the courtyard.' Chen left without answering. After a while, the door opened again.

I did not move. I thought about what they were planning for me. I knew for certain that they were not willing to let me go. No surprise there! My elder brother arrived with an old man, who walked in slowly. He had a menacing look about him. He must have been afraid that I would see it, as he kept his head low, stealing glances at me through the corner of his glasses.

Synthesis

早上，	我	靜坐了	一會兒。	陳老五	送
Zǎoshang	wǒ	jìngzuò	yīhuìer	陈老五 Chén Lǎowǔ	sòng
Early morning	I	sat quietly	a while	Mr Chén Laowu	sent

進	飯	來，	一	碗	菜，	一	碗	蒸	魚
jìn	fàn	lái	yī	wǎn	cài	yī	wǎn	zhēng	yú
in	food	arrive	a	bowl	vegetables	a	bowl	steamed	fish

這	魚	的	眼睛，	白	而且	硬，	張著
这 zhè	yú	de	yǎnjing	bái	érqiě	yìng	zhāngzhe
this	fish	part.	eyes	white	but also	hard	open

嘴，	同	那	一	夥	想	吃人	的	人
zuǐ	tóng	nà	yī	huǒ	xiǎng	chīrén	de	rén
mouth	like	that	a	crowd	think	cannibal	part.	people

一樣。	同	吃	了	几	筷，	滑溜溜	的
yīyàng	Tóng	chī	le	幾 jǐ	kuài	huáliūliū	de
same	like	eat	part.	some	chopsticks	smooth; slick	part.

不知	是	魚	是	人，	便	把
bùzhī	shì	yú	shì	rén	biàn	bǎ
don't know	is	fish	is	people	then	part.

他	兜肚連腸	的	吐出。	我	説	老五,	對
tā	dōudǔ liáncháng	de	tùchū	Wǒ	说 shuō	Lǎowǔ	对 duì
it	the whole lot	part.	vomit up	I	said	Laowu name	to

大哥	説,	我	闷	慌,	想	到	園
dàgē	说 shuō	wǒ	mèn	huāng	xiǎng	dào	yuán
older brother	said	I	dispirited	confusing	think	to go	garden

裡	走走。	老五	不	答應,	走	了;
lǐ	zǒuzǒu	Lǎowǔ	bù	dāying	zǒu	le
in	to walk	Laowu name	neg. prefix	promise	to walk	part.

停	一會,	可	就	開了	門。	我
tíng	一会 yīhuì	kě	jiù	开了 kāile	门 mén	Wǒ
to stop	a moment	can	then	to open	gate	I

也	不動,	研究	他們	如何	擺佈	我;
yě	不动 bùdòng	yánjiū	tāmen	rúhé	摆佈 bǎibù	wǒ
also	not move	considered	they	what	arrange	me

知道	他們	一定	不	肯	放鬆。	果然!
zhīdào	tāmen	yīdìng	bù	kěn	放松 fàngsōng	Guǒrán
know	they	certainly	neg. prefix	willing	let go	For sure

我	大哥	引了	一	個	老头子,	慢慢
wǒ	dàgē	yǐnle	yī	个 gè	lǎotóuzi	mànmàn
my	older brother	guided, led	an	class.	older man	slowly

走	來;	他	滿眼	凶	光,	怕	我	看出,
zǒu	lái	tā	满眼 mǎnyǎn	xiōng	guāng	pà	wǒ	kànchū
walk	arrive	he	eyes full	vicious	gleam	afraid	I	see

只是	低頭	向著地,	從	眼鏡	橫
zhǐshì	低头 dītóu	xiàngzhedì	从 cóng	眼镜 yǎnjìng	横 hèng
so	head bowed	downwards	from	spectacles	menacing

邊	暗暗	看	我。
边 biān	ànàn	kàn	wǒ
side	secret	looks	me

Notes

兜肚連腸 dōudǔ liáncháng,
兜 dōu – pouch, 肚 dǔ, dù – belly, tripe,
連腸 liáncháng – intestines

Chapter IV extract 2

大哥說，“今天你彷彿很好。”我說“是的。”大哥說，“今天請何先生來，給你診一診。”我說“可以！”其實我豈不知道這老頭子是劊子手扮的！無非借了看脈這名目，揣一揣肥瘠：因這功勞，也分一片肉吃。我也不怕；雖然不吃人，膽子卻比他們還壯。伸出兩個拳頭，看他如何下手。老頭子坐著，閉了眼睛，摸了好一會，呆了好一會；便張開他鬼眼睛說，“不要亂想。靜靜的養幾天，就好了。”

Translation 1.

'You seem to be very well today,' said my brother.

'Yes,' said I.

'I have invited Mr Ho here today,' said my brother, 'to examine you.'

'All right,' said I. Actually I knew quite well that this old man was the executioner in disguise! He simply used the pretext of feeling my pulse to see how fat I was; for by so doing he would receive a share of my flesh. Still I was not afraid. Although I do not eat men, my courage is greater than theirs. I held out my two fists, to see what he would do. The old man sat down, closed his eyes, fumbled for some time and remained still for some time; then he opened his shifty eyes and said, 'Don't let your imagination run away with you. Rest quietly for a few days, and you will be all right.'

<u>*Translation 2.*</u>

My elder brother said, 'You seem better today.' I replied, 'Yes.' 'Today, I've invited Dr. He to come and give you a check up,' he announced. I replied, 'Fine!' However, I did not realize that this old man was to be my executioner! He was simply checking my pulse as a pretext to feel how plump I was. For this service, he would probably be given a piece of my flesh to eat. I am not afraid. Even though I'm not a cannibal, I'm still more courageous than them. I extended both my fists to see what he would do. The old man sat down and closed his eyes. He felt my wrist for a while, then sat expressionless for a moment. Finally, he opened his crafty eyes and said, 'Relax. Take it easy for a few days and you'll feel better.'*

<u>Synthesis</u>

大哥	說，	今天	你	彷彿	很	好。
Dàgē	说 shuō	jīntiān	nǐ	fǎngfú	hěn	hào
older brother	said	today	you	seem	very	well

我	說，	是的。	大哥	說，	今天	請
Wǒ	说 shuō	shìde	Dàgē	说 shuō	Jīntiān	qǐng
I	said	yes	Older brother	said	today	ask

何先生	來，	給	你	診一診。	我
Hé xiānsheng	lái	jǐ	nǐ	诊一诊 zhěnyīzhěn	wǒ
Mr He	to come	give	you	check-up	I

* Cannibalism – this an allegory to oppression

説,	可以!	其實	我	豈不	知道	這
说 shuō	Kěyǐ	Qíshí	wǒ	qǐbù	zhīdào	这 zhè
said	can	In fact	I	could not	know	this

老头子	是	劊子手	扮	的!	無非
lǎotóuzi	shì	刽子手 guìzishǒu	bàn	de	Wúfēi
old fellow	is	executioner	disguise	part.	Nothing but

借了	看	脈	這	名目,	揣一揣	肥瘠:
jiè	kàn	mài	这 zhè	míngmù	chuǎiyīchuǎi	féijí
pretext	to see	arteries	this	procedure	to estimate	fat or thin

因	這	功勞,	也	分	一片	肉	吃。
yīn	这 zhè	gōngláo	yě	fèn	yīpiàn	ròu	chī
because	this	service	also	share	piece	flesh	to eat

我	也	不怕;	雖然	不	吃人,	膽子
Wǒ	yě	bùpà	虽然 suīrán	bù	chīrén	dǎnzi
I	also	not afraid	although	neg.prefix	cannibal	courage

卻比	他們	還	壯。	伸出	兩個	拳頭,
quèbì	他们 tāmen	还 hái	zhuàng	Shēnchū	两个 liǎnggè	拳头 quántou
more than	they	even	stronger	Extend	both	fists

看	他	如何	下手。	老头子	坐著,	閉了
kàn	tā	rúhé	xiàshǒu	Lǎotóuzi	zuòzhe	闭 bìle
watch	him	what way	to start	Old fellow	sat down	closed

眼睛,	摸了	好一會;	呆了	好一會;	便
yǎnjing	mōle	好一会 hǎo	dāile	好一会 hǎo	biàn
eyes	feeling	some time	expressionless	some time	then

張開	他	鬼	眼睛,	説,	不要	亂想。
张开 zhāngkāi	tā	guǐ	yǎnjing	说 shuō	bùyào	乱想 luànxiǎng
opened	his	crafty	eyes	said	don't be	paranoid

靜靜	的	養	幾天,	就	好了。
静静 Jìngjìng	de	养 yǎng	几天 jǐtiān	jiù	hǎole
Quiet	part.	take care	few days	then	well

Chapter IV extract 3

不要亂想，靜靜的養！養肥了，他們是自然可以多吃；我有什麼好處，怎麼會“好了”？他們這群人，又想吃人，又是鬼鬼祟祟，想法子遮掩，不敢直截下手，真要令我笑死。我忍不住，便放聲大笑起來，十分快活。自己曉得這笑聲裏面，有的是義勇和正氣。老頭子和大哥，都失了色，被我這勇氣正氣鎮壓住了。

Translation 1.

Don't let your imagination run away with you! Rest quietly for a few days! When I have grown fat, naturally they will have more to eat; but what good will it do me, or how can it be 'all right'? All these people wanting to eat human flesh and at the same time stealthily trying to keep up appearances, not daring to act promptly, really made me nearly die of laughter. I could not help roaring with laughter, I was so amused. I knew that in this laughter were courage and integrity. Both the old man and my brother turned pale, awed by my courage and integrity.

Translation 2.

Don't be paranoid! Take it easy! Relax and fatten up, they will naturally have more of me to eat. But, how does that help me? How can that make me 'feel better'? Not only do they want to eat people, slyly, underhanded, trying to hide it. They don't dare do anything too overtly. It almost makes me want to die laughing. I could not stand it anymore and burst out in uncontrollably laughter. I knew that my laughter was filled with courage and honesty. The old man and my elder brother paled, awed by my courage and honesty.

Synthesis

不要	亂想,	靜靜	的	養!	養	肥
Bùyào	乱想 luànxiǎng	静静 jìngjìng	de	养 yǎng	养 Yǎng	féi
Don't be	paranoid	quiet	part.	take care	Take care	fat

了,	他們	是	自然	可以	多	吃;
le	他们 tāmen	shì	zìrán	kěyǐ	duō	chī
part.	they	are, will	naturally	can, be able	much	to eat

我	有	什麼	好處,	怎麼	會	好了?
wǒ	yǒu	什么 shénme	好处 hǎochu	怎么 zěnme	会 huì	hǎole
I	have	what	benefit	how	can	better

他們	這	群人,	又	想	吃人,	又是
他们 tāmen	这 zhè	qúnrén	yòu	xiǎng	chīrén	yòushì
they	this	gang	also	want	eat people	yet

鬼鬼祟祟,	想法子	遮掩,	不敢	直截	下手,
guǐguǐsuìsuì	xiǎngfǎzi	zhēyǎn	bùgǎn	zhíjié	xiàshǒu
slyly	trying	conceal	not dare to	openly	do it

真要	令	我	笑	死。	我	忍不住,
zhēn yāo	lìng	wǒ	xiào	sǐ	Wǒ	rěnbuhù
really want	to make	me	laugh	to die	I	couldn't help

便	放聲	大笑	起來,	十分	快活。	自己
biàn	放声 fàngshēng	dàxiào	qǐlai	shí fēn	kuàihuo	Zìjǐ
then	burst	laugh heartily	begin	greatly	amused	one

曉得	這	笑聲	裏面,	有的是	義勇	和
晓得 xiǎode	这 zhè	xiàoshēng	里面 lǐmiàn	yǒudeshì	义勇 yìyǒng	hé
to know	this	laughter	inside	a lot of	courage	and

正氣。	老头子	和	大哥,	都	失了色,	被
正气 zhèngqì	Lǎotóuzi	hé	dàgē	dōub	shīlesè	bèi
integrity	Old fellow	and	older brother	both	paled	by

我	這	勇氣	正氣	鎮壓住了。
wǒ	这 zhè	勇气 yǒngqì	正气 zhèngqì	镇压住了 zhènyāzhùle
my	this	courage	integrity	put down

Chapter IV extract 4

但是我有勇氣，他們便越想吃我, 沾光一點這勇氣。老頭子跨出門，走不多遠， 便低聲對大哥説道，“趕緊吃罷！”大哥點點頭。原來也有你！這一件大發見, 雖似 意外，也在意中：合夥吃我的人, 便是我的哥哥！

吃人的是我哥哥！

我是吃人的人的兄弟！

我自己被人吃了，可仍然是吃人的人的兄弟！

Translation 1.

But just because I am brave they are the more eager to eat me, in order to acquire some of my courage. The old man went out of the gate, but before he had gone far he said to my brother in a low voice, 'To be eaten at once!' And my brother nodded. So you are in it too! This stupendous discovery, although it came as a shock, is yet no more than I had expected: the accomplice in eating me is my elder brother!

The eater of human flesh is my elder brother!

I am the younger brother of an eater of human flesh!

I myself will be eaten by others, but none the less I am the younger brother of an eater of human flesh!

Translation 2.

However, the more courage I displayed, the more they wanted to eat me so as to absorb my courage. The old man left. Then, just outside the door, he said to my elder brother in a low voice, 'Hurry up and eat!'

My elder brother nodded in agreement. So you are in this too! This enormous revelation, however unexpected, was in fact predictable. My elder brother is one of those cannibals!

My elder brother is one of them!

I am the brother of a person who eats people!

I will be eaten by others, but I still remain the brother of a person who eats people!

Synthesis

但是	我	有	勇氣,	他們	便	越	想
Dànshì	wǒ	yǒu	yǒngqì	他们 tāmen	biàn	yuè	xiǎng
However	I	have	courage	they	then	more	want

吃	我,	沾光	一點	這	勇氣。	老头子
chī	wǒ	zhānguāng	一点 yīdiǎn	这 zhè	yǒngqì	Lǎotóuzi
to eat	me	benefit	a little	this	courage	Old fellow

跨出	門,	走	不	多	遠,	便	低聲
kuà	门 mén	zǒu	bù	duō	远 yuǎn	biàn	低声 dīshēng
stepped out	gate	walk	not	too	far	then	low voice

對	大哥,	説道,	趕緊	吃	罷!	大哥
对 duì	dàgē	说道 shuōdào	赶紧 gǎnjǐn	chī	罢 ba	Dàgē
to	older brother	said	hurriedly	eat	final part.*	Older brother

點點	頭。	原來	也	有	你!	這	一
点点 diǎndiǎn	头 tóu	原来 Yuánlái	yě	yǒu	nǐ	这 zhè	yī
nodded	head	So	also	there is	you	this	a

件	大	發見,	雖似	意外,	也	在意中:
jiàn	dà	发见 fā jiàn	虽似 suīsì	yìwài	yě	zàiyìzhōng
class.	huge	discovery	though	unexpected	also	expected

合夥	吃	我	的	人,	便	是	我的	哥哥!
合伙 héhuǒ	chī	wǒ	de	rén	biàn	shì	wǒde	gēgē
partners	eat	me	part.	people	then	is	my	brother

吃人的	我的	哥哥!	我	是	吃人的	人的
Chīrénde	wǒde	gēgē	Wǒ	shì	chīrénde	rénde
Cannibal	my	brother	I	am	cannibal	people's

兄弟!	我	自己	被	人吃了,	可	仍然
xiōngdì	Wǒ	zìjǐ	bèi	rénchīle	kě	réngrán
brother	I	myself	pass. voice	eaten by people	can	nevertheless

是	吃人的	人的	兄弟!
shì	chīrénde	rénde	xiōngdì
be	cannibal	people's	brother

* 罷 (罢) final particle

Chapter V

這幾天是退一步想：假使那老頭子不是劊子手扮的，真是醫生，也仍然是吃人的 人。他們的祖師李時珍做的“本草什麼”上，明明寫著人肉可以煎吃；他還能說自己不吃人麼？

至於我家大哥，也毫不冤枉他。他對我講書的時候，親口説過可以“易子而食”； 又一回偶然議論起一個不好的人，他便説不但該殺，還當“食肉寢皮”。我那時年紀還小，心跳了好半天。前天狼子村佃戶來説吃心肝的事，他也毫不奇怪，不住的點頭。 可見心思是同從前一樣狠。既然可以“易子而食”，便什麼都易得，什麼人都吃得。 我從前單聽他講道理，也胡塗過去；現在曉得他講道理的時候，不但唇邊還抹著人油， 而且心裡滿裝著吃人的意思。

Translation 1.

These few days I have been thinking again: suppose that old man were not an executioner in disguise, but a real doctor; he would be none the less an eater of human flesh. In that book on herbs, written by his predecessor Li Shih-chen, it is clearly stated that men's flesh can he boiled and eaten; so can he still say that he does not eat men?

As for my elder brother, I have also good reason to suspect him. When he was teaching me, he said with his own lips, 'People exchange their sons to eat.' And once in discussing a bad man, he said that not only did he deserve to be killed, he should 'have his flesh eaten and his hide slept on....' I was still young then, and my heart beat faster for some time, he was not at all surprised by the story that our tenant from Wolf Cub Village told us the other day about eating a man' s heart and liver, but kept nodding his head. He is evidently just as cruel as before. Since it is possible to 'exchange sons to eat,' then anything can be exchanged, anyone can be eaten. In the past I simply listened to his explanations, and let it go at that; now I know that when he explained it to me, not only was there human fat at the corner of his lips, but his whole heart was set on eating men.

Translation 2.

These past few days I've thought about it objectively, 'Even if that old man was not an executioner in disguise, but really a doctor, he is nevertheless a cannibal.' In the encyclopedia, 'Herbal Medicines', written by their founder Li Shizhen, it clearly states that human flesh can be fried and eaten; how can he still say that he himself doesn't eat people?

As for my elder brother, I haven't treated him unfairly at all. When he was teaching me, he would say things like: one can 'exchange children and eat them.[*]*' Another time, while discussing an unsavoury person, he said that not only should he be killed, but in addition he should be 'eaten and flayed.' I was still quite young at the time and it set my heart beating for hours. The other day, when the tenant farmer from Wolf Cub Village talked about eating hearts and livers, he did not seem to think it was strange at all as he kept nodding his head. It is evident that his mind is as vicious now as it was then. Since if you can 'exchange children to be eaten', then you can exchange anything and eat anyone. His previous attempts to reason with me had always left me confused. Now, I know that when he was endeavouring to reason with me, not only were his lips dripping with the fat of human flesh, he was also hiding the fact his heart and mind were filled with the desire to eat people.*

<u>Synthesis</u>

這幾天	是	退	一步	想:	假使	那
这几天 Zhèjǐtiān	shì	tuì	yībù	xiǎng	jiǎshǐ	nà
These few days	are	to retreat	a step	to think	if	that

老头子	不是	劊子手	扮	的,	真	是
lǎotóuzi	bùshì	刽子手 guìzishǒu	bàn	de	zhēn	shì
old fellow	is not	executioner	disguise	part.	really	is

* Expression dating from Lie Zi (Taoist classic) referring to siege of Song Kingdom 4th century BC

醫生，	也	仍然	是	吃人的人。	他們的
医生 yīshēng	yě	réngrán	shì	chīrénde	他们的 Tāmen
doctor	also	nevertheless	is	man-eating person	Their

祖師	李時珍	做	的	“本草什麼”	上，
祖师 zǔshī	李时珍 lǐshízhēn	zuò	de	本草什么 Běncǎo Shénme	shàng
founder	Lǐ Shízhēn	made	part.	“Herbal Medicines”	on

明明	寫著	人肉	可以	煎	吃；	他	還
míngmíng	写着 xiězhe	rénròu	kěyǐ	jiān	chī	tā	还 hái
clearly	wrote	human flesh	may	fried	eaten	he	still

能	說	自己	不吃人	麼？	至於	我
néng	说 shuō	zìjǐ	bùchīrén	么 má	至于 Zhìyú	wǒ
be able	to say	oneself	not eat people	how ?	as for	my

家	大哥，	也	毫不	冤枉	他。	他
jiā	dàgē	yě	háobù	yuānwang	tā	Tā
a person	older brother	also	hardly	unfair	him	He

對	我	講書	的	時候，	親口	說過
对 duì	wǒ	讲书 jiǎngshū	de	时候 shíhou	亲口 qīnkǒu	说过 shuōguò
to	me	teach	part.	time	personally	said

可以	“易子而食”；	又一回	偶然	議論起
kěyǐ	yìzǐérshí	yòuyīhuí	ǒurán	议论 yìlùn qǐ
can	exchange sons as food	and once	casually	commenting on

一	個	不好	的	人，	他	便	說	不但
yī	gè	bùhǎo	de	rén	tā	biàn	说 shuō	búdàn
a	class.	no good	part.	person	he	then	said	not only

該	殺，	還	當	“食肉寢皮”。	我
该 gāi	杀 shā	还 hái	当 dāng	shíròuqǐnpí	Wǒ
ought	to kill	in addition	should	eaten and flayed	I

那時	年紀	還小，	心跳了好	半天。
那时 nàshí	年纪 niánjì	还小 háixiǎo	xīntiàolehǎo	bàntiān
at that time	age	still young	heartbeat fast	half a day

前天	狼子村	佃戶	來	説	吃
Qiántiān	Lángzīcūn	diànhù	lái	说 shuō	chī
Two days before	Wolf Cub Village	tenant farmer	came	to tell	eat

心肝	的	事，	他	也	毫不	奇怪，
xīngān	de	shì	tā	yě	háobù	qíguài
heart liver	part.	story	his	too	scarcely	strange

不住的	點頭。	可見	心思	是	同	從前
bùzhùde	点头 diǎntóu	Kějiàn	xīnsi	shì	tóng	从前 cóngqián
continuously	nod	It is evident	mind	is	same	before

一样	狠。	既然	可以	“易子而食”，	便
yīyàng	hěn	Jìrán	kěyǐ	yì zǐ ér shí	biàn
same	vicious	Since	can	exchange sons as food	then

什麼	都	易得，	什麼人	都	吃得。	我
什么 shénme	dōu	yìde	什么 shénme	dōu	chī	Wǒ
anything	even	exchanged	anybody	all	eaten	I

從前	單聽	他	講道	理，	也	胡塗
从前 cóngqián	单听 dānting	tā	讲道 jiǎngdào	lǐ	yě	hútu
previously	listen to	his	lecture	logic	also	confused

過去；	現在	曉得	他	講道	理	的
过去 guòqu	现在 xiànzài	晓得 xiǎode	tā	讲道 jiǎngdào	lǐ	de
in the past	now	know	his	lecture	logic	part.

時候，	不但	唇	邊	還	抹著	人油，
时候 shíhou	bùdàn	chún	边 biān	还 hái	抹着 mǒzhe	rényóu
when	not only	lips	edges	still	smeared	human fat

而且	心裡	滿裝著	吃人	的	意思。
érqiě	xīnli	满装着 mǎnzhuāngzhe	chīrén	de	yìsi
but also	heart	filled	eat people	part.	ideas

Notes

退一步想 tuì yībù xiǎng – to think over

李时珍 Lǐ Shízhēn (1518-1593) – Ming botanist and pharmacologist, author of *Herbal Medicines*

Chapter VI

黑漆漆的，不知是日是夜。趙家的狗又叫起來了。

獅子似的凶心，兔子的怯弱，狐狸的狡猾，……

Translation 1.

Pitch dark. I don't know whether it is day or night. The Chao family dog has started barking again.

The fierceness of a lion, the timidity of a rabbit, the craftiness of a fox....

Translation 2.

It's pitch black; I am not sure whether it's night or day. The Zhao family's dog is barking again.

It reminds me of the ferocity of a lion, the timidity of a rabbit, or the cunning of a fox....

Synthesis

黑漆漆的，	不知	是	日	是	夜。	趙家
Hēiqīqī	bùzhī	shì	rì	shì	yè	赵 Zhào jiā
Black as paint (pitch)	don't know	is	day	is	night	Zhao family

的	狗	又	叫起來了。	獅子	似的	凶心，
de	gǒu	yòu	jiàoqǐlaile	Shīzi	shide	xiōngxīn
part.	dog	again	starts barking	Lion	as	fierce

兔子的	怯弱，	狐狸的	狡猾，
tùzi	qièruò	húli	jiǎohuá
rabbit	timid	fox	cunning

Chapter VII extract 1

我曉得他們的方法，直捷殺了，是不肯的，而且也不敢，怕有禍祟。所以他們大家聯絡，佈滿了羅網，逼我自戕。試看前幾天街上男女的樣子，和這幾天我大哥的作為，便足可悟出八九分了。最好是解下腰帶，掛在樑上，自己緊緊勒死；他們沒有殺人的罪名，又償了心願，自然都歡天喜地的發出一種嗚嗚咽咽的笑聲。否則驚嚇憂愁死了，雖則略瘦，也還可以首肯幾下。

Translation 1.

I know their way; they are not willing to kill anyone outright, nor do they dare, for fear of the consequences. Instead they have banded together and set traps everywhere, to force me to kill myself. The behaviour of the men and women in the street a few days ago, and my elder brother's attitude these last few days, make it quite obvious. What they like best is for a man to take off his belt, and hang himself from a beam; for then they can enjoy their heart's desire without being blamed for murder. Naturally that sets them roaring with delighted laughter. On the other hand, if a man is frightened or worried to death, although that makes him rather thin, they still nod in approval.

Translation 2.

I know their methods. They are unwilling to kill me outright. They dare not do that, for fear of the consequences. Thus, they have all conspired with each other to lay a trap, to force me into killing myself. One can surmise most of this simply by observing the behaviour of the men and women on the street these last few days, along with the way my brother is acting. The best thing would be to undo my belt and hang myself from the rafters. That way, they would be satisfied, without feeling guilty of murder. This would of course make them howl with laughter. On the other hand, if I was driven to death by fear and worry, they would still nod in approval; even if it meant that I became thinner.

Synthesis

我	曉得	他們	的	方法,	直捷	殺	了,
Wǒ	晓得 xiǎode	他们 tāmen	de	fāngfǎ	zhíjié	杀 shā	le
I	know	they	part.	method	directly	to kill	part.

是	不肯	的,	而且	也	不敢,	怕	有
shì	bukěn	de	érqiě	yě	bùgǎn	pà	yǒu
are	not prepared to	part.	but	not	dare	afraid	there are

禍祟。	所以	他們	大家	聯絡,	佈満	了
祸祟 huòsuì	Suǒyǐ	他们 tāmen	dàjiā	联络 liánluò	佈满 bùmǎn	le
consequences	so	they	all	get together	cast	part.

羅網,	逼	我	自戕。	試	看	前幾天
罗网 luówǎng	bī	wǒ	zìqiāng	试 Shì	kàn	qiánjǐtiān
net	to force	me	suicide	Try	to see	a few days before

街上	男女	的	樣子,	和	这幾天	我
jiēshang	nánnǚ	de	样子 yàngzi	hé	这几天 qiánjǐtiān	wǒ
on the street	men women	part.	manner	and	the past few days	me

大哥	的	作為,	便	足	可	悟	出
dàgē	de	作为 zuòwéi	biàn	zú	kě	wù	chū
eldest brother	part.	conduct	then	ample	can	understand	comp.

八九分	了。	最好	是	解下	腰帶,
bā jiǔ fēn	le	Zuìhǎo	shì	jiěxià	腰带 yāodài
eight or nine tenths	part.	Best	is	untie	belt

掛	在	樑	上,	自己	緊緊	勒死;
挂 guà	zài	liáng	shàng	zìjǐ	紧紧 jǐnjǐn	lēisǐ
to hang	at	roof beam	on	oneself	tightly	strangle

他們	沒有	殺人	的	罪名,	又	償了
他们 tāmen	没 méiyǒu	杀 shārén	de	zuìmíng	yòu	chángle
they	not	murder	part.	be accused	and	to pay

心願,	自然	都	歡天喜地	的	發出
心愿 xīnyuàn	zìrán	dōu	欢天喜地 huāntiānxǐdì	de	发出 fāchū
craving	naturally	all	delighted	part.	start

一種	嗚嗚咽咽	的	笑聲。	否則	驚嚇
yīzhǒng	呜呜咽咽 wūwūyèyè	de	笑声 xiàoshēng	Fǒuzé	jīngxià
a kind of	crying	part.	laughter	If	frightened

憂愁	死了,	雖則	略瘦,	也	還	可以
yōuchóu	sǐle	虽则 suīzé	lüèshòu	yě	还 hái	kěyǐ
worried	die	however	slim	also	still	can

首肯	幾下。
shǒukěn	几下 jǐxià
nod approval	several times

Notes

佈滿了羅網　bùmǎnle luówǎng – cast the net, set a trap

Chapter VII extract 2

他們是只會吃死肉的！——記得什麼書上説，有一種東西，叫"海乙那"的，眼光和樣子都很難看；時常吃死肉，連極大的骨頭，都細細嚼爛，嚥下肚子去，想起來也教人害怕。"海乙那"是狼的親眷，狼是狗的本家。前天趙家的狗，看我幾眼，可見他也同謀，早已接洽。老頭子眼看著地，豈能瞞得我過。

最可憐的是我的大哥，他也是人，何以毫不害怕；而且合夥吃我呢？還是歷來慣 了，不以為非呢？還是喪了良心，明知故犯呢？

我詛咒吃人的人，先從他起頭；要勸轉吃人的人，也先從他下手。

<u>Translation 1.</u>

They only eat dead flesh! I remember reading somewhere of a hideous beast, with an ugly look in its eye, called ‘hyena’ which often eats dead flesh. Even the largest bones it grinds into fragments and swallows: the mere thought of this is enough to terrify one. Hyenas are related to wolves, and wolves belong to the canine species. The other day the dog in the Chao house looked at me several times; obviously it is in the plot too and has become their accomplice. The old man's eyes were cast down, but that did not deceive me!

The most deplorable is my elder brother. He is also a man, so why is he not afraid, why is he plotting with others to eat me? Is it that when one is used to it he no longer thinks it a crime? Or is it that he has hardened his heart to do something he knows is wrong?

In cursing man-eaters, I shall start with my brother, and in dissuading man-eaters, I shall start with him too.

<u>*Translation 2.*</u>

They can only eat dead meat! I remember a book that described something called a 'hyena,' the eyes and appearance of which were both hideous. It normally eats dead meat, even to the point of chewing up and swallowing large bones. It is quite frightening to think about. The 'hyena' is a member of the wolf family. Dogs are also members of the wolf family. Judging by the way the Zhao family's dog was looking at me the other day, it has been in connivance with the others for quite some time. It cannot fool me by staring at the ground.

The saddest part is my brother. He is a man. How is it he not even the least bit afraid of joining with the others in eating me? Has he become so used to the idea that he does not think of it as being something wrong? Or, has he wilfully rejected all morality, knowing full well that it is wrong? I curse all those who eat people. In cursing those who eat people, I shall start with him. If I were to dissuade people from eating people, then I would start with him.

<u>Synthesis</u>

他們	是	只會	吃	死	肉	的!	記得
他们 Tāmen	shì	zhǐhuì	chī	sǐ	ròu	de	记得 Jìde
They	are	only	eat	dead	meat	part.	Remember

什麼	書	上	說,	有	一種	東西,
什么 shénme	书 shū	shàng	说 shuō	yǒu	yīzhǒng	东西 dōngxi
some	book	on	said	have	a kind	thing

叫	"海乙那"	的,	眼	光	和	樣子
jiào	hǎiyǐnà	de	yǎn	guāng	hé	样子 yàngzi
called	hyena transliteration	part.	eyes	gleam	and	looks

都	很	難看;	時常	吃	死	肉,
dōu	hěn	难看 nánkàn	时常 shícháng	chī	sǐ	ròu
entirely	very	ugly	often	eat	dead	meat

連	極大的	骨頭,	都	細細	嚼	爛,
连 lián	jídàde	骨头 gǔtou	dōu	细细 xìxì	jiáo	烂 làn
even	enormous	bone	all	fine	chew	thoroughly

嚥	下	肚子	去,	想起來	也	教人
yàn	xià	dùzi	qù	xiǎngqilai	yě	jiāo rén
swallow	down	belly	compli.*	think of	and	cause people

害怕。	“海乙那”	是	狼的	親眷,	狼
hàipà	Hǎiyǐnà	shì	lángde	亲 qīnjuàn	láng
fear	Hyena - transliteration	is	wolf's	relative	wolf

是	狗的	本家。	前天	趙家	的	狗,
shì	gǒude	běnjiā	Qiántiān	赵家 Zhào jiā	de	gǒu
is	dog	family	Before yesterday	Zhao family	part.	dog

看	我	幾	眼,	可見	他	也	同謀,
kàn	wǒ	儿 jǐ	yǎn	kějiàn	tā	yě	tóngmóu
look	me	several	looks	obvious	he	also	conspire with sb.

早已	接洽。	老頭子	眼,	看著	地,	豈
zǎoyǐ	jiēqià	老头子 Lǎotóuzi	yǎn	看着 kànzhe	dì	岂 qǐ
long time	arranged	Old fellow	eyes	looked	ground	how

能	瞞得	我	過。	最	可憐	的	是
néng	瞒得 mánde	wǒ	过 guò	Zuì	kělián	de	shì
can	conceal from	me	suffix*	The most	lamentable	part.	is

是	我的	大哥,	他	也	是	人,	何以
shì	wǒ	dàgē	tā	yě	shì	rén	héyǐ
is	my	elder brother	he	also	is	man	so

毫不	害怕;	而且	合夥	吃	我	呢?
háobù	hàipà	érqiě	合伙 héhuǒ	chī	wǒ	ne
not at ally	afraid	besides	others	eat	me	part.

* 去 compliment, 過 (过) guò suffix

還是	歷來	慣	了,	不	以為	非	呢?
还是 háishì	历来 lìlái	惯 guàn	le	bù	以为 yǐwéi	fēi	ne
but	always been	used to	part.	not	believing	wrong	part.

還是	喪	了	良心,	明知故犯	呢?
还是 Háishì	sàng	le	liángxīn	míngzhīgùfàn	ne
or	lost	part.	scruples	willfully idiom.	part.

我	詛咒	吃人的人,	先從	他	起頭;
Wǒ	诅咒 zǔzhòu	chīrénde rén	先从 xiāncóng	tā	起头 qǐtóu
I	curse	cannibal people	first	him	begin

要勸	轉	吃人的人,	也	先從	他
要劝 yāoquàn	转 zhuǎn	chīrénde rén	yě	先从 xiāncóng	tā
persuade	then onto	cannibal people	so	first	him

下手。
xiàshǒu
to start

<u>Chapter VIII extract 1</u>

其實這種道理，到了現在，他們也該早已懂得，……

忽然來了一個人；年紀不過二十左右，相貌是不很看得清楚，滿面笑容，對了我點頭，他的笑也不像真笑。我便問他，“吃人的事，對麼？”他仍然笑著說，“不是 荒年，怎麼會吃人。”我立刻就曉得，他也是一夥，喜歡吃人的；便自勇氣百倍，偏要問他。

“對麼？”

“這等事問他什麼。你真會……說笑話。……今天天氣很好。”

天氣是好，月色也很亮了。可是我要問你，“對麼？”

Translation 1.

Actually, such arguments should have convinced them long ago....

Suddenly someone came in. He was only about twenty years old and I did not see his features very clearly. His face was wreathed in smiles, but when he nodded to me his smile did not seem genuine. I asked him 'Is it right to eat human beings?'

Still smiling, he replied, 'When there is no famine how can one eat human beings?'

I realized at once, he was one of them; but still I summoned up courage to repeat my question:

'Is it right?'

'What makes you ask such a thing? You really are fond of a joke.... It is very fine today.'

'It is fine, and the moon is very bright. But I want to ask you: Is it right?'

Translation 2.

As a matter of fact, they should have understood this kind of reasoning a long time ago...

Suddenly, someone came in. He was about twenty years of age, but I could not make out his face clearly. He wore a broad smile on his face, but it was not a real smile. He nodded his head toward me. I asked him, 'Is it right to eat people?' Still smiling, he replied, 'There is no famine, why would anyone want eat somebody?' With that, I knew that he was with the rest of them. He liked to eat people. Then I summoned up my courage and repeated the question.

'Is it right?'

‘Why do you ask such a thing? You must be fond of making jokes.... The weather is nice today.’

‘The weather is nice indeed. The moon is also very bright. But, I want to ask you something else.’

‘Is it right?’

Synthesis

其實	這種	道理,	到了	現在,	他們	也
其实 Qíshí	这种 zhèzhǒng	dàolǐ	dàole	现在 xiànzài	他们 tāmen	yě
In fact	this kind of	approach	finally	now	they	also

該	早已	懂得,	忽然	來了	一個人;
该 gāi	zǎoyǐ	懂得 dǒngde	hūrán	láile	yīgèrén
should	long ago	understood	suddenly	arrived	someone

年紀	不過	二十	左右,	相貌	是	不很
年纪 niánjì	bùguò	èrshí	zuǒyòu	xiàngmào	shì	bùhěn
aged	only	twenty	approximately	appearance	is	not very

看得	清楚,	滿面	笑容,	對了	我	點頭,
kànde	qīngchu	满面 mǎnmiàn	xiàoróng	对 duìle	wǒ	点头 diǎntóu
see	clear	face full	smile	towards	me	nod

他的	笑	也	不像	真	笑。	我	便	問	他,
tā	xiào	yě	bùxiàng	zhēn	xiào	Wǒ	biàn	问 wèn	tā
his	smile	also	not seem	real	smile	I	then	ask	him

“吃人的	事,	對麼?”	他	仍然	笑著	說,
chīrénde	shì	对么 duìmá	Tā	réngrán	xiàozhe	说 shuō
men-eating	business	eh?	he	still	smiling	said

“不是	荒年,	怎麼	會	吃人。”	我	立刻
bùshì	huāng nián	怎么 zěnme	会 huì	chīrén	Wǒ	likè
no	famine	how	can	eat people	I	instantly

就	曉得,	他	也	是	一夥,	喜歡
jiù	xiǎode	tā	yě	shì	一伙 yīhuǒ	喜欢 xǐhuan
then	knew	he	also	is	one of them	like

吃人的;	便	自勇氣	百倍,	偏要	問	他。
chīrénde	biàn	zìyǒngqì	bǎibèi	piānyào	问 wèn	tā
cannibals	then	courage	a hundredfold	insist	ask	him

"對麼?"	這	等事	問	他什麼。	你	真	會
对么 Duìmá	这 Zhè	děngshi	问 wèn	tā shénme	Nǐ	zhēn	会 huì
Is it right?	This	thing	ask	is what	You	really	can

會	説	笑話。	今天	天氣	很好。	天氣
会 huì	说 shuō	xiàohuà	Jīntiān	tiānqì	hěnhào	Tiānqì
can	tell	joke	Today	weather	nice	Weather

很好.	月色	也	很	亮	了。	可是	我
hěnhào	yuèsè	yě	hěn	liàng	le	Kěshì	wǒ
nice	moonlight	also	very	bright	part.	But	I

要	問	你,	"對麼?"
yāo	问 wèn	nǐ	对么 Duìmá?
want	ask	you	Is it right?

Chapter VIII extract 2

他不以為然了。含含糊胡的答道，“不……”

“不對？他們何以竟吃？！”

“沒有的事……”

“沒有的事？狼子村現吃；還有書上都寫著，通紅斬新！”

他便變了臉，鐵一般青。睜著眼說，“有許有的，這是從來如此……”

“從來如此，便對麼？”

“我不同你講這些道理；總之你不該説，你説便是你錯！”

我直跳起來，張開眼，這人便不見了。全身出了一大片汗。他的年紀，比我大哥小得遠,居然也是一夥；

這一定是他娘老子先教的。還怕已經教給他兒子了；所以連小孩子，也都惡狠狠的看我。

Translation 1.

He looked disconcerted, and muttered: 'No....'

'No? Then why do they still do it?'

'What are you talking about?'

'What am I talking about? They are eating men now in Wolf Cub Village, and you can see it written all over the books, in fresh red ink.'

His expression changed, and he grew ghastly pale. 'It may be so,' he said, staring at me. 'It has always been like that....'

'Is it right because it has always been like that?'

'I refuse to discuss these things with you. Anyway, you shouldn't talk about it. Whoever talks about it is in the wrong!'

I leaped up and opened my eyes wide, but the man had vanished. I was soaked with perspiration. He was much younger than my elder brother, but even so he was in it. He must have been taught by his parents. And I am afraid he has already taught his son: that is why even the children look at me so fiercely.

Translation 2.

Disconcerted, he replied with a vaguely annoyed grumble: 'No....'

'If it's not right, then why do they continue to eat people?'

'I don't know what you're talking about...'

'You don't? People are being eaten in Wolf Cub Village

as we speak. It's also written in all the books in blood-red ink!'

His facial expression changed. He became quite pale. He stared at me and said: 'That may be. But, it's always been that way....'

'Does the fact that it's always been that way make it right?'

'I'm not going to talk about these things with you. In any case, you shouldn't talk about this. It's wrong to talk about it!'

I jumped up and opened my eyes, but he had disappeared. I broke out into a sweat all over my body. He was much younger than my older brother, yet he was a part of their group. This was definitely something that he learnt from his parents. I fear he may have already taught it to his son as well. That's why the little children are glaring at me with that look of hatred.

<u>Synthesis</u>

他	不以為然	了。	含	含糊	胡	的
Tā	不以为然 bùyǐwéirán	le	Hán	hánhú	hú	de
he	disconcerted (idiom)	part.	Muttered	vaguely	offended	part.

答道,	不…	不對?	他們	何以	竟	吃?!
dādào	bù	不对 bùduì	他们 tāmen	héyǐ	jìng	chī
in reply	no	No?	They	why	go as far as	eating

没有的事…	没有的事?	狼子村	現	吃;
méiyǒudeshì	méiyǒudeshì	Lángzǐcūn	现 xiàn	chī
They don't….	They don't?	Wolf Cub Village	now	eat

還有	書	上	都	寫著,	通紅	斬新!
还有 háiyǒu	shū	shàng	dōu	写着 xiězhe	通红 tōnghóng	斩新 zhǎnxīn
furthermore	book	on	*even*	written	very red	freshly beheaded

他 便 變了 臉, 鐵 一般 青。
tā biàn 变了 biànle 脸 liǎn 铁 tiě yì bān qīng
he then changed face iron a sort of greenish black

睜著 眼 說, 有許有的, 這 是 從來
睁 Zhēngzhe yǎn 说 shuō 有许有的 yǒuxǔyǒude 这 zhè shì 从来 cónglái
Opened eyes said maybe this is always

如此… 從來 如此, 便 對麼? 我 不同
rúcǐ 从来 cónglái rúcǐ biàn 对么 duì Wǒ bùtóng
so always so then right? I not agree

你 講 這些 道理; 總之 你 不該
nǐ 讲 jiǎng 这些 zhèxiē dàolǐ 总之 zǒngzhī nǐ 不该 bùgāi
you say these ideas anyway you should not

說, 你 說 便 是 你 錯! 我 直
说 shuō nǐ 说 shuō biàn shì nǐ 错 cuò Wǒ zhí
talk you said then is you wrong I directly

跳起來, 張開 眼, 這 人 便 不見 了。
tiàoqǐlai 张 zhāngkāi yǎn 这 zhè rén biàn 不见 bùjiàn le
jumped up open up eyes this person then not see part.

全身 出了 一大 片 汗。他的 年紀, 比
Quánshēn chūle yī dà piàn hàn Tāde 年纪 niánjì bì
Entire body go out a big class.* sweat His age compared

我 大哥 小 得 遠, 居然 也 是
wǒ dàgē xiǎo de 远 yuǎn jūrán yě shì
my eldest brother small part. far unexpectedly also is

一夥; 這 一定 是 他 娘 老子
yīhuǒ 这 zhè yīdìng shì tā niáng lǎozi
one of them this certainly is his mother father

先 教的。 還 怕 已經 教 給 他
xiān jiāode 还 Hái pà 已经 yǐjīng jiāo 给 gěi tā
first taught What is more fear already teach give his

兒子	了;	所以	連	小孩子,	也	都
儿子 érzi	le	suǒyǐ	连 lián	xiǎoháizi	yě	dōu
son	part.	therefore	connection	children	also	all

惡狠狠	的	看	我。
恶狠狠 èhěnhěn	de	kàn	wǒ
very fierce	part.	look	me

*片 classifier

Chapter IX

自己想吃人，又怕被別人吃了，都用著疑心極深的眼光，面面相覷。……

去了這心思，放心做事走路吃飯睡覺，何等舒服。這只是一條門檻，一個關頭。 他們可是父子兄弟夫婦朋友師生仇敵和各不相識的人，都結成一夥，互相勸勉，互相 牽掣，死也不肯跨過這一步。

Translation 1.

Wanting to eat men, at the same time afraid of being eaten themselves, they all look at each other with the deepest suspicion....

How comfortable life would be for them if they could rid themselves of such obsessions and go to work, walk, eat and sleep at ease. They have only this one step to take. Yet fathers and sons, husbands and wives, brothers, friends, teachers and students, sworn enemies and even strangers, have all joined in this conspiracy, discouraging and preventing each other from taking this step.

仇官仇富的"仇恨标签"不要随便贴

没有反思就没有人性的复苏

"安全"决定仕途是大势所趋

环保也需"走基层"

一条寻狗微博的"娱乐至死"

Page 2 of the February 20, 2013, edition of China Youth Daily.
See article by Zhang Ming 张鸣 on the right-hand side.
没有反思就没有人性的复苏

There are many people [in our country] who yearn for a repeat of the Cultural Revolution, for another violent convulsion. This should send shivers through us all. If we refuse to review and re-examine the Cultural Revolution, we might still be a society of cannibals. And if we are such a society, it doesn't matter how bright we might seem on the outside, or how fully we enjoy the fruits of civilisation — *we are still a den of cannibals.* (authors italics)

Translation 2.

They themselves want to eat people, but do not want to be eaten by others. They all look at each other with suspicion and fear....

If they could just rid themselves of these ideas, they could work, eat and sleep without worrying. How pleasant that would be. A single step. Yet, fathers, sons, husbands, wives, friends, teachers, students, enemies and even strangers have banded together, agreeing they would rather die than take this one step.

Synthesis

自己	想	吃	人,	又	怕	被	别人	吃了,
Zìjǐ	xiǎng	chī	rén	yòu	pà	bèi	biérén	chīle
Oneself	want	eat	people	and	fear	pass.voice	other people	eaten

都	用	著	疑心	極深	的	眼光,
dōu	yòng	着 zhe	yíxīn	极深 jíshēn	de	yǎnguāng
all	therefore	part.	suspicion	deep	part.	looked

面面相覷。	去了	這	心思,	放心	做事
miànmiànxiāngqù	Qùle	这 zhè	xīnsi	fàngxīn	zuòshì
look in dismay (idiom)	Take away	this	idea	relieved	to work

走路	吃飯	睡覺,	何等	舒服。	這	只是
zǒulù	吃饭 chīfàn	睡觉 shuìjiào	héděng	shūfu	这 Zhè	zhǐshì
to walk	to eat	to sleep	how	comfortable	This	simply

一	條	門檻,	一	個	關頭。	他們	可是
yī	tiáo	门槛 ménkǎn	yī	个	关头 guāntóu	他们 Tāmen	kěshì
a	class.	step	a	gè	moment	They	however

父子	兄弟	夫婦	朋友	師生	仇敵
fùzǐ	xiōngdì	夫妇 fūfù	péngyou	shīshēng	chóudí
father & son	brothers	couples	friend	teachers & students	enemy

和	各	不相識的人,	都	結成	一夥,	互相
hé	gè	不相识的人 bùxiāngshíderén	dōu	jiéchéng	一伙 yīhuǒ	hùxiāng
and	every	stranger	all	form	group	mutually

勸勉,	互相	牽掣,	死	也不	肯	跨過
劝勉 quànmiǎn	hùxiāng	牵掣 qiān chè	sǐ	yěbù	kěn	跨过 kuàguò
counsel	mutually	discourage	die	than	agree	cross

這	一	步。
这 zhè	yī	bù
this	one	step

Chapter X extract 1

大清早，去尋我大哥；他立在堂門外看天，我便走到他背後，攔住門，格外沉靜， 格外和氣的對他說，

“大哥，我有話告訴你。”

“你說就是，” 他趕緊回過臉來，點點頭。

“我只有幾句話，可是說不出來。大哥，大約當初野蠻的人，都吃過一點人。後來因為心思不同，有的不吃人了，一味要好，便變了人，變了真的人。有的卻還吃，—— 也同蟲子一樣，有的變了魚鳥猴子，一直變到人。有的不要好，至今還是蟲子。這吃人的人比不吃人的人，何等慚愧。怕比蟲子的慚愧猴子，還差得很遠很遠。

Translation 1.

Early this morning I went to look for my elder brother. He was standing outside the hall door looking at the sky, when I walked up behind him, stood between him and the door, and with exceptional poise and politeness said to him:

'Brother, I have something to say to you.'

'Well, what is it?' he asked, quickly turning towards me and nodding.

'It is very little, but I find it difficult to say. Brother, probably all primitive people ate a little human flesh to begin with. Later, because their outlook changed, some of them stopped, and because they tried to be good they changed into men, changed into real men. But some are still eating, just like reptiles. Some have changed into fish, birds, monkeys and finally men; but some do not try to be good and remain reptiles still. When those who eat men compare themselves with those who do not, how ashamed they must be. Probably much more ashamed than the reptiles are before monkeys.'

<u>*Translation 2.*</u>

Early this morning, I went to look for my older brother; he was standing just outside the hall door looking at the sky. I walked up behind him in the doorway. The very calmly and cautiously said to him, 'I have something I want to tell you.'

He quickly turned around and nodded.

'I just have a few things to say, but I don't know quite how to put it. I'm sure all primitive humans ate a little human flesh at first. Then, later on, some of them stopped eating human flesh because their thinking changed. They because they simply wanted to be better, change into human beings, real human beings. However, there were some that refused to stop eating human flesh. The same as with insects, some of which later became fish, birds,

monkeys and eventually, humans. Some of them did not want to become better, and remain insects even today. How ashamed these people who eat human flesh must feel compared to those that do not. I'm sorry to say they must feel far more ashamed than insects are compared to monkeys.'

Synthesis

大清早,	去	尋	我	大哥;	他	立	在
Dàqīngzǎo	qù	寻 xún	wǒ	dàgē	tā	lì	zài
Early morning	go	look for	my	elder brother	he	stand	at

堂	門	外	看	天,	我	便	走	到
táng	门 mén	wài	kàn	tiān	wǒ	biàn	zǒu	dào
hall	door	outside	looking	sky	I	then	walk	to

他	背後,	攔住	門,	格外	沉靜,	格外
tā	bèihòu	拦住 lánzhù	门 mén	géwài	chénjìng	géwài
him	behind	stop	door	especially	softly	especially

和氣	的	對	他	説,	大哥,	我	有
héqi	de	对 duì	tā	说 shuō	dàgē	wǒ	yǒu
politely	part.	to	him	said	elder brother	I	have

話	告訴	你。	你	説	就是,	他
话 huà	告诉 gàosu	nǐ	Nǐ	说 shuō	jiùshì	tā
words	to tell	you	You	say	namely	he

趕緊	回過	臉來,	點點頭。	我	只有
赶紧 gǎnjǐn	回过 huíguò	脸来 liǎnlái	点点头 diǎndiǎntóu	Wǒ	zhǐyǒu
hurriedly	turning around	to face	nodded	I	only

幾	句	話	可是	説	不	出來。
几 jǐ	句 jù	话 huà	kěshì	说 shuō	bù	chūlái
a few	class.	words	but	talk	not	come out

大哥,	大約	當初	野蠻	的	人,	都	吃過
Dàgē	大约 dàyuē	dāngchū	野蛮 yěmán	de	rén	dōu	吃过 chīguò
Elder brother	about	that time	barbarian	part.	people	all	ate

一點	人。	後來	因為	心思	不同，	有的
一点 yīdiǎn	rén	后来 Hòulái	因为 yīnwèi	xīnsi	bùtóng	yǒude
a bit of	men	Later	because	ideas	changed	some

不	吃	人	了，	一味	要好，	便	變	了	人，
bù	chī	rén	le	yíwèi	yàohǎo	biàn	变 biàn	le	rén
not	eat	people	part.	simply	be better	then	change	part.	people

變	了	真的	人。	有的	卻	還	吃，	也
变 biàn	le	zhēnde	rén	Yǒude	却 què	还 hái	chī	yě
change	part.	really	people	Some	however	still	eat	also

同	蟲子	一樣，	有的	變了	魚	鳥	猴子，
tòng	虫子 chóngzi	一样 yīyàng	yǒude	变了 biànle	鱼 yú	鸟 niǎo	hóuzi
like	insects	same	some	changed	fishes	birds	monkeys

一直	變到	人。	有的	不要好，	至今	還是
yīzhí	变到 biàndào	rén	Yǒude	yàohǎo	zhìjīn	还是 háishì
directly	becoming	men	Some	not better	until now	still

蟲子。	這	吃人的	人，	比	不吃人的
虫子 chóngzi	这 Zhè	chīrénde	rén	bǐ	chīrénde
insects	These	cannibal	people	compared to	non man-eating

人，	何等	慚愧。	怕	比	蟲子	的
rén	héděng	惭愧 cánkuì	Pà	bǐ	虫子 chóngzi	de
people	how	shamefull	Afraid	than	insects	part.

慚愧	猴子，	還	差得	很遠很遠。
惭愧 cánkui	hóuzi	还 hái	chàde	很远很远 hěnyuǎn hěnyuǎn
shame	monkeys	still	worse	by far

Chapter X extract 2

“易牙蒸了他兒子，給桀紂吃，還是一直從前的事。誰曉得從盤古開闢天地以後， 一直吃到易牙的兒子；從易牙的兒子，一直吃到徐錫林；從徐錫林，又一直吃到狼子村捉住的人。去年城裡殺了犯人，還有一個生痨病的人，用饅頭蘸血舐。

“他們要吃我，你一個人，原也無法可想；然而又何必去入夥。吃人的人，什麼事做不出；他們會吃我，也會吃你，一夥裏面，也會自吃。但只要轉一步，只要立刻改了，也就是人人太平。雖然從來如此，我們今天也可以格外要好，説是不能！大哥， 我相信你能説，前天佃戶要減租，你説過不能。”

<u>Translation 1.</u>

'In ancient times Yi Ya boiled his son for Chieh and Chou to eat; that is the old story. But actually since the creation of heaven and earth by Pan Ku men have been eating each other, from the time of Yi Ya's son to the time of Hsu Hsi-lin, and from the time of Hsu Hsi-lin down to the man caught in Wolf Cub Village. Last year they executed a criminal in the city, and a consumptive soaked a piece of bread in his blood and sucked it.

'They want to eat me, and of course you can do nothing about it single-handed; but why should you join them? As man-eaters they are capable of anything. If they eat me, they can eat you as well; members of the same group can still eat each other. But if you will just change your ways immediately, then everyone will have peace. Although this has been going on since time immemorial, today we could make a special effort to be good, and say this is not to be done! I'm sure you can say so, brother. The other day when the tenant wanted the rent reduced, you said it couldn't be done.'

盤古氏

Pangu 盘古 'the first man, who opened up heaven and earth' (p82)

Translation 2.

'We all know the ancient story about Yi Ya cooking his son for the tyrant kings, Jie and Zhou, to eat. Anybody knows from the time Pangu created the heavens and earth, down to Yi Ya's son, and then from Xu Xilin to the man caught in Wolf Cub Village, people have continued to eat other people? Last year when a criminal was executed in town, a man suffering from tuberculosis even dipped his steamed bun into the blood so that he could lick it.

'They want to eat me. I know that there's nothing you can do about it as an individual. But, why do you have to join them? A person that eats others is capable of anything. If they can eat me, they can eat you as well as each other. But, if you change your ways today, everyone can live in peace. Even if it's always been like this, we could make a special effort and try to be better, starting today; say that this is unacceptable! I believe you can say such a thing. The other day, when the tenant farmer asked for his rent be reduced, you said it was unacceptable.'

Synthesis

易牙	蒸了	他	兒子,	給	桀	紂	吃,
Yì Yá	zhēng	Tā	儿子 érzi	给 gěi	Jié	Zhòu	chī
name	boiled	his	son	gave	a tyrant	a tyrant	to eat

還是	一直從前	的	事。	誰	曉得
háishì	一直从前 yīzhí cóngqián	de	Shì	谁 Shéi	晓得 xiǎode
however	ancient	part.	business	Anybody	knows

從	盤古	開闢	天地	以後,	一直
从 cóng	盘古 Pángǔ	开辟 kāipì	tiāndì	以后 yǐhòu	yīzhí
since	the Creator	created	heaven and earth	after	then

吃到	易牙	的	兒子;	從	易牙	的	兒子,
chī	Yì Yá	de	儿子 érzi	从 cóng	Yì Yá	de	儿子 érzi
eat	name	part.	son	from	name	part.	son

一直	吃到	徐錫林;	從	徐錫林,	又
yīzhí	chī	徐锡林 Xú Xīlín	从 cóng	徐锡林 Xú Xīlín	yòu
then	eat	name	since	name	also

一直	吃到	狼子村	捉住	的	人。	去年
yīzhí	chī	Lángzǐcūn	zhuōzhù	de	rén	Qùnián
then	eat	Wolf Cub Village	caught	part.	people	Last year

城裡	殺了	犯人,	還有	一	個	生癆病
chénglǐ	杀了 shāle	fànrén	还有 háiyǒu	yī	gè	生痨病 shēngláobìng
in town	killed	convict	furthermore	a	class.	consumptive

的	人,	用	饅頭	蘸	血	舐。	他們	要
de	rén	yòng	馒头 mántou	zhàn	xuè	shì	Tāmen	yāo
part.	man	used	steamed bun	to dip	blood	to lick	They	want

吃	我,	你	一個人,	原	也	無法
chī	wǒ	nǐ	yīgèrén	yuán	yě	无法 wúfǎ
to eat	me	you	an individual, one person	then	besides	unable

可想;	然而	又	何必	去	入	夥。	吃人的,
kěxiǎng	ránér	yòu	hébì	qù	rù	huǒ	Chīrénde
to imagine	however	also	no need	go	join	crowd	Cannibal

人,	什麼事	做不出;	他們	會	吃	我,
rén	什么事 shénmeshì	zuòbùchū	tāmen	会 huì	chī	wǒ
people	such a thing	impossible	they	could	eat	me

也	會	吃	你,	一	夥	裏面,	也
yě	会 huì	chī	nǐ	yī	huǒ	里面 lǐmiàn	yě
also	could	to eat	you	a	crowd	inside	and

會	自	吃。	但	只要	轉	一步,
会 huì	zì	chī	Dàn	zhǐyào	转 zhuǎn	一步 yībù
could	themselves	eat	But	provided	change direction	one step

只要	立刻	改了,	也	就是	人人	太平。
zhǐyào	lìkè	gǎile	yě	jiùshì	rénrén	tàipíng
then	at once	transformed	and	only then	everyone	peace & security

雖然	從來	如此,	我們	今天	也	可以
虽 Suīrán	从来 cónglái	rúcǐ	我们 wǒmen	jīntiān	yě	kěyǐ
Though	always	this way	we	today	also	can

格外	要好,	說	是	不能!	大哥,	我
géwài	yàohǎo	说 shuō	shì	bùnéng	dàgē	我 wǒ
especially	harmonious	say	is	not possible	big brother	I

相信	你	說,	前天	佃戶	要	減	租,
xiāngxìn	nǐ	说 shuō	qiántiān before	diànhù	yāo	jiǎn	zū
convinced	you	say	yesterday	tenant farmer	asked	to lower	rent

你	說過	不能。
nǐ	说過 shuō	bùnéng
you	said	not possible

Notes

桀紂 Jie and Zhou – tyrants of the Three Dynasties Period

盤古 Pángǔ – The first living being and creator according to Chinese mythology

<u>Chapter X extract 3</u>

當初，他還只是冷笑，隨後眼光便兇狠起來，一到說破他們的隱情，那就滿臉都變成青色了。大門外立著一夥人，趙貴翁和他的狗，也在裏面，都探頭探腦的挨進來。 有的是看不出面貌，似乎用布蒙著；有的是仍舊青面獠牙，抿著嘴笑。我認識他們是一夥，都是吃人的人。可是也曉得他們心思很不一樣，一種是以為從來如此，應該吃的；一種是知道不該吃，可是

仍然要吃，又怕别人説破他，所以聽了我的話，越發氣憤不過，可是抿著嘴冷笑。

這時候，大哥也忽然顯出凶相，高聲喝道，

Translation 1.

At first he only smiled cynically, then a murderous gleam came into his eyes, and when I spoke of their secret his face turned pale. Outside the gate stood a group of people, including Mr Chao and his dog, all craning their necks to peer in. I could not see all their faces, for they seemed to be masked in cloths; some of them looked pale and ghastly still, concealing their laughter. I knew they were one band, all eaters of human flesh. But I also knew that they did not all think alike by any means. Some of them thought that since it had always been so, men should be eaten. Some of them knew that they should not eat men, but still wanted to; and they were afraid people might discover their secret; thus when they heard me they became angry, but they still smiled their. cynical, tight-lipped smile.

Suddenly my brother looked furious, and shouted in a loud voice:

Translation 2.

At first, he just simply sneered. Then, a malicious gleam appeared in his eyes, But when I began to talk about their secrets, his face turned green. A large crowd of people was standing outside the door. Zhao Guiweng and his dog amongst them. They were all pressing in straining to have a look. There were some whose faces I could not distinguish. It was as if they had covered their faces with a cloth. There were others who had that ferocious look. Their lips were pursed. I realized that they were a part of that group of cannibals. However, they each behaved differently. Some felt that things had always been this way, and that men should be eaten. Others knew that one should not eat men, but wanted to eat them anyway. These were afraid that I might try to talk them out of it. They became even more angry when they heard my words. Keeping their lips shut tight with their sneering smiles.

It was at that point that my older brother suddenly appeared and shouted furiously:

Synthesis

當初,	他	還	只是	冷笑,	隨後	眼光
当初 Dāngchū	tā	还 hái	zhǐshì	lěngxiào	随后 suíhòu	yǎnguāng
Then	he	just	simply	sneered	soon after	gleam

便	兇狠	起來,	一到	説	破	他們	的
biàn	xiōnghěn	qǐlai	yí dào	说 shuō	pò	他们 tāmen	de
angry	malicious	appeared	or	speak	expose	they	part.

隱情,	那就	滿臉	都	變成	青色	了。
隐情 yǐnqíng	nà jiù	满脸 mǎnliǎn	dōu	变成 biànchéng	青色 qīngsè	le
secrets	then	face	all	change	green	part.

大門	外	立著	一夥人,	趙貴翁	和
Dàmén	wài	立着 lìzhe	yīhuǒrén	赵贵翁 Zhào Guìwēng	hé
Main door	outside	stood	a crowd	person's name	and

他的	狗,	也	在	裏面,	都	探頭探腦
tāde	gǒu	yě	zài	里面 lǐmiàn	dōu	探头探脑 tàntóutànnǎo
his	dog	and	at	inside	all	idiom – straining to see

的	挨	進來。	有的是	看不出	面貌，
de	āi	进来 jìnlái	有的是 Yǒudeshì	kànbuchū	miànmào
part.	by turns	in	Some	cannot see	faces

似乎	用	布	蒙著;	有的是	仍舊
sìhū	yòng	bù	蒙着 mēngzhe	有的是 yǒudeshì	仍旧 réngjiù
as if	using	cloth	cover	some	still though

青面獠牙，	抿著	嘴笑。	我	認識	他們
qīngmiànliáoyá	抿着 mǐnzhe	zuǐxiào	Wǒ	认识 rènshi	他们 tāmen
idiom – ferocious-looking	pursed (lips)	smile	I	know	they

是	一	夥，	都	吃人的人。	可是	也	曉得
shì	yī	huǒ	dōu	chīrénderén	Kěshì	yě	晓得 xiǎode
are	a	gang	all	cannibals	But	also	know

他們	心思	很	不一樣，	一種	是	以為
他们 tāmen	xīnsi	hěn	不一样 bùyīyàng	一种 yīzhǒng	shì	以为 yǐ wéi
their	ideas	very	different	a kind	are	think, believe

從來	如此，	應該	吃的;	一種	是	知道
从来 cónglái	rúcǐ	应该 yīnggāi	chīde	一种 yīzhǒng	shì	zhīdào
always	in this way	should	eaten	a kind	are	know

不該	吃，	可是	仍然	要	吃，	又	怕
不该 bùgāi	chī	kěshì	réngrán	yāo	chī	yòu	pà
should not	eat	but	yet	want	eat	and	fear

別人	說	破	他，	所以	聽了	我的
biérén	说 shuō	pò	tā	suǒyǐ	听了 tīngle	wǒde
others	talk	expose	it	consequently	heard	my

話，	越發	氣憤	不過，	可是	抿著	嘴
话 huà	越发 yuèfā	气愤 qìfèn	不过 búguò	kěshì	抿着 mǐnzhe	zuǐ
words	more and more	furious	only	but	tight	mouth

冷笑。	這	時候，	大哥	也	忽然	顯出
lěngxiào	这 Zhè	时候 shíhòu	dàgē	yě	hūrán	显出 xiǎnchū
sneer	Zhis	time	elder brother	also	suddenly	appeared

凶相，	高聲	喝道，
xiōngxiàng	高声 gāoshēng	喝道 hèdào
furious	loudly	shouted out

Chapter X extract 4

"都出去！瘋子有什麼好看！"

這時候，我又懂得一件他們的巧妙了。他們豈但不肯改，而且早已佈置；預備下一個瘋子的名目罩上我。將來吃了，不但太平無事，怕還會有人見情。佃戶說的大家吃了一個惡人，正是這方法。這是他們的老譜！

陳老五也氣憤憤的直走進來。如何按得住我的口，我偏要對這夥人說，

"你們可以改了，從真心改起！要曉得將來容不得吃人的人，活在世上。

Translation 1.

'Get out of here, all of you! What is the point of looking at a madman?'

Then I realized part of their cunning. They would never be willing to change their stand, and their plans were all laid; they had stigmatized me as a madman. In future when I was eaten, not only would there be no trouble, but people would probably be grateful to them. When our tenant spoke of the villagers eating a bad character, it was exactly the same device. This is their old trick.

Old Chen came in too, in a great temper, but they could not stop my mouth, I had to speak to those people:

'You should change, change from the bottom of your hearts!' I said. 'You most know that in future there will be no place for man-eaters in the world.'

<u>*Translation 2.*</u>

'Get out of here! What's so interesting about a madman!'

It was also at this point that I began to realize how artful they were. Not only are they unwilling to change, they had this all arranged. They had made sure that I was marked as a madman. In the future, when they eat me, not only will nobody take question this, they will probably be grateful. When the tenant farmer told the story about how they had eaten the criminal in this way. It was part of their old ways.

Chen Laowu angrily stormed in. No matter how hard they tried to keep me from speaking, I could not hold myself back, insisting:

'You can change. You can make a change in your hearts! You know the world will not tolerate those who eat others in the future.'

<u>Synthesis</u>

都	出去!	瘋子	有	什麼	好看!	這
Dōu	chūqù	fēngzi	yǒu	什么 shénme	hǎokàn	这 Zhè
All	out!	Madman	has	what	appealing	This

時候,	我	又	懂得	一	件	他們	的
时候 shího	wǒ	yòu	dǒngde	yī	jiàn	他们 tāmen	de
time	I	also	understand	a	part	they	part.

巧妙	了。	他們	豈但	不	肯	改,
qiǎomiào	le	他们 Tāmen	岂但 kǎidàn	bù	kěn	gǎi
ingenuity	part.	They	not only	not	willing	to change

而且	早已	佈置;	預備	下	一	個	瘋子
érqiě	zǎoyǐ	布置 bùzhì	预备 yùbèi	xià	yī	个 gè	疯子 fengzi
but also	long since	settled	fix	under	a	class.	madman

的	名目	罩上	我。	將來	吃了,	不但
de	míng mù	zhào	wǒ	将来 Jiānglái	chīle	bùdàn
part.	name	cover	me	In the future	eaten	not only

太平無事,	怕	還	會	有	人	見情。
太平无事 tàipíngwúshì	pà	还 hái	会 huì	yǒu	rén	见情 jiànqíng
idiom – all is well	fear	still	can	have	people	grateful

佃戶	說	的	大家	吃了	一	個	惡人,
佃户 Diànhù	说 shuō	de	dàjiā	chīle	yī	个 gè	恶人 èrén
Tenant farmer	said	part.	everyone	eaten	a	class.	evil person

正是	這	方法。	這	是	他們	的	老譜!
zhèngshì	这 zhè	fāngfǎ	这 Zhè	shì	他们 tāmen	de	老谱 lǎopǔ
exactly	this	way	This	is	they	part.	old ways

陳老五	也	氣憤憤	的	直走	進來。
陈老五 Chén Lǎowǔ	yě	气愤愤 qìfènfèn	de	zhízǒu	进来 jìnlái
Mr Chén Laowu	also	furious	part.	directly	came in

如何	按得住	我	的	口,	我	偏要	對
Rúhé	àndezhù	wǒ	de	kǒu	wǒ	piānyào	对 duì
In any case	restrain	my	part.	mouth	I	insist	infront

這	夥	人	說,	你們	可以	改	了,	從
这 zhè	huǒ	rén	说 shuō	你们 nǐmen	kěyǐ	gǎi	le	cóng
this	crowd	people	said	you	can	change	part.	from

真心	改起!	要	曉得	將來	容不得
zhēnxīn	gǎiqǐ	Yāo	晓得 xiǎode	将来 jiānglái	róngbudé
sincerely	change	want	to know	in the future	unacceptable

吃人的人,	活	在	世上。
chīrénderén	huó	zài	shìshàng
cannibals	to live	at (on)	on earth

The last Emperor of Shang Dynasty, Di Xin 帝辛,
also known as King Zhou 紂王
His was considered one of the most infamous reigns (1075-1046 BC)
in all Chinese history, notably for its for decadence and corruption

Chapter X extract 5

"你們要不改，自己也會吃盡。即使生得多，也會給真的人除滅了，同獵人打完狼子一樣！——同蟲子一樣！"

那一夥人，都被陳老五趕走了。大哥也不知那裡去了。陳老五勸我回屋子裡去。屋裡面全是黑沉沉的。橫樑和椽子都在頭上發抖；抖了一會，就大起來，堆在我身上。

萬分沉重，動彈不得；他的意思是要我死。我曉得他的沉重是假的，便掙紮出來，出了一身汗。可是偏要說，

"你們立刻改了，從真心改起！你們要曉得將來是容不得吃人的人，……"

Translation 1.

'If you don't change, you may all be eaten by each other. Although so many are born, they will be wiped out by the real men, just like wolves killed by hunters. Just like reptiles!'

Old Chen drove everybody away. My brother had disappeared. Old Chen advised me to go back to my room. The room was pitch dark. The beams and rafters shook above my head. After shaking for some time they grew larger. They piled on top of me.

The weight was so great, I could not move. They meant that I should die. I knew that the weight was false, so I struggled out, covered in perspiration. But I had to say:

'You should change at once, change from the bottom of

your hearts! You must know that in future there will be no place for man-eaters in the world....'

Translation 2.

'If you do not change, you will be eaten yourselves. Even if more of you are born, you will eventually be exterminated by real humans, just as wolves were hunted into extinction...like insects!'

The crowd of onlookers was driven off by Chen Laowu. My older brother disappeared as well. Chen Laowu urged me to go home, to return to my room. Inside it was pitch black inside. Above my head, the beams and rafters were shaking. After a while, they became larger and piled down on top of me.

They were so heavy I could not move an inch. His intention was clearly to kill me. I knew that the weight was not real and began to struggle more. I broke out into a sweat. Despite this, I could not help but saying, 'You can change. Make a change in your hearts! You know that in the future, the world will not tolerate those who eat others....'

Synthesis

你們	要	不改，	自己	會	也	吃	盡。
你 Nǐmen	yào	bùgǎi	zìjǐ	会 huì	yě	chī	尽 jìn
You	if	not change	oneself	can	also	eat	end

即使	生得	多，	也	會	給	真的	人
Jíshǐ	Shēngde	duō	yě	会 huì	给 gěi	zhēnde	rén
Even if	born	many	also	can	give	real	people

除滅	了,	同	獵人	打完	狼子	一樣!
除灭 chúmiè	le	tóng	猎人 lièrén	dǎwán	lángzi	一样 yīyàng
eliminate	part.	like	hunters	finish off	wolves	the same

同	蟲子	一樣!	那	一夥人,	都	被
tóng	虫子 chóngzi	一样 yīyàng	nà	yīhuǒrén	dōu	bèi
like	insect	the same	that	crowd	all	by

陳老五	趕走了。	大哥	也	不知	那裡
陈老五 Chén Lǎowǔ	赶走了 gǎnzǒule	Dàgē	yě	zhī	nǎli
Mr Chén Laowu	driven out	Big brother	also	not know	where

去了。	陳老五	勸	我	回	屋子	裡去。
qùle	陈老五 Chén Lǎowǔ	劝 quàn	wǒ	huí	wūzi	lǐqù
gone	Mr Chén Laowu	urged	me	return	house	go inside

屋	裡面	全	是	黑沉沉	的。	橫樑
Wū	lǐmiàn	quán	shì	hēichēnchēn	de	Hèngliáng
House	inside	all	is	pitch-black	part.	Beams

和	椽子	都	在	頭上	發抖;
hé	chuánzi	dōu	zài	头上 tóushàng	发抖 fādǒu
and	rafters	all	at (located)	overhead	tremble

抖了	一會,	就	大起來,	堆	在	我	身
dǒule	一会 yīhui	jiù	dàqǐlai	duī	zài	wǒ	shēn
tremble	a moment	then	became bigger	piled	at (on)	my	body

上。	萬分	沉重,	動彈不得;	他	的
shàng	万分 Wànfēn	沉重 chénzhòng	动弹不得 dòngtanbudé	tā	de
on	extremely	heavy	idiom – unable to move	it	part.

意思	是要	我	死。	我	曉得	他	的
yìsi	shìyāo	wǒ	sǐ	Wǒ	晓得 xiǎode	tā	de
meant	should	I	die	I	know	it	part.

沉重	是	假的,	便	掙紮	出來,	出了
沉重 chénzhòng	shì	jiǎde	biàn	挣扎 zhēngzā	chūlái	chūle
weight	is	not real	so	struggled	out	out

一身汗。	可是	偏要	說,	你們	立刻	改了,
yīshēnhàn	Kěshì	piānyào	说 shuō	你们 nǐmen	lìkè	gǎile
in a sweat	But	insist on	saying	you	at once	change

從	真心	改起!	你們	要	曉得	將來
从 cóng	zhēnxīn	gǎiqǐ	你们 nǐmen	yāo	晓得 xiǎode	将来 jiānglái
from	sincere	change	you	want	to know	in the future

是	容不得	吃人的人,
shì	róngbudé	chīrénderén
will be	unacceptable	cannibalism

Chapter XI

太陽也不出，門也不開，日日是兩頓飯。

我捏起筷子，便想起我大哥；曉得妹子死掉的緣故，也全在他。那時我妹子才五歲，可愛可憐的樣子，還在眼前。母親哭個不住，他卻勸母親不要哭；大約因為自己吃了，哭起來不免有點過意不去。如果還能過意不去，……

妹子是被大哥吃了，母親知道沒有，我可不得而知。

母親想也知道；不過哭的時候，卻並沒有說明，大約也以為應當的了。記得我四五歲時，坐在堂前乘涼，大哥說爺娘生病，做兒子的須割下一片肉來，煮熟了請他吃， 才算好人；母親也沒有說不行。一片吃得，整個的自然也吃得。但是那天的哭法，現在想起來，實在還教人傷心，這真是奇極的事！

Translation 1.

The sun does not shine, the door is not opened, every day two meals.

I took up my chopsticks, then thought of my elder

brother; I know now how my little sister died: it was all through him. My sister was only five at the time. I can still remember how lovable and pathetic she looked. Mother cried and cried, but he begged her not to cry, probably because he had eaten her himself, and so her crying made him feel ashamed. If he had any sense of shame....

My sister was eaten by my brother, but I don't know whether mother realized it or not.

I think mother must have known, but when she cried she did not say so outright, probably because she thought it proper too. I remember when I was four or five years old, sitting in the cool of the hall, my brother told me that if a man's parents were ill, he should cut off a piece of his flesh and boil it for them if he wanted to be considered a good son; and mother did not contradict him. If one piece could be eaten, obviously so could the whole. And yet just to think of the mourning then still makes my heart bleed; that is the extraordinary thing about it!

Translation 2.

The sun has not come out and the door has not opened. I have been getting two meals a day.

Taking up my chopsticks, I started thinking about my older brother; I realized that he was the sole cause of my little sister's death. At the time, my little sister was no more than five years old. I can still see her adorable, pathetic, face in my mind's eye. My mother would not stop crying. He begged my mother to stop crying. It was probably because he had eaten her. When she started crying, he could not help but feeling remorse. If, that is, he was still capable of feeling remorse....

I have no way of knowing whether my mother knew

that my little sister was eaten by my older brother. I think she knew. However, she did not admit it at the time, probably because she also thought that things were as they should be. I remember being four or five years old and enjoying the shade of the hall, when my older brother told me that when one's parents fall ill, the son should cut off a piece of his own flesh, cook it, and feed it to them. This was the mark of a good person. My mother never said this was unacceptable. If one can eat a piece of flesh, one can naturally eat the whole thing. Although, to be honest, when I think of how she cried that day, it still pains me. How truly remarkable!

<u>Synthesis</u>

太陽	也不	出，	門	也不	開，	日日
太阳 tàiyáng	也不 yěbù	出 chū	门 mén	也不 yěbù	kāi	rìrì
Sun	doesn't	come out	door	doesn't	open	everyday

是	兩	頓	飯。	我	捏起	筷子，	便
shì	两 liǎng	顿 dùn	饭 fàn	Wǒ	niēqǐ	kuàizi	biàn
are	two	class.	meals	I	pick up	chopsticks	then

想起	我	大哥；	曉得	妹子	死掉	的
xiǎngqǐ	wǒ	dàgē	晓得 xiǎode	mèizi	sǐdiào	de
think of	my	older brother	know	younger sister	died	part.

緣故，	也	全	在	他。	那時	我	妹子	才
缘 yuángù	yě	quán	zài	tā	Nàshí	wǒ	mèizi	cái
reason	also	entirely	due to	him	Then	my	sister	only

五	歲，	可愛	可憐	的	樣子，	還	在眼前。
wǔ	suì	kěài	可怜 kělián	de	样子 yàngzi	还 hái	zàiyǎnqián
five	class.	adorable	sad	part.	air	still	now

母親	哭	個	不住，	他	卻	勸	母親	不要
Mǔqīn	kū	个 gè	bú zhù	tā	却 què	劝 quàn	mǔqīn	bùyào
Mother	wept	class.	endlessly	he	but	begged	mother	not to

哭;	大約	因為	自己	吃了,	哭起來	不免
kū	大约 dàyuē	因为 yīnwèi	zìjǐ	chīlc	kūqǐlai	bùmiǎn
cry	probably	because	himself	eaten	crying	inevitably

有點	過意不去。	如果	还	能	過意不去,
有点 yǒudiǎn	过意不去 guòyìbùqù	Rúguǒ	hái	néng	过意不去 guòyìbùqù
a little	feel very apologetic	If	still	able	to feel very apologetic

妹子	是	被	大哥	吃了,	母親	知道
mèizi	shì	bèi	dàgē	chīle	mǔqīn	zhīdào
younger sister	is	by	older brother	eaten	mother	know

沒有,	我	可	不得而知。	母親	想	也
méiyǒu	wǒ	kě	bùdéérzhī	Mǔqīn	xiǎng	yě
not	I	can	not know	Mother	think	also

知道;	不過	哭	的	時候,	卻並	沒有
zhīdào	不过 bùguò	kū	de	时候 shíhou	却并 quèbìng	méiyǒu
know	only	cry	part.	moment	but	not

說明,	大約	也	以為	應當的了。	記得
说明 shuōmíng	大约 dàyuē	yě	以为 yǐwéi	应当的了 yīngdāng	记得 jìde
explain	probably	also	believe	should have	Remember

我	四五	歲時,	坐	在	堂	前	乘涼,
wǒ	sìwǔ	岁时 suìshí	zuò	zài	táng	qián	chéngliáng
I	four or five	aged	sitting	at	main hall	in front of	cool in shade

大哥	說,	爺娘	生病,	做	兒子	的	須
dàgē	说 shuō	爷娘 yéniáng	shēngbìng	zuò	儿子 érzi	de	须 xū
older brother	said	parents	fall ill	to do	son	part	must

割	下	一片	肉	來,	煮熟了	請	他	吃,
gē	xià	yīpiàn	ròu	来 lái	zhǔshóule	请 qǐng	tā	chī
to cut	off	a slice	flesh	compli.	boil	ask	him	eat

才	算	好人;	母親	也	沒有	說,	不行。
cái	suàn	hàorén	mǔqīn	yě	méiyǒu	说 shuō	bùxíng
only then	consider	good man	mother	also	not	say	not wrong

一片	吃得，	整個	的	自然	也	吃得。
Yīpiàn	chīle	整个 zhěnggè	de	zìrán	yě	chīle
a piece	eaten	all	part.	naturally	also	eaten

但是	那天	的	哭	法，	現在	想起來，
Dànshì	nàtiān	de	kū	fǎ	现在 xiànzài	xiǎngqilai
however	that day	part.	crying	way	now	remembering

實在	還	教	人	傷心，	這	真	是	奇
shízài	还 hái	jiāo	rén	伤心 shāngxīn	zhè	zhēn	shì	qí
really	in addition	teaches	people	mourning	this	really	is	strange

極	的	事！
jí	de	shì
most	part.	thing

Chapter XII

不能想了。

四千年來時時吃人的地方，今天才明白，我也在其中混了多年；大哥正管著家務， 妹子恰恰死了，他未必不和在飯菜裡，暗暗給我們吃。

我未必無意之中，不吃了我妹子的幾片肉，現在也輪到我自己，……

有了四千年吃人履歷的我，當初雖然不知道，現在明白，難見真的人！

Translation 1.

I can't bear to think of it.

I have only just realized that I have been living all these years in a place where for four thousand years they have been eating human flesh. My brother had just taken over the charge of the house when our sister died, and he may well have used her flesh in our rice and dishes, making us eat it unwittingly.

It is possible that I ate several pieces of my sister's flesh unwittingly, and now it is my turn....

How can a man like myself, after four thousand years of man-caring history, even though I knew nothing about it at first, ever hope to face real men?

<u>*Translation 2.*</u>

I cannot think about it.

It is only now that I understand that I have been dwelling in a land where people have been eating people for the last four thousand years. Since my older brother was in charge of the family affairs, I cannot rule out the possibility that he secretly mixed some of my little sister's flesh into my food after she died.

It is possible that I, unknowingly, ate a few pieces of my little sister's flesh. Now it's my turn to be eaten....

Even though I was unaware of it at first, I am the product of four thousand years of humans eating humans. Now that I know, I cannot bear to face real people!

<u>Synthesis</u>

不能	想了。	四千	年	來	時時	吃人的
Bùnéng	xiǎngle	Sìqiān	nián	来 lái	shíshí	chīrénde
cannot	imagine	4,000	years	since	regularly	cannibal

地方,	今天	才	明白,	我	也	在其中
dìfang	jīntiān	cái	míngbai	wǒ	yě	zàiqízhōng
place	today	only	obvious	I	too	amongst

混了	多年;	大哥	正	管著	家務,	妹子
hùnle	duōnián	大哥 dàgē	zhèng	管着 guǎnzhe	jiāwù	mèizi
mixed	many years	older brother	just	in charge	household	sister

恰恰	死了,	他	未必不	和	在	飯菜	裡,
qiàqià	sǐle	tā	wèibìbù	hé	zài	饭菜 fàncài	lǐ
just	died	he	not unlikely	with	in	food	in

暗暗	給	我們	吃。	我	未必	無意
ànàn	给 gěi	我们 wǒmen	chī	Wǒ	wèibì	无意 wúyì
secretly	gave	us	to eat	I	not certain	inadvertently

之中,	不吃了	我	妹子的	幾	片	肉,
zhīzhōng	bùchīle	wǒ	mèizide	几 jǐ	piàn	ròu
myself included	did not eat	my	sister's	some	pieces	flesh

現在	也	輪到	我	自己,	有了	四千	年
现在 xiànzài	yě	轮到 lúndào	wǒ	zìjǐ	yǒule	sìqiān	nián
now	also	turn	my	own	for	4,000	years

吃人	履歷的	我,	當初	雖然	不知道,
chīrénde	履历 lǚlìde	wǒ	当初 dāngchū	虽然 suīrán	bùzhīdào
cannibal(ism)	history	my	at that time	although	not know

現在	明白,	難	見	真的	人!
现 xiànzài	míngbai	难 nán	见 jiàn	zhēnde	rén
today	clear	difficult	to see	really	people

Chapter XIII

沒有吃過人的孩子，或者還有？
救救孩子……

Translation 1.

Perhaps there are still children who have not eaten men? Save the children....

Translation 2.

Perhaps there are still children who have not eaten people.

Save the children....

Synthesis

沒有	吃過人的	孩子,	或者	還有?	救救
Méiyǒu	吃过人的 chīguòrénde	háizi	huòzhě	还有 háiyǒu	Jiùjiù
never	eaten men	children	or	are there?	save

孩子...
háizi
children

Notes

Ku Chiu means 'Ancient Times'. Lu Xun had in mind the long history of feudal oppression in China.

A famous pharmacologist (1518-1593), author of Bencao gangmu (本草綱目).

These are quotations from the old classic Zuo Zhuan.

According to ancient records, Yi Ya cooked his son and presented him to Duke Huan of Chi who reigned from 685 to 643 B.C. Chieh and Chou were tyrants of an earlier age. It seems the madman made a mistake here.

'Hsu Hsi-lin was sentenced to death and decapitated for assassinating a Qing official. His heart was offered to as a sacrifice to the spirit of the official he had killed and his liver was eaten by soldiers who expected in this way to receive a portion of the courage which had characterized the assassin's deeds.' (The Star, New Zealand ,Tuesday, October 20, 1908)

狂人日記

I

今天晚上，很好的月光。

我不見他，已是三十多年；今天見了，精神分外爽快。才知道以前的三十多年， 全是發昏；然而須十分小心。不然，那趙家的狗，何以看我兩眼呢？

我怕得有理。

II

今天全沒月光，我知道不妙。早上小心出門，趙貴翁的眼色便怪：似乎怕我，似乎想害我。還有七八個人，交頭接耳的議論我，又怕我看見。一路上的人，都是如此。其中最兇的一個人，張着嘴，對我笑了一笑；我便從頭直冷到腳跟，曉得他們布置，都已妥當了。

我可不怕，仍舊走我的路。前面一夥小孩子，也在那裡議論我；眼色也同趙貴翁一樣，臉色也鐵青。我想我同小孩子有什麼仇，他也這樣。忍不住大聲説，“你告訴我！”他們可就跑了。

我想：我同趙貴翁有什麼仇，同路上的人又有什麼仇；只有廿年以前，把古久先生的陳年流水簿子，踹了一腳，古久先生很不高興。趙貴翁雖然不認識他，一定也聽到風聲，代抱不平；約定路上的人，同我作冤對。但是小孩子呢？那時候，他們還沒有出世，何以今天也睜著怪眼睛，似乎怕我，似乎想害我。這真教我怕，教我納罕而且傷心。

我明白了。這是他們娘老子教的！

III

晚上總是睡不著。凡事須得研究，才會明白。

他們——也有給知縣打枷過的，也有給紳士掌過嘴的，也有衙役佔了他妻子的， 也有老子娘被債主逼死的；他們那時候的臉色，全沒有昨天這麼怕，也沒有這麼凶。

最奇怪的是昨天街上的那個女人，打他兒子，嘴裡說道，“老子呀！我要咬你幾 口才出氣！”他眼睛卻看著我。我出了一驚，遮掩不住；那青面獠牙的一夥人，便都 哄笑起來。陳老五趕上前，硬把我拖回家中了。

拖我回家，家裡的人都裝作不認識我；他們的臉色也全同別人一樣。進了書房 ，便反扣上門，宛然是關了一隻雞鴨。這一件事，越教我猜不出底細。

前幾天，狼子村的佃戶來告荒，對我大哥說，他們村裡的一個大惡人，給大家打 死了；幾個人便挖出他的心肝來，用油煎炒了吃，可以壯壯膽子。我插了一句嘴，佃 戶和大哥便都看我幾眼。今天才曉得他們的眼光，全同外面的那夥人一模一樣。

想起來，我從頂上直冷到腳跟。

他們會吃人，就未必不會吃我。

你看那女人“咬你幾口”的話，和一夥青面獠牙人的笑，和前天佃戶的話，明明 是暗號。我看出他話中全是毒，笑中全是刀。他們的牙齒，全是白厲厲的排著，這就 是吃人的傢夥。

照我自己想，雖然不是惡人，自從踹了古家的簿子，可就難說了。他們似乎別有 心思，我全猜不出。況且他們一翻臉，便說人是惡人。我還記得大哥教我做論，無論 怎樣好人，翻他幾句，他便打上幾個圈；原諒壞人幾句，他便說“翻天妙手，與眾不 同”。我那裡猜得到他們的心思，究竟怎樣；況且是要吃的時候。

凡事總須研究，才會明白。古來時常吃人，我也還記得，可是不甚清楚。我翻開 歷史一查，這歷史沒有年代，歪歪斜斜的每頁上都寫著“仁義道德”幾個字。我橫豎 睡不著，仔細看了半夜，才從字縫裡看出字來，滿本都寫著兩個字是“吃人”！

書上寫著這許多字，佃戶說了這許多話，卻都笑吟吟的睜著怪眼看我。

我也是人，他們想要吃我了！

IV

早上，我靜坐了一會兒。陳老五送進飯來，一碗菜一碗蒸魚；這魚的眼睛，白 而且硬，張著嘴，同那一夥想吃人的人一樣。吃了幾筷，滑溜溜的不知是魚是人，便 把他兜肚連腸的吐出。

我說“老五，對大哥說，我悶得慌，想到園裡走走。”老五不答應，走了；停一 會，可就來開了門。

我也不動，研究他們如何擺佈我；知道他們一定不肯放鬆。果然！我大哥引了一 個老頭子，慢慢走來；他滿眼凶光，怕我看出，只是低頭向著地，從眼鏡橫邊暗暗看我。大哥說，“今天你彷彿很好。”我說“是的。”大哥說，“今天請何先生來，給 你診一診。”我説“可以！”其實我豈不知道這老頭子是劊子手扮的！無非借了看脈 這名目，揣一揣肥瘠：因這功勞，也分一片肉吃。我也不怕；雖然不吃人，膽子卻比 他們還壯。伸出兩個拳頭，看他如何下手。老頭子坐著，閉了眼睛，摸了好一會，呆 了好一會；便張開他鬼眼睛説，“不要亂想。靜靜的養幾天，就好了。”

不要亂想，靜靜的養！養肥了，他們是自然可以多吃；我有什麼好處，怎麼會“好 了”？他們這群人，又想吃人，又是鬼鬼祟祟，想法子遮掩，不敢直截下手，真要令 我笑死。我忍不住，便放聲大笑起來，十分快活。自己曉得這笑聲裏面，有的是義勇 和正氣。老頭子和大哥，都失了色，被我這勇氣正氣鎮壓住了。

但是我有勇氣，他們便越想吃我，沾光一點這勇氣老頭子跨出門，走不多遠， 便低聲對大哥説道，“趕緊吃罷！”大哥點點頭。原來也有你！這一件大發見，雖似 意外，也在意中：合夥吃我的人，便是我的哥哥！

吃人的是我哥哥！

我是吃人的人的兄弟！

我自己被人吃了，可仍然是吃人的人的兄弟！

V

這幾天是退一步想：假使那老頭子不是劊子手扮的真是醫生，也仍然是吃人的 人。他們的祖師李時珍做的“本草什麼”上，明明寫著人肉可以煎吃；他還能説自己 不吃人麼？

至於我家大哥，也毫不冤枉他。他對我講書的時候，親口説過可以“易子而食”； 又一回偶然議論起一個不好的人，他便說不但該殺，還當“食肉寢皮”。我那時年紀 還小，心跳了好半天。前天狼子村佃戶來說吃心肝的事，他也毫不奇怪，不住的點頭。 可見心思是同從前一樣狠。既然可以“易子而食”，便什麼都易得，什麼人都吃得。 我從前單聽他講道理，也胡塗過去；現在曉得他講道理的時候，不但唇邊還抹著人油， 而且心裡滿裝著吃人的意思。

VI

黑漆漆的，不知是日是夜。趙家的狗又叫起來了。

獅子似的凶心，兔子的怯弱，狐狸的狡猾，……

VII

我曉得他們的方法，直捷殺了，是不肯的，而且也不敢，怕有禍祟。所以他們大 家聯絡，佈滿了羅網，逼我自戕。試看前幾天街上男女的樣子，和這幾天我大哥的作 為，便足可悟出八九分了。最好是解下腰帶，掛在樑上，自己緊緊勒死；他們沒有殺 人的罪名，又償了心願，自然都歡天喜地的發出一種嗚嗚咽咽的笑聲。否則驚嚇憂愁 死了，雖則略瘦，也還可以首肯幾下。

他們是只會吃死肉的！——記得什麼書上說，有一種東西，叫"海乙那"的，眼光 和樣子都很難看；時常吃死肉，連極大的骨頭，都細細嚼爛，嚥下肚子去，想起來也 教人害怕。"海乙那"是狼的親眷，狼是狗的本家。前天趙家的狗，看我幾眼，可見他 也同謀，早已接洽。老頭子眼看著地，豈能瞞得我過。

最可憐的是我的大哥，他也是人，何以毫不害怕；

而且合夥吃我呢？還是歷來慣 了，不以為非呢？還是喪了良心，明知故犯呢？

我詛咒吃人的人，先從他起頭；要勸轉吃人的人，也先從他下手。

VIII

其實這種道理，到了現在，他們也該早已懂得，……

忽然來了一個人；年紀不過二十左右，相貌是不很看得清楚，滿面笑容，對了我 點頭，他的笑也不像真笑。我便問他，“吃人的事，對麼？”他仍然笑著說，“不是 荒年，怎麼會吃人。”我立刻就曉得，他也是一夥，喜歡吃人的；便自勇氣百倍，偏 要問他。

“對麼？”

“這等事問他什麼。你真會……說笑話。……今天天氣很好。”

天氣是好，月色也很亮了。可是我要問你，“對麼？”

他不以為然了。含含糊胡的答道，“不……”

“不對？他們何以竟吃？！”

“沒有的事……”

“沒有的事？狼子村現吃；還有書上都寫著，通紅斬新！”

他便變了臉，鐵一般青。睜著眼說，“有許有的，這是從來如此……”

“從來如此，便對麼？”

“我不同你講這些道理；總之你不該說，你說便是你錯！”

我直跳起來，張開眼，這人便不見了。全身出了一大片汗。他的年紀，比我大哥 小得遠，居然也是一夥；這一定是他娘老子先教的。還怕已經教給他兒子了；所以連 小孩子，也都惡狠狠的看我。

IX

自己想吃人，又怕被別人吃了，都用著疑心極深的眼光，面面相覷。……

去了這心思，放心做事走路吃飯睡覺，何等舒服。這只是一條門檻，一個關頭。 他們可是父子兄弟夫婦朋友師生仇敵和各不相識的人，都結成一夥，互相勸勉，互相 牽掣，死也不肯跨過這一步。

X

大清早，去尋我大哥；他立在堂門外看天，我便走到他背後，攔住門，格外沉靜， 格外和氣的對他說，

"大哥，我有話告訴你。"

"你說就是，" 他趕緊回過臉來，點點頭。

"我只有幾句話，可是說不出來。大哥，大約當初野蠻的人，都吃過一點人。後 來因為心思不同，有的不吃人了，一味要好，便變了人，變了真的人。有的卻還吃，—— 也同蟲子一樣，有的變了魚鳥猴子，一直變到人。有的不要好，至今還是蟲子。這吃 人的人比不吃人的人，何等慚愧。怕比蟲子的慚愧猴子，還差得很遠很遠。

"易牙蒸了他兒子，給桀紂吃，還是一直從前的事。誰曉得從盤古開闢天地以後， 一直吃到易牙的兒子；從易牙的兒子，一直吃到徐錫林；從徐錫林，又一直

吃到狼子 村捉住的人。去年城裡殺了犯人，還有一個生痨病的人，用饅頭蘸血舐。

"他們要吃我，你一個人，原也無法可想；然而又何必去入夥。吃人的人，什麼 事做不出；他們會吃我，也會吃你，一夥裏面，也會自吃。但只要轉一步，只要立刻 改了，也就是人人太平。雖然從來如此，我們今天也可以格外要好，說是不能！大哥， 我相信你能說，前天佃戶要減租，你說過不能。"

當初，他還只是冷笑，隨後眼光便兇狠起來，一到說破他們的隱情，那就滿臉都 變成青色了。大門外立著一夥人，趙貴翁和他的狗，也在裏面，都探頭探腦的挨進來。 有的是看不出面貌，似乎用布蒙著；有的是仍舊青面獠牙，抿著嘴笑。我認識他們是 一夥，都是吃人的人。可是也曉得他們心思很不一樣，一種是以為從來如此，應該吃 的；一種是知道不該吃，可是仍然要吃，又怕別人說破他，所以聽了我的話，越發氣 憤不過，可是抿著嘴冷笑。

這時候，大哥也忽然顯出凶相，高聲喝道，

"都出去！瘋子有什麼好看！"

這時候，我又懂得一件他們的巧妙了。他們豈但不肯改，而且早已佈置；預備下 一個瘋子的名目罩上我。將來吃了，不但太平無事，怕還會有人見情。佃戶說的大家 吃了一個惡人，正是這方法。這是他們的老譜！

陳老五也氣憤憤的直走進來。如何按得住我的口，我偏要對這夥人說，

"你們可以改了，從真心改起！要曉得將來容不得吃人的人，活在世上。

"你們要不改，自己也會吃盡。即使生得多，也會給真的人除滅了，同獵人打完狼子一樣！——同蟲子

一樣！”

那一夥人，都被陳老五趕走了。大哥也不知那裡去了。陳老五勸我回屋子裡去。

屋裡面全是黑沉沉的。橫樑和椽子都在頭上發抖；抖了一會，就大起來，堆在我身上。萬分沉重，動彈不得；他的意思是要我死。我曉得他的沉重是假的，便掙紮出來，出了一身汗。可是偏要說，

“你們立刻改了，從真心改起！你們要曉得將來是容不得吃人的人，……”

XI

太陽也不出，門也不開，日日是兩頓飯。

我捏起筷子，便想起我大哥；曉得妹子死掉的緣故也全在他。那時我妹子才五 歲，可愛可憐的樣子，還在眼前。母親哭個不住，他卻勸母親不要哭；大約因為自己 吃了，哭起來不免有點過意不去。如果還能過意不去，……

妹子是被大哥吃了，母親知道沒有，我可不得而知。

母親想也知道；不過哭的時候，卻並沒有說明，大約也以為應當的了。記得我四 五歲時，坐在堂前乘涼，大哥說爺娘生病，做兒子的須割下一片肉來，煮熟了請他吃， 才算好人；母親也沒有說不行。一片吃得，整個的自然也吃得。但是那天的哭法，現 在想起來，實在還教人傷心，這真是奇極的事！

XII

不能想了。

四千年來時時吃人的地方，今天才明白，我也在其

中混了多年；大哥正管著家務， 妹子恰恰死了，他未必不和在飯菜裡，暗暗給我們吃。

我未必無意之中，不吃了我妹子的幾片肉，現在也輪到我自己，……

有了四千年吃人履歷的我，當初雖然不知道，現在明白，難見真的人！

XIII

沒有吃過人的孩子，或者還有？

救救孩子……

一九一八年四月。

Zhou Erfu

MORNING IN SHANGHAI

上海的早晨

Morning in Shanghai

上海的早晨

This voluminous saga-like novel written by Zhou Erfu (1914-2004) was published in 1958 (part I) and 1962 (part II). It was set in Shanghai, under Mao's Communist government, in the period immediately following the country's long drawn out civil war, which ended with the Nationalists fleeing to Taiwan in 1949.

Morning in Shanghai paints a panoramic image of life in the city after the Communist victory, which emerged relatively intact after the battle. Under the early Communist government capitalism flourished, competing with state-owned businesses. However, by 1956 more than two thirds of all important industrial enterprises were state-owned, with the remainder under joint public-private ownership. Zhou Erfu's novel is interesting in that it is one of the few that describes capitalism during this period. It was of course written and published during the Mao period and as such conforms with the ideology of that time; when the Communist Party and workers fought unbridled capitalism and reformed its leaders.

To modern Western readers the style may be seen as somewhat ingenuous, whilst the proses are repetitive and long winded, as is the translation of A.C.Barnes, which no doubt remains *deliberately* close to Zhou Erfu's original Chinese work. A more modern approach is illustrated by an alternative translation, which is perhaps more suggestive of present day styles.

As in the preceding sections this presentation consists of excerpts of the original text broken down into short bites. As the novel is voluminous, the author of this present book has chosen the simple path of taking the introductory chapter, which nevertheless gives students an insight into the style and subject of the story. The Chinese texts are accompanied by pinyin pronunciation and suggested English dictionary equivalents. The choice of the latter is broad and sometimes challenging, which often leads to confusion for students of the Chinese language.

One of the difficulties that confront many students is Chinese names, both those of the persons and places. Confusion is added in that the contemporary translations do not employ pinyin equivalents. In addition translators have followed the original texts by reiterating whole names; it is as if we were to write for example John Fitzgerald Kennedy each time he is mentioned in a book, rather than referring to John, Kennedy, JFK, the president, or some other convenient tag, without losing sight of the person being talked about.

Contemporary translations have unfortunately discouraged many readers from discovering and enjoying novels that paint a unique picture of the tumultuous post imperial years in China, as seen through the eyes of the Chinese authors who themselves lived through those turbulent times.

What is remarkable is that capitalism survived the excesses of the revolution thanks to Hongkong, Macao and Taiwan, and of course the overseas Chinese. The Communist government in Beijing united the Mainland and in spite of its terrible aberrations, notably the *Great Leap Forward* and the *Cultural Revolution*, created the indispensable conditions necessary for the re-emergence of capitalism.

It goes without saying that the extraordinary movement of countless Chinese peasants drawn to the cities and industrial centres in those times provided the labour needed to build modern China. Equally remarkable are the parallels can be drawn between *Morning in Shanghai* and today's China, where capitalism is often as ruthless as that described in the novel through the exploits of Wu Sunfu.

In the presentation of these extracts, the author has taken certain liberties in his approach, which is neither a reflection on Zhou Erfu's work, nor A.C.Barnes' vast effort of translation. It should be remembered that the original work was written at a time when Mao's Communist ideology allowed no deviation and writers served the system.

When in 1958, Mao's *Great Leap Forward* was launched, its objective was to transform China into a modern communist society through a process of industrialization and collectivization of land. Private business of any nature was prohibited, and those engaged in it were labelled as counter revolutionaries and persecuted. By the time the part II of *Morning in Shanghai* was published, the *Great Leap Forward* had wreaked havoc on China's economy, bringing death and famine to countless millions.

Extract 1 from Chapter 1

一辆黑色的小奥斯汀汽车远远驶来，在柏油路上发出轻轻嗞嗞声。马路两边是整齐的梧桐树，树根那部分去年冬天涂上去的白石灰粉已开始脱落，枝头上宽大的绿油油的叶子，迎风轻微摆动着。马路上行人很少，没有声思。天空晴朗，下午的阳光把法国梧桐的阴影印在柏油路上，仿佛是一张整的图案画。小奥斯汀穿过了横马路，降低了速速，在梧桐的阴影上开过来。

Translation 1.

Its tires hissing softly over the asphalt surface of the road, a little black Austin car was approaching in the distance. The avenue was lined with neatly-spaced plane trees, the lime-wash applied last winter already beginning to flake off the bottoms of their trunks, and their broad, rich green leaves fluttering in the breeze. The avenue was almost deserted and not a sound disturbed its tranquil calm. From a clear, cloudless sky the afternoon sun threw the shadows of the plan trees on the roadway in a neat pattern. Passing over an interesting avenue, the little Austin slackened its pace and came running across the shadows of the trees.

Translation 2.

A small black Austin appeared in the distance, it was moving fast, making a soft whistling sound over the macadam. The road were lined with plane trees, the previous winter the lower trunks had been painted with lime was peeling off. The branches were covered with broad deep green leaves that swayed gently in the wind. There were few people on the road, barely a sound. The sky was bright and clear, the afternoon sun shone casting shadows of the trees on the road, it was like a perfect painting. The small Austin passed over the shadows and slowed down.

Synthesis

一	辆	黑色	的	小	奥斯汀	汽车	远远
Yī	liàng	hēisè	de	xiǎo	àosītīng	qìchē	yuǎnyuǎn
A	classifier	black	of	small	Austin	car; auto	distant

驶	来，	在	柏油路	上	发出	轻轻
shǐ	lái	zài	bǎiyóulù	shàng	fāchū	qīng
fast	to come	at	tarred road	on	to issue	softly

嗞嗞声。	马路	两边	是	整齐	的	梧桐树
sīsīshēng	Mǎlù	liǎngbian	shì	zhěngqí	de	wútóngshù
whistling sound	Road	both sides	to be	neatly	part.	parasol tree

树根	那	部分	去年	冬天	涂	上去	的
shùgēn	nǎ	bùfèn	qùnián	dōngtiān	tú	shàngqù	de
tree roots	this	part	last year	winter	to apply	to go up	of

白	石灰	粉	已	开始	脱落,	枝	头上
bái	shíhuī	fěn	yǐ	kāishǐ	tuōluò	zhī	tóushàng
white	lime	powder	already	start	drop off	branch	above

宽大	的	绿油油	的	叶子，	迎风	轻微	摆动
kuāndà	de	lǜyóuyóu	de	yèzi	yíngfēng	qīngwēi	bǎidòng
wide	part.	lush green	part.	leaf, foliage	in wind	slight	sway

着。	马路	上行	人	很	少,	没有	声
zhe	Mǎlù	shàngxíng	rén	hěn	shǎo	méiyǒu	shēng
particle	Road	on, up	person	very	few	not have	sound

思。	天空	晴朗，	下午	的	阳光	把	法国
sī	Tiānkōng	qínglǎng	xiàwǔ	de	yángguāng	bà	fǎguó
think	Sky	cloudless	afternoon	part.	sunshine	part.	French

梧桐	的	阴影	印	在	柏油路	上，	仿佛
wútóng	de	yīnyǐng	yìn	zài	bǎiyóulù	shàng	fǎngfú
plane tree	part.	shadow	print	at	tarred road	on	to seem; as if

是	一	张	整	的	图案	画。	小	奥斯汀穿
shì	yī	zhāng	zhěng	de	túàn	huà	Xiǎo	àosītīng
to be	one	class.	exact	part.	pattern	picture	Small	Austin

穿过	了	横	马路,	降低	了	速速,	在
chuānguò	le	hèng	mǎlù	jiàngdī	le	sùsù	zài
pass	part.	harsh	road	reduce	part.	speed	at

梧桐	的	阴影	上	开	过来。
wútóng	part.	yīnyǐng	shàng	kāi	guòlái
plane tree		shadow	on	open	pass

<u>Notes</u>

柏油　　bǎiyóu – asphalt / tar / pitch / macadam
梧桐树　wútóngshù – Chinese plane tree

Illustration from Morning in Shanghai
1981 edition Foreign Language Press, Beijing

Extract 2 from Chapter 1

在一片红色砖墙的当中，俩扇黑漆大铁门紧紧闭着铁门上两个狮子头的金色的铁环，在太阳里闪闪发着金光。小奥斯汀的喇叭对着黑漆大门交了两声。黑漆大铁门开了，迎面站出来的是身上穿着银色卡叽布制服的门房老刘。他伸开右手，向里面指着，让小奥斯汀开了进去。她旋即关紧了大门，好像防备坏人跟再汽车后面溜进来似的。他过来拉开奥斯汀的车门，里面跳下一个四十开外的中年人。

Translation 1.

A large, black-painted double iron gate stood securely closed in the middle of a red brick wall, its two lion-headed, gilded iron rings glinting gold in the sunlight. The little Austin sounded its horn twice at the black gate. The gate opened and out stepped Old Liu the gatekeeper, in a silver-grey drill uniform. He held out his right hand and signalled the little Austin in, shutting the gate tight behind it the moment it had passed through, as if afraid that some evil-doer might slip in behind it. He then came over and opened the car door and a middle-aged man in his forties stepped out.

Translation 2.

Standing in the middle of a red brick wall was a pair of tightly shut black iron gates, surmounted by golden lion heads set in iron hoops that glittered brightly in the sun. The small Austin sounded its horn a couple of times. The gates opened and Liu, the gatekeeper, dressed in a grey serge uniform, appeared. He raised a hand and beckoned the car in. He carefully shut the gates, as if to prevent undesirables from following the car in. Liu then opened the door of the small Austin and a man of about forty jumped out.

Synthesis

在	一片	红色	砖	墙	的	当中，	俩
Zài	yīpiàn	hóngsè	zhuān	qiáng	de	dāngzhōng	liàng
At	a + class.	red	brick	wall	of	in middle	classifier

扇	黑	漆	大	铁	门	紧紧	闭
shàn	hēi	qī	da	tiě	mén	jǐnjǐn	bi
panel	black	paint	big	iron	door	tight	close

着。	铁	门	上	两	个	狮子头	的
zhe	Tiě	mén	shàng	liǎng	gè	shīzitóu	de
part.	Iron	door	on	pair	class.	lion head	of

金色	的	铁环，	在	太阳	里	闪闪	发
jīnsè	de	tiěhuán	zài	tàiyáng	lǐ	shǎnshǎn	fā
golden	part.	iron hoops	at	sun	in	glittering	emit

着	金	光。	小	奥斯汀	的	喇叭	对	着
zhe	jīn	guāng	Xiǎo	àosītīng	de	lǎba	duì	zhe
part.	gold	shine	Small	Austin	part.	horn	before	part.

黑	漆	大门	交	了	两	声。	黑	漆
hēi	qī	dàmén	jiāo	le	liǎng	shēng	Hēi	qī
black	paint	main door	call	part.	couple	sound	Black	paint

大	铁	门	开	了，	迎面	站	出来	的	是
da	tiě	mén	kāi	le	yíngmiàn	zhàn	chūlái	de	shì
big	iron	door	start	part.	directly	to stand	to go out	part.	to be

身上	穿	着	银色	卡叽布	制服	的	门	房
shēnkāi	chuān	zhe	yínsè	qiǎjībù	zhìfú	de	mén	fáng
stretch	dress	part.	silver	serge cloth	uniform	of	door	house

老	刘。	他	伸开	右手,	向	里面	指	着,	让
lǎo	Liú	Tā	shēnkā	yòushǒu	xiàng	lǐmiàn	zhǐ	zhe	ràng
old	name	He	reach out	righthand	direct	inside	finger	part.	let

小	奥斯汀	开	了	进去。	她	旋即	关紧	了
xiǎo	àosītīng	kāi	le	jìnqù	Tā	xuánjí	guānjǐn	le
small	Austin	start	part.	in	He	shortly	closed	part.

好像	防备	坏人	跟	再	汽车	后面	溜
hǎoxiàng	fángbèi	huàirén	gēn	zài	qìchē	hòumian	liū
as if	prevent	undesirables	with	again	car	behind	slip in

进来	似的。	他	过来	拉开	奥斯汀	的	车门,
jìnlái	shìde	Tā	guòlái	lākāi	Aosītīng	de	chēmén
come in	as if	He	come over	opened	Austin	of	car door

里面	跳	下	一	个	四十	开外	的	中年	人。
lǐmiàn	tiào	xià	yī	yī	sìshí	kāiwài	de	zhōngnián	rén
inside	jump	out	one	class.	forty	about	part.	middle age	man

Notes

卡叽布 qiǎjībù – serge; a type of cloth

老刘 lǎo – prefix used before the surname of a person or a numeral indicating the order of birth of the children in a family or to indicate affection or familiarity. In this case Liú, i.e. Lao Liu.

Remark

In Chinese, because names are common or similar, descriptions are frequently employed to indicate a person i.e. his or her age: young, old, middle aged; his facial features: long, square, round, thin, pale etc.; his corpulence i.e. tall, slim, short, fat etc.; his or her clothing; his or her family relationship i.e. husband, wife, son, daughter etc.; profession, rank etc.

Extract 3 from Chapter 1

他穿的着一身浅灰色底子淡蓝色条子的西装，打着一条瑰红的领带；长型的脸庞微笑着，两腮露出两个酒酒，鼻鼻梁上架着一副玳瑁边框子的散光眼镜，眼光机灵地向四边一扫：院里没人。他橐橐地走了进去。

这个是沪江纱厂的副厂长梅佐贤，外号叫酸辣汤。这个外号的来源有一段这样的历史；梅佐贤本来并不是办沙厂的，是开饭馆出身人。

Translation 1.

He was dressed in a European-style suite of pale-grey material with pale-blue stripes and a rose red tie; his long, squarish face wore a smile, his cheeks were dimpled, and his nose was surmounted by a pair of spectacles with tortoise-shell frames. His questing gaze swept alertly all round him. There was no one in the courtyard. He marched indoors. This was Mei Zuoxain, the deputy director of the Hu Jiang Cotton Mill, know by the nickname of 'Pepper-and-Vinegar Soup'. The reason for this nickname was that he had not originally been connected with cotton mills at all, but had been in the business as a restaurateur.

Translation 2.

He was dressed in a light grey pin stripe European-style suit with a rose coloured tie. He wore a smile on his long square face, his cheeks were dimpled, and perched on the bridge of his nose was a pair of tortoise shell glasses. His sharp eyes swept over the courtyard. There was not a soul in sight; the only sound was that of his footsteps as he made his way inside. He was Mei Zouxian, deputy manager of the Hujiang Cotton Factory, better known as 'Hot-sour-soup' by the factory workers.

Synthesis

他	穿	的	着	一身	浅	灰色	底子	淡蓝色
Tā	chuān	de	zhe	a suit	qiǎn	huīsè	dǐzi	tiáozidí
he	to wear	of	part.	yīshēn	light	grey	background	light blue

条子	的	西装，	打着	一	条	瑰	红	的
tiáozi	de	xīzhuāng	dǎzhuó	yī	tiáo	guī	hóng	de
stripes	of	West. style	dressed	one	class.	rose	red	of

领带；	长	型	的	脸庞	微笑	着，	两	腮
lǐngdài	cháng	xíng	de	liǎnpáng	wēixiào	zhuó	liǎng	sāi
neck tie	long	style	of	face	smile	wear	two	cheek

露出	两	个	酒窝，	鼻梁	上	架	着
lùchū	liǎng	gè	jiǔwō	bíliáng	shàng	ji	zhuó
show	two	class.	dimple	nose bridge	on	support	wear

一	副	玳瑁	边框	子	的	散光	眼镜，
yī	fù	dàimào	biānkuàng	suff.	de	sànguāng	yǎnjing
one, a	pair	tortoise shell	frame	zi*	of	corrective	glasses

眼光	机灵	地	向	四边	一	扫：	院	里
yǎnguāng	jīlíng	dì	xiàng	sìbiān	yī	sǎo	yuàn	lǐ
looked	clever	part.	toward	four sides	one	sweep	courtyard	in

没	人。	他	橐橐	地	走	了	进去。	这	个
méi	rén	Tā	tuótuó	dì	zǒu	le	jìnqù	Zhè	ge
not	person	He	footsteps	part.	to go	par.	go in	This	class.

是	沪江纱厂	的	副厂长	梅佐贤，
shì	Hùjiāng Shāchǎng	de	fùchǎngzhǎng	Méi Zuǒxián
to be	Hùjiāng Cotton Mill	of	deputy director	name

外号	叫	酸辣汤。	这	个	外号	的	来源
wàihào	jiào	suānlàtāng	Zhè	ge	wàihào	de	láiyuán
nickname	call	hot-sour-soup	This	class.	nickname	of	originate

有	一	段	这	样	的	历史;	梅佐贤
yǒu	yī	yī	zhè	yàng	de	lìshǐ	Méi Zuǒxián
to have	one	class.	this	kind	part.	history	name

本来	并不	是	办	沙厂	的,	是	开	饭馆
běnlái	bìngbù	shì	bàn	shāchǎng	de	shì	kāi	fànguǎn
originally	not at all	to be	manage	cotton mill	part.	to be	run	restaurant

出身	人。
chūshēn	rén
family	person

* 子 noun suffix

Notes

橐橐 tuótuó the sound of footsteps – (onomatopoeia)
的西装 Western style (clothing)
玳瑁 dàimào – hawksbill turtle /tortoiseshell
散光 sǎnguāng – astigmatism

一身浅灰色底子淡蓝色条子 a light grey striped suit

Extract 4 from Chapter 1

他的表哥裘学良是沪江纱厂的厂长，就凭这个亲戚关系到厂里来的，起先是担任事务住任的工作，最近升了副厂长。裘学良经常病在家, 不来上班。梅佐贤这个副厂长, 几乎就是正厂长。他在纱厂工作和他开饭馆一样, 钱经过梅佐贤的手, 他总要弄点油水。比如说厂里发代办米吧， 本来应该向上海粮食公司采办的，但是没有油水可捞，他就向庆丰米号采办，沪江纱厂总管理处的职员和厂里职员家属的代办米，

Translation 1.

His cousin Qiu Xueliang was the director of the Hu Jiang Cotton Mill, and it had been purely on the strength of this family relationship that he had come to the mill; his first post had been as head of the general office and recently he had been promoted to deputy director. Since Qiu Xueliang spent most of his time ill at home and did not come in to the mill, Mei Zuoxian, as deputy director, was virtually running the mill himself. He behaved in his present job the way he always had as a restaurateur; no money could pass through his hands without some of it finding its way into his pocket in the form of 'squeeze'. For example, the rice issued by the mill in part-payment of wages should originally have been obtained from the Shanghai Foodstuffs Corporation but there was no scope for squeeze under this arrangement so he changed over to Qing Feng Rice Store. All the rice issued to families of the head-office and mill staff was supplied by the Qing Feng Rice Store;

Translation 2.

His cousin Qiu Xueliang was the director of the Hu Jiang Cotton Mill, thanks to which he joined the factory. His first position was head of the administrative office then, more recently, he was promoted to deputy manager. However, Qiu was at home sick much of the time that meant Mei effectively controlled the mill. He ran the business as he had run the family restaurant; raking-off a cut from from every deal he handle. For example, the rice that was distributed to the workers in part-payment of wages should have been provided by the Shanghai

Foodstuffs Corporation, however, there was nothing in this for Mei, so he transferred the business to the Qing Feng Rice Company.

Synthesis

他	的	表哥	裘学良	是	沪江纱厂	的
Tā	de	biǎogē	Qiú Xuéliáng	shì	hùjiāngshāchǎng	de
His	poss.	cousin	name	is	Hù Jiāng Cotton Mill	of

厂长，	就	凭	这	个	亲戚	关系到	厂
chǎngzhǎng	jiù	píng	zhè	ge	qīnqi	guānxìdào	chǎng
director	thus	rely on	this	class.	relative	relations	factory

里	来	的，	起先	是	担任	事务	住任的
lǐ	lái	de	qǐxiān	shì	dānrèn	shìwù	zhùrènde
in	arrive	part.	at first	to be	to serve	affairs	to live at

工作，	最近	升	了	副厂长。	裘学良	经常
gōngzuò	zuìjìn	shēng	le	fùchǎngzhǎng	Qiú Xuéliáng	jīngcháng
work	recently	rise	part.	deputy director	name	often

病	在	家，	不	来	上班。	梅佐贤
bìng	zài	jiā	bù	lái	shàngbān	Méi Zuǒxián
sick	at	home	not	to come	go to work	name

这个	副厂长，	几乎	就是	正	厂长。
zhègè	fùchǎngzhǎng	jīhū	jiùshì	zhèng	chǎngzhǎng
this	deputy director	almost	*emphatic*	main	factory director

他	在	纱厂	工作	和	他	开	饭馆
Tā	zài	shāchǎng	gōngzuò	huò	tā	kāi	fànguǎn
his	at	cotton mill	job	and	his	run	restaurant

一样，	钱	经过	梅佐贤	的	手，	他	总要
yīyàng	qián	jīngguò	Méi Zuǒxián	de	shǒu	tā	zǒngyào
the same	money	passed	name	of	hand	his	nevertheless

弄	点	油水。	比如	说	厂里	发	代办
nòng	diǎn	yóu	Bǐrú	shuì	chǎnglǐ	fā	dàibàn
manage	some	profits	for example	persuade	factory	send	agent

米	吧，	本来	应该	向	上海粮食公司
mǐ	ba	běnlái	yīnggāi	xiàng	Shànghǎi Liángshi Gōngsī
rice	particle	at first	must	to	Shanghai Foodstuffs Co.

采办	的，	但是	没有	油水	可	捞，	他	就
cǎibàn	de	dànshì	méiyǒu	yóu	kě	lāo	tā	jiù
purchase	part.	but	not	profits	able	gain	he	then

向	庆丰米号	采办，	沪江纱厂	总管理处
xiàng	qìngfēngmǐháo	cǎibàn	hùjiāngshāchǎng	zǒngguǎnlǐchù
towards	Qing Feng Rice Co.	purchase	Hùjiāng Cotton Mill	offices, HQ

的	职员	和	厂里职员	家属	的	代办	米，
de	zhíyuán	huò	chǎnglǐzhíyuán	jiāshǔ	de	dàibàn	mǐ
of	workers	with	factory workers	family	of	representatives	rice

Notes

开 kāi – run, operate

号 háo – business house; company

Extract 5 from Chapter 1

...都是庆丰送去的；有时，在梅佐贤的默许之下，还掺杂一些霉米进去；那时候，梅佐贤所得到的油水当然就更多了。大家吃代办米发现霉味，自然有些不不满，甚至于发了牢骚, 梅佐贤表现得更不满，他当着职员的面骂庆丰，说这样做生意是自寻；可是下一次的代办米仍然是要庆丰送出。一任事务主任，梅佐贤捞到的油水不少， 他同人合伙，开了一家碾米厂。

Translation 1.

Sometimes, with Mei Zuoxian's tacit consent, some mildewed rice would be mixed in with it. At such times Mei Zuoxian's squeeze would naturally increase. And, naturally enough, there would be a certain amount of discontent and even grumbling when people found their rice tasted mildewy. Mei Zuoxian pretended to be even more upset than they were and abused Qing Feng Rice Store in front of his staff, saying that this was a suicidal way of doing business; yet the next issue of rice would be supplied by the Qing Feng Rice Store as before. As the head of the general office, Mei Zuoxian was able to line his pockets with squeeze; later he clubbed together with some other people to set up a rice-hulling mill.

Translation 2.

Sometimes, with Mei's tacit consent, mouldy rice was mixed in with the good, thus adding to Mei's rake-off. Naturally people complained when they tasted the mould. Mei pretended to be angry and accused the Qing Feng company of profiteering in front of his staff, in spite of that the next delivery was supplied by the same firm. As head of the company's general office, Mei was thus able to line his pockets and later invest in a new rice mill together with his cronies.

Synthesis

都是	庆丰	送去	的；	有时，	在	梅佐贤
Dōushì	Qìng Fēng	sòngqù	de	yǒushí	zài	Méi Zuǒxián
All	name	send	part.	sometimes	at	name

的	默许	之下，	还	掺杂	一些	霉	米
de	mòxǔ	zhīxià	hái	chānzá	yīxiē	méi	mǐ
part.	tacit	under	also	mixing	some	moldy	rice

进去；	那时候，	梅佐贤	所得	到	的	油水
jìnqù	nàshíhou	Méi Zuǒxián	suǒdé	dào	de	yóushuǐ
go in	at the same time	name	acquired	comp.	of	profit

当然	就	更多	了。	大家	吃	代办	米
Dāngrán	jiù	gèngduō	le	Dàjiā	chī	dàibàn	mǐ
naturally	then	even more	part.	Everybody	eat	representatives	rice

发现	霉	味，	自然	有些	不	不满，	甚至于
fāxiàn	méi	wèi	zìrán	yǒuxiē	bù	bùmǎn	shènzhìyú
find	moldy	taste	of course	somewhat	not	discontent	so much so

发	了	牢骚，	梅佐贤	表现	得	更	不满，
fā	le	láosāo	Méi Zuǒxián	biǎoxiàn	de	gèng	bùmǎn
develope	part.	discontent	name	display	part.	very	discontent

他	当着	职员	的	面	骂	庆丰，
tā	dāngzhe	zhíyuán	de	miàn	mà	Qìng Fēng
he	in presence of	staff	part.	face	cursed	name

说	这样	做生意	是	自寻；	可是	下一次
shuō	zhèyàng	zuòshēngyì	shì	zìxún	kěshì	xiàyīcì
said	this kind of	to do business	to be	self seeking	however	next time

的	代办	米	仍然	是	要	庆丰	送出。
de	dàibàn	mǐ	réngrán	shì	yāo	Qìngfēng	sòngchū
part.	act for	rice	still	to be	ask	name	send

一任	事务	主任，	梅佐贤	捞到的	油水
Yīrèn	shìwù	zhǔrèn	Méi Zuǒxián	lāodàode	yóushuǐ
Allowed	business	director	name	make	profit

不少,	他	同人	合伙,	开	了	一	家	碾米厂。
bùshǎo	tā	tóngrćn	hćhuǒ	kāi	lc	yī	jiā	niǎnmǐchǎng
a lot	his	colleagues	jointly	start	part.	one	class.	rice mill

Notes

碾米厂 niǎnmǐchǎng – rice hulling mill

Extract 6 from Chapter 1

工人说，蛋糕到了梅佐贤的手里也要小一圈。这个比喻并不过火。在上海解放前夕，厂里的刚丝针布，皮带皮, 棉纱等等东西，直往他家里搬，起初说是保存起来，以后就变成梅佐贤的了。

他做这些事本总经理并不是不得，但他不在乎。因为总经理要更大的油水，梅佐贤可以在这个方面献出他的才能智慧。只要总经里的眉毛一动，

Translation 1.

The workers said even an egg would shrink on its way through his hands, an analogy that was far from being an exaggeration. When Shanghai was liberated, wire-cloth, leather belting, yarn and so on were shifted to his home, at first for the alleged purpose of looking after it, though later it bccamc Mci Zuoxian's own.

It was not that the general manager did not know of these activities of his, but he did not care. For the general manager was interested in bigger slices of squeeze than this, and Mei was able to contribute his abilities and his wits to these larger issues. The merest twitch of an eyebrow,

Translation 2.

The workers said even an egg would shrink as it passed through his hands, an analogy that was far from being exaggerated. On the eve of Shanghai's liberation, carding-wire, leather belting, yarn and other goods were moved for safekeeping to Mei's home. These were soon considered by Mei's as his own property. The general manager overlooked this, since he was interested in bigger things and Mei's talents would be of help. The merest twitch of an eyebrow ...

Synthesis

工人	说,	鸡蛋	到了	梅佐贤	的	手里	也
Gōngrén	shuō	jīdàn	dàole	Méi Zuǒxián	de	shǒulǐ	yě
Workers	said	egg	arrive	name	part.	in hand	also

要	小	一圈。	这个	比喻	并不	过火。	在
yāo	xiǎo	yījuàn	Zhège	bǐyù	bìngbù	guòhuǒ	Zài
would	small	round	This	analogy	not at all	exaggerated	At

上海	解放	前夕,	厂里	的	刚丝针布,	皮带皮,
shànghǎi	jiěfàng	qiánxī	chǎnglǐ	de	gāngsīzhēnbù	pídàipí
Shanghai	liberate	eve	in factory	part	carding wire	leather belt

棉纱	等等	东西,	直往	他	家里	搬,	起初
miánshā	děngděng	dōngxi	zhíwǎng	tā	jiālǐ	bān	qǐchū
cotton yarn	etcetera	things	directly	his	home	move	at first

说	是	保存	起来,	以后	就	变成	梅佐贤
shuō	shì	bǎocún	qǐlai	yǐhòu	jiù	biànchéng	Méi Zuǒxián
said	to be	to conserve	adverb	after	then	become	name

的了。	他	做	这些	事	本	总经理	并不
de le	Tā	zu	zhèxiē	shì	běn	zǒngjīnglǐ	bìngbù
particles	He	make	these	things	class.	general manager	not at all

是	不得,	但	他	不在乎。	因为	总经理
shì	bùdé	dàn	tā	bùzàihu	Yīnwèi	zǒngjīnglǐ
to be	not allowed	however	he	doesn't care	Because	general manager

要	更大	的	油水,	梅佐贤	可以	在	这个
yā	gèngdà	de	yóushuǐ	Méi Zuǒxián	kěyǐ	zài	zhège
want	bigger	part.	profit	name	could	at	this

方面	献出	他	的	才能	智慧。	只要
fāngmiàn	xiànchū	tā	de	cáinéng	zhìhui	Zhǐyào
aspect	offer	his	part.	ability	knowledge	If

总经里	的	眉毛	一动,
zǒngjīnglǐ	de	méimao	yīdòng
gen.manager	part.	eyebrow	moved

Notes

The battle for Shanghai took place in 1949, with the Communist forces of Mao opposing Chiang Kai-shek's Nationalist government. The Communist victory is commemorated in China today as the 'Liberation of Shanghai'. The city emerged relatively intact in spite of the Nationalist's attempted scorch-earth policy thanks to the populations resistance to the destruction.

刚丝针布，皮带皮, 棉纱 technical terms employed in the cotton industry

Extract 7 from Chapter 1

他就晓得总经里在动脑筋。丹是总经理要办的事，假如别人办不到，只要找梅做贤，没有一件不能完成的。而且, 有些事只要总经理稍为暗示一下，他就懂得因为怎样去办。他的另外一绰号叫做总经理肚里的蛔虫，就是这样得来的。因为字太长，又只能说明他的一个方面，就是说不恨贴切，叫的人比较少，也不经常。酸辣汤的外号在厂里是无人不知的。

Translation 1.

...was enough to tell him what was going on in the general manager's mind. If the general manager wanted something done and no one else was able to tackle it he had only to entrust it to Mei Zuoxian, who put anything through. Furthermore, it only needed a hint from the general manager for him to know how certain matters should be handled. He had another nickname, 'Round-worm in the general manager's belly', which had been given to him for this reason. But since it was rather long and not very very apt in the sense that it only described one aspect of him, it was not used by many people and was not often heard. But there was no one in the factory who did not know his other nickname 'Pepper-and-Vinegar Soup'.

Translation 2.

...was enough to tell him what was going on the the general manager's mind. Anything special was entrusted to Mei Zuoxian, for whom the slightest hint was sufficient to understand how certain matters should be handled. This resulted in another sobriquet, the parasite (the worm in the general manager's belly), but for simplicity he was generally called 'Sour-soup' by most of the the factory workers.

Synthesis

他	就	晓得	总经里	在	动脑筋。	凡是
tā	jiù	xiǎode	zǒngjīnglǐ	zài	dòngnǎojīn	Fánshì
He	then	to know	general manager	at	using his brain	All

总经理	要	办	的	事，	假如	别人
zǒngjīnglǐ	yāo	bàn	de	shì	jiǎrú	biérén
general manager	want	manage	part.	business	if	other people

办不到，	只要	找	梅做贤，	没有	一	件
bànbudào	zhǐyào	zhǎo	Méi Zuǒxián	méiyǒu	yī	jiàn
impossible	as long as	look for	name	had not	a, one	item

不能	完成	的。	而且，	有些	事	只要
bùnéng	wánchéng	de	Erqiě	yǒuxiē	shì	zhǐyào
cannot	complete	part.	But	some	matters	as long as

总经理	稍为	暗示	一下，	他	就	懂得
zǒngjīnglǐ	shāowèi	yīnshì	yīxià	tā	jiù	dǒngde
general manager	somewhat	hint	a little	he	then	understood

因为	怎样	去办。	他	的	另外	一	绰号
yīnwèi	zěnyàng	qùbàn	Tā	de	lìngwài	yī	chuòhào
because	this	way	His	part.	besides	a, one	nickname

叫做	总经理	肚里	的	蛔虫，	就是
jiàozuò	zǒngjīnglǐ	dùlǐ	de	huíchóng	jiùshì
called	general manager	stomach	part.	roundworm	this is

这样	得	来的。	因为	字	太长，	又	只能
zhèyàng	děi	láidí	Yīnwèi	zì	tàicháng	yòu	zhǐnéng
why this	must	come about	Because	word	too long	also	can

说明	他的	一	个	方面，	就是说	不	恨
shuōmíng	tāde	yī	gè	fāngmiàn	jiùshìshuō	bù	hèn
explain	his	a, one	class.	attitude	in other words	not	hate

贴切，	叫	的	人	比较	少，	也不	经常。
tiēqiè	jiào	de	rén	bǐjiào	shǎo	yěbù	jīngcháng
closest	call	part.	man	comparatively	small	neither nor	daily often

酸辣汤	的	外号	在厂里	是	无人不知	的。
Suānlàtāng	de	wàihào	zàichǎnglǐ	shì	wúrénbùzhī	de
hot sour soup	part.	nickname	in the factory	to be	known to all	part.

Notes

肚里的蛔虫 dǔlǐ de huíchóng - roundworm belly, wormy belly, parasite

Extract 8 from Chapter 1

他自然并非不晓得这个外号，有时听到了倒反而很得意：我梅佐贤就是酸辣汤，你把我怎么样？现在从事务主任爬到副厂长的地位，是总经理面前的一位红人，谁也奈何他不得。

梅佐贤走进了客厅。穿着白卡叽布制服的王揍着一个托盘经经走过来，把得坐在双人纱发里，就像在自己家里一样，他向老王望了一眼，谦和地问道：

“总经理回来了吗？”

Translation 1.

Naturally enough he was far from being ignorant of the fact he was known by this nickname, and sometimes he would overhear it being used and derive considerable satisfaction from hearing it; what can you do about it if I am Sour-soup? For now that he had climbed up from the position of head of the general office to that of director of the mill he was a great a great favourite with the general manager and there was nothing anybody could do about him.

Mei Zuoxian went into the drawing room and Old

Wang, in a uniform of white drill, came over noiselessly with a tray and put on a low round table in front of Mei Zuoxian some superior grade Lion Peak Longjing tea that he had just made. Mei Zuoxian planted himself nonchalantly on a settee, making himself thoroughly at home, then glanced at Old Wang and enquired amiably:

'Is the general manager back yet?'

Translation 2.

Naturally he was far from ignoring this and sometimes he would overhear it being used, deriving a certain satisfaction. What can I do about it? he asked himself. He climbed up to being manager of the general office to mill general manager and nobody could touch him.

Mei went into the reception room and Old Wang, dressed in a white serge uniform, appeared silently with a tray and a pot of the best Lion Peak Longjing tea which he placed on a low table. Mei nonchalantly planted himself on a sofa, then glancing towards Wang asked:

'Has the general manager returned?'

Synthesis

他	自然	并非	不	晓得	这个	外号，	有时
Ta	zìrán	bìngfēi	bù	xiǎode	zhège	wàihào	yǒushí
He	naturally	does not	not	know	this	nickname	sometimes

听到	了	倒反	而	很	得意：	我	梅佐贤
tīngdào	le	dàofǎn	ér	hěn	déyì	wǒ	Méi Zuǒxián
to hear	part.	on the contrary	and is	very	proud	I	name

就是	酸辣汤，	你	把	我	怎么样？	现在
jiùshì	Suānlàtāng	nǐ	bà	wǒ	zěnmeyàng	Xiànzài
am	Hot sour soup	you	part.	I	what can do?	Now

从	事务	主任	爬	到	副厂长	的	地位,
cóng	shìwù	zhǔrèn	pá	dào	fùchǎngzhǎng	de	dìwèi
from	business	director	climb	to	deputy director	part.	position

是	总经理	面前	的	一位	红人,	谁	也
shì	zǒngjīnglǐ	miànqián	de	yīwèi	hóngrén	shéi	yě
to be	general manager	in front	part.	a person	favorite	who	also

奈何	他	不得。	梅佐贤	走进	了
nàihé	tā	bùdé	Méi Zuǒxián	zǒujìn	le
do something to	he, him	may, must not	name	went in	part

客厅。	穿着	白	卡叽布	制服	的	老王	捧
kètīng	Chuānzhe	bái	qiǎjībù	zhìfú	de	lǎowàng	pěng
reception	Wearing	white	serge cloth	uniform	of	Lao Wang	holding

着	一	个	托	盘	轻轻	走过来,	把	得
zhe	yī	class.	tuō	tray	qīngqīng	zǒuguòlái	bà	dé
part.			hold	pán	softly	walked in	parti.	taking

坐	在	双人	纱发	里	就	像	在	自己	家里
zuò	zài	shuāngrén	shāfā	lǐ	jiù	xiàng	zài	zìjǐ	jiālǐ
sit	at	two-peron	sofa	in	then	seem	at	one's	home

一样,	他	向	老王	望	了	一眼,	谦和
yīyàng	tā	xiàng	Lǎo Wàng	wàng	le	yīyǎn	qiānhé
like	he	towards	name	look	part.	a glance	modestly

地	问道:	"总经理	回来了	吗?"
de	wèndào	Zǒngjīnglǐ	huílaile	mǎ
part.	asked	General manager	returned	question

Extract 9 from Chapter 1

"刚回来，在楼上洗脸。"

"请你告诉他，我来看他。如果他有事，我在这里多等一歇没有关系。"

老王点了点头，去了。梅佐贤揭开矮圆桌上的那听三五牌香烟，他抽了支出来，就从西袋口袋里掏出一

个银色的烟盒子，很自然地把三五牌的香烟往自己的烟盒子里袋。然后拿起矮圆桌上的银色的朗生打火机，

Translation 1.

'He's just got back. He's upstairs having a wash.'

'I'd like you to tell him I've come to see him. If he's busy I don't mind waiting.'

Old Wang nodded and went off. Mei Zuoxian took the lid off a tin of State Express cigarettes on the little round table and after taking one fished out a silver-coloured cigarette case from the pocket of his European-style suit and calmly filled it from the tin. Then he picked up the silver-coloured Ronson lighter that was on the table,

Translation 2.

'He's just got back. He's upstairs freshening up.'

'Can you tell him I here. If he's busy I can wait.'

Wang nodded and left. Mei open a tin of State Express 555 cigarettes on the small table and after taking one out, pulled a silver cigarette case from his suit-pocket and proceeded to fill it from the tin. Then, taking the silver Ronson lighter that lay on the table,

Synthesis

刚	回来,	在	楼上	洗	脸。	请	你
Gāng	huílai	zài	lóushàng	xǐ	liǎn	Qǐng	nǐ
Just	to return	at	upstairs	wash	face	Please	you

告诉	他,	我	来看	他。	如果	他	有事,
gàosu	tā	wǒ	láikàn	tā	Rúguǒ	tā	yǒushi
tell	he	I	come to see	him	If	he	busy

我	在	这里	多	等	一	歇	没有关系。
wǒ	zài	zhèlǐ	duō	děng	yī	xiē	méiyǒuguānxi
I	at	here	a lot	wait	a, one	rest	no problem

老王	点了,	点头	去了。	梅佐贤	揭开	矮
Lǎo	diǎnle	diǎntóu	qùle	Méi Zuǒxián	jiēkāi	ǎi
Wàng	a little	nod	went	name	open	low

圆桌	上	的	那	听	三五	牌	香烟,
yuánzhuō	shàng	de	nà	tìng	sānwǔ	pái	xiāngyān
round table	on	part.	part.	tin*	555	class.	cigarettes

他	抽	了	支	出来,	就	从	西袋口	袋里
tā	chōu	le	zhī	chūlái	jiù	zòng	xīdài	inside
he	draw	part.	class.	out	then	from	breast pocket	dàilǐ

掏出	一	个	银色	的	烟	盒子,	很	自然
tāochū	yī	gè	yínsè	de	yān	hézi	hěn	zìrán
pulled out	a, one	class.	silver	part.	cigarette	case	very	naturally

地	把	三五	牌	的	香烟	往	自己	的	烟
di	bà	sānwǔ	pái	de	xiāngyān	wǎng	zìjǐ	de	yānhézi
part.	put	555	class.	part.	cigarettes	to	self	part.	cigarette

盒子	里袋。	然后	拿起	矮	圆桌	上	的
hézi	lǐdài	Ránhòu	náqǐ	ǎi	yuánzhuō	shàng	de
case	inside	Then	took	low	round table	on	part.

银色	的	朗生	打火机,
yínsè	de	lǎngshēng	dǎhuǒjī
silver	part.	Ronson*	lighter

*三五 State Express 555 cigarettes in a tin box, 听 tìng – tin (p.139)

Extract 10 from Chapter 1

燃着了烟在抽，怡然地望着客厅角落里的那架大钢琴。后面是落地的大玻璃窗，透过乳白色绢子的团花窗帷，他欣赏着窗外花团里翠绿的龙柏。

Translation 1.

...lit his cigarette and sat there smoking, looking contentedly across at the grand piano in the corner of the room. There was a large window extending right down to the floor behind the piano and he was enjoying the emerald green cypresses in the garden outside through the milk-white silk curtains patterned with circular designs.

*朗生 Lǎngshēng – Ronson (a cigarette lighter) transliteration (p.139)

Translation 2.

...lit his cigarette and sat there smoking, gazing contentedly at the grand piano in the corner of the room. The windows behind were hung with white embroidered silk curtains and in the garden beyond he admired the flowers amongst the deep green cypresses and junipers.

Synthesis

燃着	了	烟	在	抽，	怡然	地	望着
ránzhuó	le	yān	zài	chōu	yírán	dì	wàngzhuó
light	part.	cigarette	at	draw	contentedly	part.	gazed

客厅	角落	里	的	那	架	大钢琴。	钢琴
kètīng	jiǎoluò	lǐ	de	nǎ	jià	dàgāngqín	Gāngqín
reception room	corner	in	part.	there	class.	grand piano	Piano

后面	地	大	玻璃	窗，	透过	乳白色	绢
hòumian	dì	dà	bōli	chuāng	tòuguò	rǔbáisè	juàn
behind	part.	big	glass	window	through	milky white	silk

子	的	团花	窗帷，	他	欣赏着	窗
zi	de	tuánhuā	chuāngwéi	tā	xīnshǎngzhe	chuāng
prefix.	part.	embroidered	cutains	he	appreciated	window

外	花团	里	翠绿	的	龙柏。
wài	huātuán	lǐ	cuìlǜ	de	lóngbǎi
outside	blossom	in	emerald green	part.	junipers

Notes

绢 juàn – a kind of silk

Extract 11 from Chapter 1

楼上传来咳嗽声。梅佐贤从怡然自得的境地跳了出来，他连忙熄灭了烟，站起来拍一拍刚才落在西装裤子上的烟灰，整了一下玫瑰红的领带。他晓得总经理快下来了，目光对着客厅的门。果然楼梯上有人下来了，沉重的脚步声一步步迟缓地往下移动。梅佐贤走到门那边去，像是接待一个贵宾似的在那边等候着。

Translation 1.

A cough from upstairs brought Mei Zuoxian out of his carefree reverie with a start; he hastily stubbed out his cigarette, stood up to brush the cigarette ash off his trousers and adjusted his rose-red tie. He knew that the general manager would soon be down and his eyes were on the door of the room. Sure enough someone was coming down the stairs with heavy steps that moved down slowly a step at a time. Mei Zuoxian went over to the door and waited there as if to receive an honoured guest.

<u>*Translation 2.*</u>

A cough from upstairs brought Mei out of his reverie with a start; he hastily put out his cigarette, stood up, brushed the cigarette ash off his trousers and straightened his tie. He fixed his eyes on the door, the general manager would be down any moment. Then, sure enough he heard the heavy steps on the stairs. Mei went over to the door, where he waited as if to receive an honoured guest.

<u>Synthesis</u>

楼上	传来	咳嗽	声。	梅佐贤	从	怡然自得
Lóushàng	chuánlái	késou	shēng	Méi Zuǒxián	cóng	yíránzìde
Upstairs	came	cough	sound	name	mood	happy content

的	境地	跳了	出来，	他	连忙	熄灭	了
de	jìngdì	tiàole	chūlái	tā	liánmáng	xīmiè	le
part.	circumstances	bounded	up	he	at once	put out	part.

烟，	站起来	拍一拍	刚才	落在	西装裤子
yān	zhànqǐlai	pāiyīpāi	gāngcái	luòzài	xīzhuāngkùzi
cigarette	to stand up	patted	just	drop on,	Western trousers

上	的	烟灰，	整了一下	玫瑰红的	领带。
shàng	de	yānhuī	zhěngleyīxià	méiguīhóngde	lǐngdài
on	part.	cigarette ash	straightened	rose coloured	tie

他	晓得	总经理	快	下来了，	目光	对着
Tā	xiǎode	zǒngjīnglǐ	kuài	xiàlaile	mùguāng	duìzhe
he	know	general manager	about to	to come down	look	towards

客厅	的	门。	果然	楼梯上	有人	下来了,
kètīng	de	mén	Guǒrán	lóutī	yǒurén	xiàlaile
reception	part.	door	Sure enough	upstairs	somebody	coming down

沉重	的	脚步	声	一步步	迟缓	地	往下
chénzhòng	de	jiǎobù	shēng	yībùbù	chíhuǎn	de	wǎngxià
heavy	part.	footstep	sound	step by step	slow	-ly	down

移动。	梅佐贤	走	到	门	那边去,	像	是
yídòng	Méi Zuǒxián	zǒu	dào	mén	nàbianqù	xiàng	shì
movement	name	walk	to	door	over to	seem	to be

接待	一	个	贵宾	似的	在	那边	等候着。
jiēdài	yī	gè	guìbīn	shìde	zài	nàbian	děnghòuzhe
receive	a	class.	honoured guest	as if	at	there	waiting

Notes

从 — cóng – attitude, mood

怡然自得 — yíránzì (idiom) – happy, to be pleased with oneself

Extract 12 from Chapter 1

　一个矮胖的中年人走到客厅门口，容光焕发，脸胖得像一个圆球，下巴的肉往下垂着，使人担心这肉随时可以掉下来。看上去年纪不过四十左右，实际上他已是靠五十的人了。头上没有一根白发，修理得很整齐，油光发亮，镜子似的，苍蝇飞上去也要滑下来的。头上没有一根白发，他很得意自己没有一根白发，用谦虚的语气经常在朋友面前夸耀自己：

Translation 1.

A short, fat, middle-aged man appeared in the doorway, his almost spherical face plump and shinning and his double chin hanging down in an alarming way that made one fear that it might drop off at any moment. He did not give the impression of being more than about forty, but in actual fact he was close on fifty. There was not a single grey hair on his head and his hair was smoothed down to such a gleaming, mirror-like surface that an alighting fly would have skidded off it. He was rather proud of the fact that he had not a single grey hair on his head and he was always boasting to his friends in a modest tone of voice:

Translation 2.

A short, overweight, middle aged man appeared at the door, his plump round faced beamed, his fleshy chin sagged so much one feared it would fall off at any moment. He appeared to be about forty, though in fact he was already going-on fifty. His carefully groomed hair shone like a mirror, it was so smooth a fly would have slipped off. With not a single grey hair on his head he felt intensely proud of himself. Using the falsely modest tone he employed when boasting to friends, he told them:

Synthesis

一	个	矮胖	的	中年	人	走	到	客厅
Yī	gè	ǎipàng	de	zhōngnián	rén	zǒu	dào	kètīng
A	class.	short thickset	part.	middle-aged	man	walk	to	reception

门口	容光焕发,	脸	胖	得	像	一	个
ménkǒu	róngguānghuànfā	liǎn	pàng	děi	xiàng	yī	gè
doorway	beaming	face	plump	part.	resemble	a, one	class.

圆球,	下巴	的	肉	往	下垂	着,	使
yuánqiú	xiàba	de	ròu	wǎng	xiàchuí	zhe	shǐ
ball	chin	part.	fleash	direction	sag	part.	to cause

人	担心	这	肉	随时	可以	掉下	来。
rén	dānxīn	zhè	ròu	suíshí	kěyǐ	diàoxià	lái
people	worry	this	flesh	any time	could	drop	to come

看上去	年纪	不过	四十	左右,	实际上	他
kànshangqu	niánjì	bùguò	sìshí	zuǒyòu	shíjìshàng	tā
It would appear	young	only	forty	about	in fact	he

已	是	靠	五十	的	人	了。	头上
yǐ	shì	kào	wǔshí	de	rén	le	Tóushàng
already	to be, is	going on	fifty	part.	person	part.	Head

没有	一	根	白发,	修理	得很	整齐,	油光
méiyǒu	yī	gēn	báifà	xiūlǐ	dehěn	zhěngqí	yóuguāng
have not	single	class.	gray hair	cut	very	neatly	glossy

发亮,	镜子	似的,	苍蝇	飞上去	也	要
fāliàng	jìngzi	shìde	cāngying	fēishàngqù	yě	yāo
shine	mirroir	as if	a fly	fly onto	also	would

滑	下来的。	头	上	没有	一	根	白发,
huá	xiàlaide	Tóu	shàng	méiyǒu	yī	gēn	báifà
slide	down	head	on	have not	a, one	class.	grey hair

他	很	得意	自己	没有	一	根	白发,
tā	hěn	déyì	zìjǐ	méiyǒu	yī	gēn	báifà
he	very	proud	oneself	have not	a, one	class.	grey hair

用	谦虚	的	语气	经常	在	朋友	面前
yòng	qiānxū	de	yǔqì	jīngcháng	zài	péngyou	miànqián
to use	modest	part.	tone	often	at	friend	in front of

夸耀	自己:
kuāyào	zìjǐ
flaunt	oneself

Extract 13 from Chapter 1

“我是蒙不白之冤，这个年纪应该有白发了。我的三个老婆对我没有一根白发是很不满意的，尤其是大老婆最恨我的头发不白。”如果朋友们凑趣地说：“那是怕你纳第三个姨太太。”那他就高兴得眼睛眯成一条缝，乐得说不出话来，只是嘻嘻地笑笑。上海解放以后，他的说法有一点修正：“我的老婆对我没有一根白发是很不满意的。”他不再提三个老婆了。

Translation 1.

‘I’m destined never to go grey; I ought to be going grey at my age. My three wives are very annoyed with me about it, and my first wife is particularly upset about it.’ If his friends then said jokingly: ‘That’s because they’re afraid you’ll take a third concubine,’ he would be so delighted that his eyes would narrow into slits and so happy that he could not speak, only chuckle to himself. After the liberation of Shanghai he made a slight modification in this remark: ‘My wife is very annoyed with me for not having a single grey hair.’ No more mention of three wives.

Translation 2.

‘I know its unjust, at my age I should have grey hair. My three wives are not at all happy with this situation, especially my first wife who detests the fact my hair is not grey.’ When his friends jokingly told him he would have to take a third concubine, his eyes narrowed with pleasure leaving him almost wordless. After the liberation of

Shanghai he changed his tone, there was no more mention of three wives, he simply explained his wife was annoyed by the fact there was not a single grey hair to be found on his head.

Synthesis

我	是	蒙	不白之冤,	这个	年纪	应该
Wǒ	shì	mēng	bùbáizhīyuān	zhège	niánjì	yīnggāi
I	am	unaware	injustice	this	age	should

有	白发	了。	我的	三	个	老婆	对
yǒu	báifà	le	Wǒ	sān	gè	lǎopó	duì
to have	grey hair	part.	My	three	class.	wife	vis-à-vis

我	没有	一	根	白发	是	很	不满意	的
wǒ	méiyǒu	yī	gēn	báifà	shì	hěn	bùmǎnyì	de
I	have not	one	class.	grey hair	are	very	dissatisfied	part.

尤其是	大老婆	最	恨	我的	头发	不	白。
yóuqíshì	dàlǎopó	zuì	hèn	wǒde	tóufa	bù	bái
especially	first wife	very	hate	my	hair	neg.	grey

如果	朋友们	凑趣	地	说:	那是	怕	你
Rúguǒ	péngyoumen	còuqù	de	shuō	nàshi of	pà	nǐ
When	friends	joking	-ly	said	course	afraid	you

纳	第三	个	姨太太。	那	他	就	高兴
nà	dìsān	gè	yítàitai	Nà	tā	jiù	gāoxìng
to receive	third	class.	concubine	Then	he	at once	happy

得	眼睛	眯	成	一	条	缝,	乐	得
de	yǎnjing	mī	chéng	yī	tiáo	fèng	lè	de
part.	eyes	squint	become	one	class.	narrow	happy	part.

说不出话来,	只是	嘻嘻	地	笑笑。	上海
shuōbùchūhuàlái	zhǐshì	xīxī	de	xiàoxiào	Shànghǎi
speechless	simply	happy	-ly*	laugh	Shanghai

解放	以后，	他	的	说法	有一点	修正：
jiěfàng	yǐhòu	tā	de	shuō fǎ	yǒu yīdiǎn	xiūzhèng
to liberate	after	he	part.	version	a little bit	modified

我的	老婆	对	我	没有	一	根	白发
wǒde	lǎopó	duì	wǒ	méiyǒu	yī	gēn	báifà
my	wife	towards	me	have not	one	class.	grey hair

是	很	不满意	的。	他	不再	提	三
shì	hěn	bùmǎnyì	de	Tā	bùzài	tí	sān
is	very	dissatisfied	part.	He	no longer	mention	three

个	老婆	了。
gè	lǎopó	le
class.	wife	part.

* 地 a structural particle like -ly

Extract 14 from Chapter 1

梅佐贤曲背哈腰迎接了沪江纱厂总经理徐义德：

"总经理，又来打扰你了。"

"来了很久吧，累你等了。"徐总经理漫不经心地瞟了他一眼。

"刚来，没啥。"

徐总经理一屁股坐在梅佐贤对面的单人沙发里，把整个沙发塞得满满的。他抽了一支烟，一对鱼眼睛望着米色的屋顶，嘴里吐出一个个圆圆的烟圈。

Translation 1.

Mei Zuoxian received Xu Yide, the general manager of the Hu Jiang Cotton Mill, with a deferential forward inclination of the body:

'I have come to disturb you again, sir.'

'Sorry to have kept you waiting for such a long time,' said the general manager, glancing briefly at him.

'It's alright, I've only just come.'

Xu Yide plumped himself down in an armchair opposite Mei Zuoxian, filling the chair completely. He lit a cigarette and sat there blowing smoke rings and gazing up at the off-white ceiling with his fish-like eyes.

Translation 2.

Mei greeted Xu Yide, the general manager of the Hu Jiang Cotton Mill, with a deferential bow.

'I'm disturbing you again Sir.'

'Sorry to have kept you waiting so long,' said Xu, glancing briefly at him.

'Not at all, I've only just arrived.'

Xu dropped into an armchair opposite Mei, filling it completely. He lit a cigarette and sat blowing smoke rings as he gazed up at the white ceiling with his fish eyes.

Synthesis

梅佐贤	曲背	哈腰	迎接	了	沪江纱厂
Méi Zuǒxián	qūbèi	hāyāo	yíngjiē	le	Hùjiāng Shāchǎng
name	bow	to bend	to greet	part.	Hùjiāng Cotton Mill

总经理	徐义德:	总经理,	又	来	打扰
zǒngjīnglǐ	Xú Yìdé	zǒngjīnglǐ	yòu	lái	dǎrǎo
general manager	name	general manager	again	come	to disturb

你	了。	来	了	很	久	吧	累	你
nǐ	le	Lái	le	hěn	jiǔ	ba	lěi	nǐ
you	part.	Come in	part.	very	time	part.	involve	you

等	了。	徐	总经理	漫不经心	地	瞟
děng	le	Xú	zǒngjīnglǐ	mànbùjīngxīn	de	piǎo
wait	part.	name	general man.	careless; heedless	-ly	cast a glance

了	一眼。	刚	来,	没	啥 (什么)。	徐
le	yīyǎn	Gāng	lái	méi	shá (dialectal)	Xú
part.	a glance	Just	come	not	matter	name

总经理	一	屁股	坐	梅佐贤	对面	的
zǒngjīnglǐ	yī	pìgu	zài	Méi Zuǒxián	duìmiàn	de
general manager	one	buttocks	at	name	opposite	part.

单人	沙发	里	把	整个	沙发	塞	得
dānrén	shāfā	lǐ	bǎ	zhěnggè	shāfā	sāi	de
sofa	sofa	in	take	whole	sofa	to squeeze in	part.

满满	的。	他	抽了	一	支烟	一对	鱼
mǎnmǎn	de	Tā	chōule	yī	zhīyān	yīdu	yú
full	part.	He	smoked	one	a cigarette	a pair	fish

眼睛	望	着	米色	的	屋顶,	嘴里	吐
yǎnjing	wàng	zhe	mǐsè	de	wūdǐng	zuǐlǐ	tǔ
eyes	gazed	part.	cream coloured	part.	ceiling	mouth	spit

出	一个个	圆圆	的	烟圈。
chū	yīgègè	yuányuán	de	yānquān
out	one by one	round	part.	smoke ring

Extract 15 from Chapter 1

梅佐贤仔细留神徐总经理的脸色，眉宇间很开朗，嘴角上时不时露出得意的微笑。他晓得今天徐总经理的情绪很好，准备好的事情可以提出来谈一谈。

“总经理，汕头的电报到了……”

徐总经理一听到汕头两个字马上就紧张起来了，他的眼光从米色的屋顶移到梅佐贤长方型的脸上：“那几批货色怎么样？”

Translation 1.

Mei Zouxian was paying close attention to the general manager’s face; his brows were unwrinkled and from time to time a satisfied smile appeared on his lips. From this he deduced that the general manager was in a good mood today, so it would be fine for him to bring up the subject he had in mind.

'We've had a telegram from Shantou, sir....'

At the mention of the word 'Shantou' Xu Yide's expression at once became tense and his eyes switched from the off-white ceiling to Mei Zuowian's long, squarish face.

'What about the goods?'

Translation 2.

Mei paid close attention to Xu's face; his brow was relaxed and from time to time a self-satisfied smile appeared on his lips. He deduced the general manager was in a good mood; it was a good moment to bring up the subject he had in mind.

'We've received a telegram from Shantou sir....'

At the mention of Shantou, Xu's expression became tense and his eyes switched from the ceiling to Mei's long face.

'How did they get on the those consignments of goods?'

Synthesis

梅佐贤	仔细留神	徐	总经理	的	脸色,
Méi Zuǒxián	zǐxì liúshén	xú	zǒngjīnglǐ	de	liǎnsè
name	careful	slow	general manager	part.	expression

眉宇间	很	开朗,	嘴	角	上	时不时
méiyǔjiān	hěn	kāilǎng	zuǐ	jiǎ	shàng	shíbùshí
brow	very	cheerful	mouth	corner	on	from time to time

露出	得意	的	微笑。	他	晓得	今天	徐
lùchū	déyì	de	wēixiào	Tā	xiǎode	jīntiān	Xú
to show	self content	part.	smile	He	know	today	name

总经理	的	情绪	很好，	准备	好的	事情
zǒngjīnglǐ	de	qíngxù	hěnhào	zhǔnbèi	hàode	shìqíng
general manager	part.	mood	very good	preparation	good	matter

可以	提出	来	谈一谈。	总经理	汕头
kěyǐ	tíchū	lái	tányītán	zǒngjīnglǐ	Shàntóu
can	to raise	to come	discuss	General manager	locality

总经理	的	电报	到了…	徐	总经理
zǒngjīnglǐ	de	diànbào	dàole	Xú	zǒngjīnglǐ general
general manager	part.	telegram	arrived	name	manager

一听到	汕头	两	个	字	马上	就	紧张
yītīng	Shàntóu	liǎng	gè	zì	mǎshàng	jiù	jǐnzhāng
hearing	locality	two	class.	word	immediately	at once	nervous

起来	了，	他	的	眼光	从	米色	的	屋顶
qǐlai	le	tā	de	yǎnguāng	cóng	mǐsè	de	wūdǐng
become	part.	he	part.	gaze	from	cream	part.	ceiling

移	到	梅佐贤	长方	型	的	脸	上：
yí	dào	Méi Zuǒxián	chángfāng	xíng	de	liǎn	shàng
shift	to	name	rectangular	style	part.	face	on

那	几	批	货色	怎么样？
nǎ	jǐ	pī	huosè	zěnmeyàng
this	how many	class.	goods	how about?

Notes

汕头 Shàntóu – Shantou, a prefecture level city in Guangdong

Extract 16 from Chapter 1

"都脱手啦。装到汕头的二十一支三百八十件，装到汉口广州的二十支一共八百三十二件全抛出了。"

"多少款子？"

"一共是一百二十五万二千四百八十块港币。"

"划到香港没有？"

"现在政府对外汇管理的紧了，不容易套。这个数目又不小，想了很多办法，靠了几家有港庄的字号才划过去。因为这个原因，电报来迟了。"

<u>Translation 1.</u>

'They've got rid of the lot. 380 bales of 21-count shipped to Shantou and a total of 832 bales of 20-count shipped to Hankou and Guangzhou; all sold.'

'How much for?'

'Altogether 1,252,480 Hongkong dollars.'

'Have you got the money across to Hongkong yet?'

'The government are tightening up on people sending money abroad and it's not easy to get around the restrictions. After all, it's no small sum and after trying many possible ways they found they could only transfer it through a number of firms having branches in Hongkong. That was the reason why the telegram was late in coming.'

<u>Translation 2.</u>

'They got rid of the lot. Three hundred and eighty bales to Shantou and a total of eight hundred and thirty two bales to Hankou and Guangzhou; all sold.'

'For how much?'

'Altogether 1,252,480 Hongkong dollars.'

'Have you got the money to Hongkong yet?'

'It's a lot of money. Government controls are stricter now and it's not so easy to get around foreign exchange regulations. We depend on firms with branches in Hongkong. That's why the telegram was late.'

Synthesis

都	脱手	啦。	装到	汕头	的	二十一	支
Dōu	tuōshǒu	la	Zhuāng	Shàntóu	de	èrshíyī	zhī
All	disposed of	exclam.	Shipped to	Shantou	part.	21	class.

三百八十	件，	装到	汉口	广州	的	二十
sānbǎibāshí	jiàn	zhuāng	Hànkǒu	Guǎngzhōu	de	èrshí
380	item	ship	Hankou	Canton	part.	20

支	一共	八百三十二	件	全	抛出	了。
zhī	yīgòng	bābǎisānshíèr	jiàn	quán	pāochū	le
class.	altogether	832	item	total	got out	part.

多少	款子？	一共	是	一百二十五万
Duōshao	kuǎnzi	Yīgòng	shì	1,250,000
Dow much	money class.	Altogether	is	

二千四百八十	块	港币。	划	到	香港
2,480	kuài	gǎngbì	huà	dào	Xiānggǎng
	class.	Hongkong $	Transfer	to	Hongkong

没有？	现在	政府	对	外汇管理	的	紧	了，
méiyǒu	Xiànzài	zhèngfǔ	duì	wàihuiguǎnlǐ	de	jǐn	le part.
no	now	government	to	exchange control	part.	strict	

不	容易	套	这个	数目	又	不小，	想	了
bù	róngyì	tào	zhègè	shùmù	yòu	bùxiǎo	xiǎng	le
neg.	easy	to bend	this	amount	also	a lot	think	part.

很多	办法，	靠	了	几	有	港	庄	的
hěnduō	bànfǎ	kào	le	jǐ	yǒu	gǎng	zhuāng	de
many	ways	rely on	part.	some	have	Hongkong	holding	part.

字号	才	划	过去。	因为	这个	原因，
zìhào	cái	huà	guòqu	Yīnwèi	zhègè	yuányīn
business	able	transfer	over	Because	this	reason

电报	来	迟了。
diànbào	lái	chíle
telegram	to arrive	late

Notes

汉口 Hànkǒu – Hankou, part of Wuhan at the junction of Han River and Changjiang River in Hubei

汕头 Shàntóu – Shantou in the Province of Guangdong about 250 kilometres N.E. of Hongkong

港币 gǎngbi – Hongkong dollar

港 Gǎng – common abbreviation for Hongkong

Extract 17 from Chapter 1

"他们办事总是这么慢，汕头这个码头靠香港那么近，来往又方便，还有广州客户，有啥困难？不怕政府管理多么紧，套汇的办法多的很，了不起多贴点水不就行了。"

"那是的，"梅佐贤心里想：坐在上海洋房里策划当然很容易，别人亲手经管这件事可不那么简单，一要可靠，不能叫政府发现；二要划算，汇水贴多了又要心痛。但是梅佐贤嘴里却说，

Translation 1.

'They're always so slow about things. The port of Shantou is quite close to Hongkong and access to Hongkong is easy and there are Guangzhou firms in the city, so there shouldn't be any difficulty. However much the government try to tighten up on transfers of money abroad there are always plenty of ways of getting around it, and if the worst comes to the worst a bigger discount will always do the trick.'

'Quite so.' Mei Zuoxian was thinking to himself: it's very easy for you , of course, sitting in your mansion in

Shanghai and making these plans, but it's not so simple for other people who actually have to carry them out in practice, because (a) you have to play safe so the government won't find out what you're up to, and (b) you've got to calculate the overall cost because he's going to be upset if he loses too much in discount. But Mei Zuoxian kept these thoughts to himself and said:

<u>*Translation 2.*</u>

'They're always so slow about things things. Shantou depends on Hongkong, it's very close and convenient for Cantonese customers, so where's the problem? Don't worry about controls being stricter there's always ways around them, it will just cost a little more.'

Of course, thought Mei, its easy for you sitting in your big house in Shanghai scheming, it's not so easy for those who have to do the work: first, you have to avoid getting caught by the government, and second, calculating the discount is even more difficult. However, he continued:

<u>Synthesis</u>

他们	办事	总是	这么	慢，	汕头	这个	码头
Tāmen	bànshì	zǒngshì	zhème	màn	Shàntóu	zhège	mǎtóu
they	handle	always	so much	slow	Shantou	this	port

靠	香港	那么	近，	来往	又	方便，	还有
kào	Xiānggǎng	nàme	jìn	láiwǎng	yòu	fāngbiàn	háiyǒu
depend	Hongkong	that	close	come and go	and	convenient	further

广州	客户，	有	啥	困难？	不怕	政府
guǎngzhōu	kèhù	yǒu	shá	kùnnan	Bùpà	zhèngfǔ
Canton	customer	have	what	difficulty	Don't fear	government

管理	多么	紧，	套汇	的	办法	多的很，
guǎnlǐ	duōme	jǐn	tàohuì	de	bànfǎ	duōde
control .	more	strict	bend control	part.	ways	hěn

了不起	多	贴	点水	不就行了。	那是的，
liǎobuqǐ	duō	tiē	diǎnshuǐ	bùjiùxíngle	Nàshide
excellent	more	allow	a little	just	Of course

梅佐贤	心里	想：	坐	在	上海	洋房	里
Méi Zuǒxián	xīnli	xiǎng	zuò	zài	Shànghǎi	yángfáng	lǐ
name	in one's heart	to think;	to sit	at	Shanghai	vast villa	in

策划	当然	很	容易，	别人	亲手	经管	这
cèhuà	dāngrán	hěn	róngyì	biérén	qīnshǒu	jīngguǎn	zhè
scheme	naturally	very	easy	others	personally	in charge of	these

件事	可不那么	简单，	一	要	可靠，	不能叫
jiànshì	kěbùnàme	jiǎndān	yī	yāo	kěkào	bùnéngjiào
business	not so, not as	simple	one	need	reliable	can't rely on

政府	发现；	二	要	划算，	汇水	贴
zhèngfǔ	fāxiàn	èr	yāo	huásuàn	huìshuǐ	tiē
government	to find out	two	need	to calculate	remittance fee	allow

多	了	又要	心痛。	但是	梅佐贤	嘴里
duō	le	yòuyāo	xīntòng	Dànshì	Méi Zuǒxián	zuǐlǐ
much	part.	more	heart pain	However	name	mouth

却说，
quèshuō
continued

Extract 18 from Chapter 1

“他们办事手脚太慢，心眼不灵活。不怕政府管的紧，就怕我们不下本钱，钱可通神。广东每年有很多侨汇，只要我们多贴点汇水，要多少外汇有多少外汇。”

“你的意见对。那批美棉和印棉有消息没有？”

“货已经到广州，正在接头……”

“要他们快一点脱手，脱手就买进……”徐总经理说到这里停了停，思考了一下才接着说，“买进糖。”＊

Translation 1.

‘They are very slow getting things done and they’re not very imaginative. What we have to worry about is not the government clamping down on us, but us failing to provide enough capital, because “money makes the mare go”. Every year there’s a lot of money sent back to their families in Guangdong by Chinese living abroad, and provided we can allow higher discounts we can buy as much foreign exchange as we like.’

‘I agree with you. Any news yet on that consignment of American and Indian cotton?’

‘The goods are already in Guangzhou and contacts are being made...’

‘Tell to hurry up and dispose of it, and with the proceeds to buy...’ Xu Yide paused and after a moment's thought went on: ‘to buy sugar.’*

Translation 2.

‘They’re too slow and not very imaginative. Don’t worry about government controls, our only problem is capital, because money talks. A lot of money is sent home to Guangdong by overseas Chinese and provided we can accept higher discount rates we can but as much foreign currency as we like.’

‘I agree with you. Any news about the consignment of American and India cotton?’

'The goods are already in Canton and contacts are being made...'

'Tell them to hurry up and sell it, and with the proceeds buy...' Xu paused then after a moment continued: 'buy sugar.'

Synthesis

他们	办事	手脚	太	慢，	心眼	不	灵活。
Tāmen	bànshì	shǒujiǎo	tài	màn	xīnyǎn	bù	línghuó
they	handle	hand and foot	too	slow	intention	neg.	flexible

不怕	政府	管	的	紧，	就	怕	我们	不下
bùpà	zhèngfǔ	guǎn	de	jǐn	jiù	pà	wǒmen	bùxià
Not fear	government	control	part.	strict	only	fear	we	worried

本钱，	钱可通神。	广东	每年	有	很多
běnqián	qián kě tōng shén	Guǎngdōng	měinián	yǒu	hěnduō
capital	money talks (idiom)	Guangdong	every year	to have	many

侨汇，	只要	我们	多	贴	点	汇水，
qiáo huì	zhǐyào	wǒmen	duō	tiē	diǎn	huìshuǐ
remittance	so long as	we	much	allow	some	remittance fee

要	多少	外汇	有	多少	外汇。	你	的
yāo	duōshao	wàihuì	yǒu	duōshao	wàihuì	Nǐ	de
need	how much	foreign exchange	have	how much	forex	You	part.

意见	对。	那	批	美棉	和	印棉	有
yìjiàn	duì	Nà	pī	měimián	hé	yìnmián	yǒu
idea	right	This	class.*	American cotton	and	Indian cotton	have

消息	没有？	货	已经	到	广州，	正在
xiāoxi	méiyǒu	Huò	yǐjīng	dào	guǎngzhōu	zhèngzài
news	no	Goods	already	arrive	Canton	in process

接头……	要	他们	快一点	脱手，	脱手
jiē tóu	yāo	tāmen	kuài yī diǎn	tuōshǒu	tuōshǒu
in touch with	want	them	hurry up	dispose of	dispose of

就	买进……	徐	总经理	说到	这里	停了停,
jiù	mǎijìn	Xú	zǒngjīnglǐ	shuōdào	zhèlǐ	tíngletíng
then	to purchase	name	gen. manager	mention	here	paused

思考	了	一下	才	接着	说,	“买进糖。*”
sīkǎo	le	yīxià	cái	jiē zhe	shuō	mǎijìn táng
reflect	part.	a little	then	carry on	speak	buy sugar*

* 批 classifier

Notes

侨汇 qiáohuì – immigrant remittances
暗号 ànhào – code
糖* táng – sugar, their secret code for US dollars

Extract 19 from Chapter 1

梅佐贤看他有点拿不稳，话讲完了眉头还在皱着想心思，就接上去说：

“是不是买进参*划算？这两天香港参的行情看涨，大户多买进。我们买进参一定可以得到一笔外快，这数目可不小。”

徐总经理没有思考，果断地说：

“还是糖好。香港大户做参的买卖怎么也做不过汇丰银行，这是大户中的大户，最后他吃通，我们不上那个当。

Translation 1.

Seeing that he was not quite sure of this and that he was still thinking with his brows knit together after he had said it, Mei said:

‘Wouldn’t it be more profitable to buy ginseng? The

Hongkong market ginseng market has been improving these last couple of days and the big operators are mostly buying. We can make ourselves a bit of extra profit if we buy ginseng. The sum involved is not a small one.'

Without giving this a moment's thought Xu said decisively:

'No, let's make it sugar. Even if the big operators in Hongkong are saying go in for ginseng they won't beat the Hongkong and Shanghai Banking Corporation at the game, because the Hongkong and Shanghai are the biggest of the big operators and they'll clean up in the end. We won't walk into that trap.'

Translation 2.

Seeing Xu's brow knit in thought, Mei said:

'Wouldn't it be better to buy ginseng, the prices have risen in the last few days in Hongkong and those with the money are buying into it. Like that we'll make a good profit.'

Without hesitation Xu said: 'No, buy sugar. If the big players in Hongkong are going for ginseng they won't beat the HSBC, because HSBC is the biggest and they'll clean up in the end. We won't get caught in that trap.'

Synthesis

梅佐贤	看	他	有点	拿不稳,	话讲	完了
Méi Zuǒxián	kàn	tā	yǒudiǎn	ná bu wěn	huàjiǎng	wánle
name	look	him	a little	uncertainly	speak	finish

眉头	还在	皱着	想心思	就	接上去	说：
méitóu	háizài	zhòu	xiǎngxīnsi	jiù	jiēshàngqù	shuō
brows	still	wrinkle	in his thoughts	then	continued	to speak

是不是	买进参	划算？	这	两	天
Shìbùshì	mǎijìn shēn	huásuàn	Zhè	liǎng	tiān
Why not	purchase ginseng	good value	These	couple	day

香港	参	的	行情	看涨，	大户	多
Xiānggǎng	shēn	de	hángqíng	kànzhǎng	dàhù	duō
Hongkong	ginseng	part.	market price	prices rising	the wealthy	all

买进。	我们	买进	参	一定	可以	得到	一笔
mǎijìn	wǒmen	mǎijìn	shēn	yīdìng	kěyǐ	dédào	yībǐ
buying	we	buying	ginseng	surely	can	to get	a stroke

外快，	这	数目	可不小。	徐	总经理	没有
wài kuài	zhè	shùmù	Kěbùxiǎo	Xú	zǒngjīnglǐ	méiyǒu
more profits	this	amount	a lot	name	general man.	have not

思考，	果断	地	说：	还是	糖	好。	香港
sīkǎo	guǒduàn	de	shuō	háishì	táng	hǎo	Xiānggǎng
to reflect	reflect on	part.	said	still	sugar	good	Hongkong

大户	做	参*	的	买卖	也	做	不过
dàhù	zuò	shēn	de	mǎimài	yě	zuò	bùguò
the wealthy	make	ginseng*	part.	buy and sell	also	make	as do

汇丰银行，	这是	大户	中的	大户，	最后
Huìfēng Yínháng	zhèshì	dàhù	zhòngdì	dàhù	zuìhòu
HSBC Bank	this is	the wealthy	home of	the wealthy	final; last

他	吃	通，	我们	不上	那个	当。
tā	chī	tōng	wǒmen	bùshàng	nàge	dàng
he	eat	everything	we	can't, not	that	equal

Notes

参* shēn – ginseng, their secret code for gold

汇丰银行 Huìfēng Yínháng – HSBC Bank

Extract 20 from Chapter 1

“这倒是，”梅佐贤马上改变口气，他自己没有啥主见的，只要老板高兴，他都赞成，“还是糖好，把稳。买进参可能利润大些，但是风险太大，何况总经理又不在香港。”

徐总经理点了点头。梅佐贤又说：

“要是总经理在香港，我看，汇丰银行也不一定斗得过你。你有丰富的经验，看香港市场的变化，决定自己的行动，

Translation 1.

‘You’ve got a point there,’ said Mei Zuoxian, changing his tune; he had no firm views on the subject and would agree to anything that made the boss happy. ‘Sugar would be better, safer. We might make a little profit by buying ginseng, but it’s too big a risk, especially as you’re not in Hongkong yourself, sir.’

Xu Yide nodded and Mei Zuoxian went on:

‘If you were in Hongkong yourself I don’t think that even the Hongkong and Shanghai would necessarily get the better of you. You have great experience and could decide what to do in accordance with the fluctuations of the Hongkong market;

Translation 2.

‘You’ve got a point there,’ said Mei, changing his tune; he had no fixed ideas on the subject and would agree with anything to make his boss happy. ‘Sugar would be better. Ginseng might be more profitable but the risks are higher,

in addition to that you're not in Hongkong yourself.'

Xu nodded and Mei went on:

'If you were in Hongkong, I don't see HSBC fighting you. With your long experience you could decide yourself according to market fluctuations.'

Synthesis

这倒是,	梅佐贤	马上	改变	口气,	他
Zhèdàoshi	Méi Zuǒxián	mǎshàng	gǎibiàn	kǒuqì	tā
That's so	name	immediately	to change	tone of voice	he

自己	没有	啥	主见	的,	只要	老板
zìjǐ	méiyǒu	shá	zhǔjiàn	de	zhǐyào	lǎobǎn
self	not	have	one's own view	part.	so long as	boss

高兴,	他	都	赞成,	还是	糖	好,	把稳。
gāoxìng	tā	dōu	zànchéng	háishì	táng	hào	bǎwěn
happy	he	everything	to approve	still	sugar	good	reliable

买进	参	可能	利润	大些,	但是	风险	太大,
Mǎijìn	shēn	kěnéng	lìrùn	dàxiē	dànshì	fēngxiǎn	tàidà
Buy	ginseng	might	profits	bigger	but	risk	great

何况	总经理	不又在	香港。	徐	总经理
hékuàng	zǒngjīnglǐ	yòubùzài	Xiānggǎng	Xú	zǒngjīnglǐ
besides	general manager	was not in	Hongkong	name	general manager

点了	点头。	梅佐贤	又	说:	要是	总经理
diǎnle	diǎntóu	Méi Zuǒxián	yòu	shuō	yàoshi	zǒngjīnglǐ
a little	to nod	name	and	said	if	general manager

在	香港,	我	看,	汇丰银行	也不一定	斗得
zài	Xiānggǎng	wǒ	kàn	Huìfēng Yínháng	yěbùyīdìng	dòuděi
in	Hongkong	I	to see	HSBC Bank	not certain	go against

过你。	你	有	丰富	的	经验,	看	香港
guònǐ	Nǐ	yǒu	fēngfù	de	jīngyàn	kàn	Xiānggǎng
you	You	have	abundant	part.	experience	to see	Hongkong

市场	的	变化，	决定	自己	的	行动，
shìchǎng	de	biànhuà	juédìng	zìjǐ	de	xíngdòng
market	part.	variation	to decide	self	part.	action

Extract 21 from Chapter 1

别人保不住会在汇丰手里栽跟斗，你一定会站得稳稳的。你是上海著名的铁算盘呀。”

梅佐贤几句话说得总经理心里暖洋洋的，表面上却谦虚地说：

“那也不一定。”

一阵橐橐的皮鞋声忽然传到客厅门外，旋即有一片红光闪过。梅佐贤问道：

“谁？”

“还不是那个小王八蛋，”徐总经理以充满了喜爱的口吻说，接着他对客厅门口叫道，“要进来就进来吧。”

Translation 1.

...other people might dance on the floor on the Hongkong and Shanghai’s strings but there’s no doubt you would keep your feet firmly planted on the ground. Because you are well known as a master brain in Shanghai.’

These few words of Mei Zuoxian's had brought a warm glow to Xu Yide’s mind, yet he preserved an air of modesty when he replied:

‘I wouldn’t say that at all.’

A sudden sound of footsteps of someone wearing leather shoes was heard outside the drawing-room door and a patch of red flashed by. Mei Zuoxian asked:

'Who was that?'

'That scamp of mine, of course,' said Xu Yide affectionately, then turned to the door and called out: 'Come on in if you're coming in.'

<u>*Translation 2.*</u>

'...other people might not do so well with HSBC, but you certainly can stand firm. You're known to be very adept in the market.' Mei Zuoxian's few words warmed the general managers heart. However he kept a modest face and he said: 'That's not so sure.' A clatter of shoes came into the drawing room and there was a flash of something red outside.

'Who is it? asked Mei Zuoxian.

'Is it that young son of a gun?' said Xu Yide warmly, then called out, 'If you want to come in, then come in!'

<u>Synthesis</u>

别人	保不住	会	在	汇丰	手里	栽跟斗，
Biérén	bǎobuzhù	huì	zài	Huìfēng	shǒulǐ	zāigēndòu
Others	most likely	can	at	HSBC Bank	hand	fail

你	一定	会	站得	稳稳的。	你	是	上海
nǐ	yīdìng	huì	zhànde	wěnwěnde	Nǐ	shì	Shànghǎi
you	certainly	can	stand	firmly	you	are	Shanghai

著名	的	铁算盘	呀。	梅佐贤	几句话说	得
zhùmíng	de	tiěsuànpán	ya	Méi Zuǒxián	jǐjù huàshuō	děi
famous	part	good calculators	part.	name	few words	made

总经理	心里	暖洋洋	的，	表面	上	却
zǒngjīnglǐ	xīnli	nuǎnyángyáng	de	biǎomiàn	shàng	què
general manager	bosom	warm	part.	face	on	however

谦虚	地	说:	那也不	一定。	一阵	橐橐
qiānxū	de	shuō	nàyěbù	yīdìng	Yīzhèn	tuótuó
modest	part.	said	It is not	certain	A clatter	onomatopoeia

的	皮鞋	声	忽然	传	到	客厅	门外,
de	píxié	shēng	hūrán	chuán	dào	kètīng	ménwài
part.	leather shoes	sounded	suddenly	spread	to	drawing room	from outside

旋即	有一	片	红光	闪过。	梅佐贤	问道:
xuánjí	yǒu yī	piàn	hóng guāng	shǎnguò	Méi Zuǒxián	wèndào
soon	a	class.	bright red	flashed by	name	asked

谁?	还不是	那个	小	王八蛋,	徐总经理
shéi	Háibùshì	nàge	xiǎo	wángbādàn	Xú zǒngjīnglǐ
Who is it?	Isn't it	that	little, young	sun of a gun	Xu Yide

以	充满了	喜爱	的	口吻	说,	接着
yǐ	chōngmǎnle	xǐài	de	kǒuwěn	shuō	jiēzhe
with	full of	affection	part.	tone	said,	catching

他	对	客厅	门口	叫道,	要	进来	就
tā	duì	kètīng	ménkǒu	jiàodào	yāo	jìnlái	jiù
him	before	drawing room	doorway	called out	want	to come in	then

进来	吧。
jìnlái	ba
come in	modal part.

Zhou Erfu

上海的早晨

一

一辆黑色的小奥斯汀汽车远远驶来，在柏油路上发出轻轻的嗞嗞声。马路两边是整齐的梧桐树，树根那部分去年冬天涂上去的白石灰粉已开始脱落，枝头上宽大的绿油油的叶子，迎风轻微摆动着。马路上行人很少，静幽幽的，没有声息。天空晴朗，下午的阳光把法国梧桐的阴影印在柏油路上，仿佛是一张整齐的图案画。小奥斯汀穿过了横马路，降低了速度，在梧桐的阴影上开过来。

在一片红色砖墙的当中，两扇黑漆大铁门紧紧闭着。铁门上两个狮子头的金色的铁环，在太阳里闪闪发着金光。小奥斯汀的喇叭对着黑漆大门叫了两声。黑漆大铁门开了，迎面站出来的是身上穿着银灰色卡叽布制服的门房老刘。他伸开右手，向里面指着，让小奥斯汀开了进去。他旋即关紧了大门，好像防备有坏人跟在汽车后面溜进来似的。他过来拉开小奥斯汀的车门，里面跳下一个四十开外的中年人。他穿着一身浅灰色底子淡蓝色条子的西装，打着一条玫瑰红的领带；长型的脸庞微笑着，两腮露出两个酒窝，鼻梁上架着一副玳瑁边框子的散光眼镜，眼光机灵地向四边一扫：院子里没人。他橐橐地走了进去。

这人是沪江纱厂的副厂长梅佐贤，外号叫酸辣汤。

这个外号的来源有一段这样的历史：梅佐贤本来并不是办纱厂的，是开饭馆出身的商人。他的表哥裘学良是沪江纱厂的厂长，就凭这个亲戚关系到厂里来的，起先是担任事务主任的工作，最近升了副厂长。裘学良经常生病在家，不来上班。梅佐贤这个副厂长，几乎就是正长了。他在纱厂工作也和他开饭馆一样，钱经过梅佐贤的手，他总要弄点油水。比如说厂里发代办米吧，本来应该向上海粮食公司采办的，但是没有油水可捞，他就向庆丰米号采办。沪江纱厂总管理处的职员和厂里职员家属的代办米，都是庆丰送去的；有时，在梅佐贤的默许之下，还掺杂一些霉米进去。那时候，梅佐贤所得到的油水当然就更多了。大家吃代办米发现霉味，自然有些不满，甚至于发了牢骚，梅佐贤表现得更不满，他当着职员的面骂庆丰，说这样做生意是自寻绝路；可是下一次的代办米仍然是要庆丰送去。一任事务主任，梅佐贤捞到的油水不少，他同人合伙，开了一家碾米厂。工人说，鸡蛋到了梅佐贤的手里也要小一圈。这个比喻并不过火。在上海解放前夕，厂里的钢丝针布、皮带皮、棉纱等等东西，直往他家里搬，起初说是保存起来，以后就变成梅佐贤的了。

他做这些事体总经理并不是不晓得，但他不在乎。因为总经理要更大的油水，梅佐贤可以在这方面献出他的才能和智慧。只要总经理的眉毛一动，他就晓得总经理在动啥脑筋。凡是总经理要办的事，假如别人办不到，只要找梅佐贤，没有一件不能完成的。而且，有些事只要总经理稍为暗示一下，他就懂得应该怎样去办。他的另外一个绰号叫做总经理肚里的蛔虫，就是这样得来的。

因为字太长，又只能说明他的一个方面，就是说不很贴切，叫的人比较少，也不经常。酸辣汤的外号在厂里是无人不知的。他自然并非不晓得这个外号，有时听到了倒反而很得意：我梅佐贤就是酸辣汤，你把我怎么样？现在从事务主任爬到副厂长的地位，是总经理面前的一位红人，谁也奈何他不得。

梅佐贤走进了客厅。穿着白卡叽布制服的老王捧着一个托盘轻轻走过来，把一杯刚泡好的上等狮峰龙井茶放在梅佐贤面前的矮圆桌上。梅佐贤悠然自得地坐在双人沙发里，就像在自己家里一样，他向老王望了一眼，谦和地问道：

"总经理回来了吗？"

"刚回来，在楼上洗脸。"

"请你告诉他，我来看他。如果他有事，我在这里多等一歇没有关系。"

老王点了点头，去了。梅佐贤揭开矮圆桌上的那听三五牌香烟，他抽了一支出来，就从西装口袋里掏出一个银色的烟盒子，很自然地把三五牌的香烟往自己的烟盒子里装。然后拿起矮圆桌上的银色的朗生打火机，燃着了烟在抽，怡然地望着客厅角落里的那架大钢琴。钢琴后面是落地的大玻璃窗，透过乳白色绢子的团花窗帷，他欣赏着窗外花团里翠绿的龙柏。

楼上传来咳嗽声。梅佐贤从怡然自得的境地跳了出来，他连忙熄灭了烟，站起来拍一拍刚才落在西装裤子上的烟灰，整了一下玫瑰红的领带。他晓得总经理快下来了，目光对着客厅的门。果然楼梯上有人下来了，沉重的脚步声一步步迟缓地往下移动。梅佐贤走到门那边去，像是接待一个贵宾似的在那边等候着。

一个矮胖的中年人走到客厅门口，容光焕发，脸胖得像一个圆球，下巴的肉往下垂着，使人担心这肉随时可以掉下来。看上去年纪不过四十左右，实际上他已是靠五十的人了。头上没有一根白发，修理得很整齐，油光发亮，镜子似的，苍蝇飞上去也要滑下来的。他很得意自己没有一根白发，用谦虚的语气经常在朋友面前夸耀自己："我是蒙不白之冤，这个年纪应该有白发了。我的三个老婆对我没有一根白发是很不满意的，尤其是大老婆最恨我的头发不白。"如果朋友们凑趣地说："那是怕你纳第三个姨太太。"那他就高兴得眼睛眯成一条缝，乐得说不出话来，只是嘻嘻地笑笑。上海解放以后，他的说法有一点修正："我的老婆对我没有一根白发是很不满意的。"他不再提三个老婆了。

梅佐贤曲背哈腰迎接了沪江纱厂总经理徐义德：

"总经理，又来打扰你了。"

"来了很久吧，累你等了。"徐总经理漫不经心地瞟了他一眼。

"刚来，没啥。"

徐总经理一屁股坐在梅佐贤对面的单人沙发里，把整个沙发塞得满满的。他抽了一支烟，一对鱼眼睛望着米色的屋顶，嘴里吐出一个个圆圆的烟圈。

梅佐贤仔细留神徐总经理的脸色，眉宇间很开朗，嘴角上时不时露出得意的微笑。他晓得今天徐总经理的情绪很好，准备好的事情可以提出来谈一谈。

"总经理，汕头的电报到了……"

徐总经理一听到汕头两个字马上就紧张起来了，他的眼光从米色的屋顶移到梅佐贤长方型的脸上：

"那几批货色怎么样？"

“都脱手啦。装到汕头的二十一支三百八十件，装到汉口广州的二十支一共八百三十二件全抛出了。”

“多少款子？”

“一共是一百二十五万二千四百八十块港币。”

“划到香港没有？”

“现在政府对外汇管理的紧了，不容易套。这个数目又不小，想了很多办法，靠了几家有港庄的字号才划过去。因为这个原因，电报来迟了。”

“他们办事总是这么慢，汕头这个码头靠香港那么近，来往又方便，还有广州客户，有啥困难？不怕政府管理多么紧，套汇的办法多的很，了不起多贴点水不就行了。”

“那是的，”梅佐贤心里想：坐在上海洋房里策划当然很容易，别人亲手经管这件事可不那么简单，一要可靠，不能叫政府发现；二要划算，汇水贴多了又要心痛。但是梅佐贤嘴里却说，“他们办事手脚太慢，心眼不灵活。不怕政府管的紧，就怕我们不下本钱，钱可通神。广东每年有很多侨汇，只要我们多贴点汇水，要多少外汇有多少外汇。”

“你的意见对。那批美棉和印棉有消息没有？”

“货已经到广州，正在接头……”

“要他们快一点脱手，脱手就买进……”徐总经理说到这里停了停，思考了一下才接着说，“买进糖。”

梅佐贤看他有点拿不稳，话讲完了眉头还在皱着想心思，就接上去说：

“是不是买进参②划算？这两天香港参的行情看涨，大户多买进。我们买进参一定可以得到一笔外快，这数目可不小。”

徐总经理没有思考，果断地说：

“还是糖好。香港大户做参的买卖怎么也做不过汇丰银行，这是大户中的大户，最后他吃通，我们不上那个当。”“这倒是，”梅佐贤马上改变口气，他自己没有啥主见的，只要老板高兴，他都赞成，“还是糖好，把稳。买进参可能利润大些，但是风险太大，何况总经理又不在香港。”

徐总经理点了点头。梅佐贤又说：

“要是总经理在香港，我看，汇丰银行也不一定斗得过你。你有丰富的经验，看香港市场的变化，决定自己的行动，别人保不住会在汇丰手里栽跟斗，你一定会站得稳稳的。你是上海著名的铁算盘呀。”

梅佐贤几句话说得总经理心里暖洋洋的，表面上却谦虚地说：

“那也不一定。”

一阵橐橐的皮鞋声忽然传到客厅门外，旋即有一片红光闪过。梅佐贤问道：

“谁？”

“还不是那个小王八蛋，”徐总经理以充满了喜爱的口吻说，接着他对客厅门口叫道，“要进来就进来吧。”

Mao Dun

MIDNIGHT

子夜

MIDNIGHT

子夜

Shen Yen-ping (1896-1981), who wrote under the name Mao Dun, (矛盾 - contradiction, later changed to 茅盾), was one of the most outstanding proponents of revolutionary realism to appear in China since the *New Literature Movement* of 1919. With other writers he founded the *Literary Research Society* in 1920, to promote a new vision of literature in China.

He joined the Communist movement against Chiang Kai-shek and writing under the name Mao Dun he turned his attention to exposing the ills of capitalism in China in the years that followed. After the founding of the People's Republic by Mao Zedong in 1949, Mao Dun became minister of culture and remained so until 1964.

Mao Dun's novel* is set in the late nineteen-twenties and early nineteen-thirties in and around Shanghai and clearly intends to show the decadency of the moneyed classes at that time. He himself explains in his introduction that he would have liked to dedicated more of his story to the revolutionaries, but was prevented from doing so by the censors at that time. Consequently, much of the story is told from the perspective of industrialists

* The most recent English version of Midnight contains this publishers note: This translation has been made from the Chinese edition published in May 1955 by the People's Literature Publishing House, Peking. Our sincere thanks are due to Mr A.C.BARNES who took much trouble in polishing the draft translation made by Hsu Meng-hsiung.

and business classes, both of which he savagely satirizes.

The story starts with the old generation represented by old Mr Wu, the patriarch, who arrives in Shanghai to escape the dangers in the more distant countryside caused by the Communist revolutionaries. He brings his copy of the *Supreme Book of Rewards and Punishments* with him, a Taoist religious book. Himself a revolutionary in his youth, old Mr Wu changed his ideas changed following a serious riding accident. As an old man has become seriously opposed to the decadent ways of Shanghai, and in particular what appears to him to be the debauched ways of the younger generation. At a welcoming party, he suffers an attack and dies, leaving the way open for his children and grandchildren, particularly his son Sunfu, a successful businessman.

Mao Dun satirizes Sunfu, his family and business associates; the latter speculating on stock and bond markets, both of which are highly volatile as a consequence of the ongoing political situation. In addition they also own various factories, notably silk and matches, in which they exploit the workers. Mao Dun criticizes not only the owners, but also the politicians, who have put Chinese manufacturers at a disadvantage relative to foreign competition.

Finally, the workers organize in themselves in the fight for their rights. The story becomes complicated as the Nationalist government confronts both warlords and communists in their battle to control the country.

No alternative translation is proposed in the present book for *Midnight*, as little more can be added for clarification. Mao Dun's style employs considerable detail, infused with realism, to paint a story portraying prevailing social conditions and the ongoing conflict between the workers and the businesses classes. The modernity of the translation made by Hsu Meng-hsiung and A.C.Barnes ensures clarity.

In *Crosscurrents in the Literature of Asia and the West* edited by Misayuki Akiyama and Yiu-nam Leung and published in 1997, Mao Dun, on his own admission, explains he was inspired by Zola's works, and probably *L'Argent*.

Midnight presents three groups of protagonists in Chinese society: industrialists, workers and imperialists. As a dedicated communist...and a bourgeois intellectual, his book was intended for readers of the dominant and business classes, his portrayal of the different characters is seen to be satirical and even supercilious.

Mao Dun in Shanghai in the 1930s

Extract 1 from Chapter 1

太阳刚刚下了地平线。软风一阵一阵地吹上人面，怪痒痒的。苏州河的浊水幻成了金绿色，轻轻地，悄悄地，向西流去。黄浦的夕潮不知怎的已经涨上了，现在沿这苏州河两岸的各色船只都浮得高高地，舱面比码头还高了约莫半尺。风吹来外滩公园里的音乐，却只有那炒豆似的铜鼓声最分明，也最叫人兴奋。

Translation 1.

The sun had just sunk below the horizon and a gentle breeze caressed one’s face. The muddy water of Soochow Creek, transformed to a golden green, flowed quietly westward. The evening tide from the Whangpoo had turned imperceptibly, and now an assortment of boats along both sides of the creek were riding high, their decks some six inches above the landing stages.

Faint strains of music were borne on the wind from the riverside park, punctuated by the sharp, cheerful clatter of kettledrums.

Synthesis

太阳	刚刚	下	了	地平线。	软	风	一阵
Tàiyáng	gānggang	xià	le	dìpíngxiàn	Ruǎn	fēng	yīzhèn
Sun	just	down	part.	horizon	Soft	wind	a gust

一阵	地	吹	上	人	面，	怪	痒痒	的。
yīzhèn	de	chuī	shàng	rén	miàn	guài	yǎngyang	de
a gust	part.	blow	on	man	face	bewilder	tickle	part.

苏州河	的	浊	水	幻	成了	金绿色，
Sūzhōuhé	de	zhuó	shuǐ	huàn	chéngle	jīnlǜsè
Suzhou Creek	part.	muddy	water	strange	become	golden green

轻轻地，	悄悄地，	向西	流去。	黄浦	的
qīngqīngde	qiāoqiāo	xiàngxī	liúqù	Huángpǔ	de
softly	quietly	westward	flowed	name river	part.

夕	潮	不知怎的	已经	涨上了，	现在
xī	cháo	bùzhīzěnde	yǐjīng	zhàngshàngle	xiànzài
evening	tide	somehow	already	risen	now

沿	这	苏州河	两岸	的	各色	船只
yàn	zhè	Sūzhōuhé	liǎngàn	de	gèsè	chuánzhī
riverside	this	Suzhou Creek	both sides	part.	all sorts	boats

都	浮得	高高地，	舱面	比	码头
dōu	fúde	gāogāode,	cāng miàn	bǐ	mǎtóu
all	floated	high	deck	compare	dock

还高	了	约莫	半尺。	风吹	来	外滩
háigāo	le	yuēmo	bànchǐ	Fēngchuī	lái	wàitān
higher	part.	about	half a foot	Wind	come	the Bund

公园	里	的	音乐，	却只有	那	炒豆
gōngyuán	lǐ	de	yīnyuè	quèzhǐyǒu	nà	chǎodòu
public park	in	part.	music	and	that	fried beans

似的	铜鼓	声	最	分明，	也最叫	人。
shìde	tóng gǔ	shēng	zuì	fēnmíng	yě zuì jiào	rén
the noise	bronze drum	sound	very	clear	also called	people

Notes

半尺 bànchǐ – half a Chinese foot (measurement)
外滩 Wàitān – the Shanghai Bund

Extract 2 from Chapter 1

暮霭挟着薄雾笼罩了外白渡桥的高耸的钢架，电车驶过时，这钢架下横空架挂的电车线时时爆发出几朵碧绿的火花。从桥上向东望，可以看见浦东的洋栈像巨大的怪兽，蹲在暝色中，闪着千百只小眼睛似的灯火。向西望，叫人猛一惊的，是高高地装在一所洋房顶上而且异常庞大的霓虹电管广告，射出火一样的赤光和青燐似的绿焰：Light，Heat，Power！

Translation

Whenever a tram passed over the bridge, the overhead cable suspended below the top of the steel frame threw off bright, greenish sparks. Looking east, one could see the warehouses of foreign firms on the waterfront of Pootung like huge monsters crouching in the gloom, their lights twinkling like countless tiny eyes. To the west, one saw with a shock of wonder on the roof of a building a gigantic neon sign in flaming red and phosphorescent green: LIGHT, HEAT, POWER!

Synthesis

暮霭	挟着	薄雾	笼罩	了	外白渡桥
Mùǎi	xié	bówù	lǒngzhào	le	Wàibáidù Qiáo
Evening mist	clasped	mist	shroud	part.	Waibaidu Bridge

的	高耸	的	钢架，	电车	驶过时，	这
de	gāosǒng	de	gāngjià	diànchē	shǐguòshí	zhè
part.	towering	part.	steel frame	trolleybus	crossed	this

钢架	下	横空	架挂	的	电车	线
gāngjià	xià	héngkōng	jiàguà	de	diànchē	xiàn
steel frame	downward	hanging over	suspend	part.	trolleybus	cable

时时	爆发	出	几	朵	碧绿	的	火花。
shíshí	bàofā	chū	jǐ	duǒ	bìlǜ	de	huǒhuā
constantly	break out	occur	many	class.	dark green	part.	spark

从	桥	上	向	东望,	可以	看见	浦东
Cóng	qiáo	shàng	xiàng	dōngwàng	kěyǐ	kànjiàn	Pǔdōng
from	bridge	on	direction	eastward	can	to see	Pudong

的	洋	栈	像	巨大	的	怪兽,	蹲
de	yáng	zhàn	xiàng	jùdà	de	guàishòu	dūn
part.	vast	warehouse	like	huge	part.	monster	to crouch

在	暝色	中,	闪着	千百	只	小	眼睛
zài	míngsè	zhòng	shǎn	qiānbǎi	zhī	xiǎo	yǎnjing
at, in	dark	middle	sparkling	thousands	class	small	eye

似的	灯火。	向	西望,	叫人	猛一惊	的,
shìde	dēnghuǒ	Xiàng	xīwàng	jiàorén	měngyījīng	de
like	lights	Direction	westward	one, pass.	with a shock	part.

是	高高	地	装在	一	所	洋	房顶
shì	gāogāo	de	zhuāng	yī	suǒ	yáng	fángdǐng
is	high	part.	adornment	one	class.	vast	roof

上	而且	异常	庞大	的	霓虹电管
shàng	érqiě	yìcháng	pángdà	de	níhóng diànguǎn
on	moreover	exceptional	huge	part.	neon tube

广告,	射出	火	一样的	赤	光	和
guǎnggào	shèchū	huǒ	yīyàngde	chì	guāng	hé
advertisement	emission	fire	same, like	red	light	and

青	燐	似的	绿	焰:	LIGHT, HEAT, POWER!
qīng	lín	shì de	lǜ	yàn	
green blue	phosphorus	like	green	flame	

Extract 3 from Chapter 1

这时候——这天堂般五月的傍晚，有三辆一九三〇年式的雪铁笼汽车像闪电一般驶过了外白渡桥，向西转弯，一直沿北苏州路去了。

过了北河南路口的上海总商会以西的一段，俗名唤

作"铁马路"，是行驶内河的小火轮

的汇集处。那三辆汽车到这里就减低了速率。第一辆车的汽车夫轻声地对坐在他旁边的穿一

身黑拷绸衣裤的彪形大汉说：

Translation 1.

It was a perfect May evening. Three 1930-model Citroëns flashed over the bridge, turned westwards, and headed straight along the North Soochow Road. Passing a block west of the Shanghai Chamber of Commerce Building on the corner of North Honan Road, where the creek was usually thronged with stream-launches plying upriver, the three cars slowed down. The driver of the first car said in a low voice to the hulking fellow sitting beside him in black silk:

The Waibaidu Bridge in Shanghai – early 20th century

Synthesis

这时候	这	天堂	般	五月	傍晚,	有
shíhòu	zhè	tiāntáng	bān	wǔyuè	bàngwǎn	yǒu
at that moment	this	heavenly	like	May	evening	have

三	辆	一九三〇	年	式	的	雪铁龙	汽车
sān	liàng	1930	nián	shì	de	Xuětiělǒng	car
3	class.		year	model	part.	Citroën	qìchē

像	闪电	一般	驶	过	了	外白渡桥,
xiàng	shǎndiàn	yībān	shǐ	guò	le	Wàibáidù Qiáo
like	lightning	same	gallop	cross	part.	Waibaidu Bridge

向西	转弯,	一直	沿	北苏州路	去了。
xiàngxī	zhuǎnwān	yīzhí	yàn	Běi Sūzhōu Lù	qù le
westward	to turn	straight	along	North Suzhou Road	go

过了	北河南路口	的	上海总商会	以西的
Guò	Běi Hénánlùkǒu	de	Shànghǎi Zǒngshānghuì	yǐxīde
Passing	North Henan Rd crossing	pt.	Shanghai Chamber Com.	to the west of

一段,	俗名	唤作	“铁马路”,	是	行驶
yīduàn	súmíng	huànzuò	Tiěmǎlù	shì	xíngshǐ
section	common name	be called	Tie (iron) Street	is	ply

内河	的	小火轮	的	汇集	处。	那
nèi hé	de	xiǎo huǒ lún	de	huìjí	chù	Nà
creek	part.	steam launch	part.	converge	place	These

三	辆	汽车	到	这里	就	减低了	速率。
sān	liàng	qìchē	dào	zhèlǐ	jiù	jiǎndī	sùlǜ
three	class.	car	to	here	then	reduced	speed

第一	辆	的	汽车	夫	轻声	地	对	坐
Dìyī	liàng	de	qìchē	fū	qīngshēng	de	duì	zuò
First	class.	part.	car	man	softly	-ly	opposite	sit

在	他	旁边	的	穿	一身	黑	拷绸	衣	裤
zài	tā	pángbiān	de	chuān	yīshēn	hēi	kǎochóu	yī	kù
at	his	side	part.	wear	suit	black	silk	dress	trousers

的	彪形大汉	说:
de	biāoxíngdàhàn	shuō
part.	strapping, burly	said

Notes

雪铁龙	Xuětiělóng – Citroën, a French car
拷绸	kǎochóu – a kind of silk
彪形大汉	biāoxíngdàhàn – strapping, burly, tough guy

Extract 4 from Chapter 1

“老关！是戴生昌罢？”

“可不是！怎么你倒忘了？您准是给那只烂污货迷昏了啦！”

老关也是轻声说，露出一口好像连铁梗都咬得断似的大牙齿。他是保镖的。此时汽车戛然而止，老关忙即跳下车去，摸摸腰间的勃郎宁，又向四下里瞥了一眼，就过去开了车门，威风凛凛地站在旁边。

Translation 1.

‘The Tai Sheng Chang Company, isn’t it, Kuan?’

‘Of course it is,’ replied his companion, also in a low voice.

‘Surely you haven’t forgotten already? That bitch must be making you soft in the head.’

As the bodyguard, for such he was, spoke, he showed large, strong teeth. The car jarred to a stop and Kuan quickly scrambled out, placing his hand on the Browning at his side as he did so and glancing all around. Then he went around and opened the other door and stood holding it, looking stern and forbidding.

<u>Synthesis</u>

老关!	是	戴生昌	罢?	可不是!	怎么	你
Lǎo Guān	shì	Dàishēngchāng	ba	Kě bu shì	Zěnme	nǐ
name	is	Tai Sheng Chang Co.	fin. part.	Of course it is	How	you

倒忘了?	您	准	是	给	那	只	烂污货
dào wàng le	Nín	zhǔn	shì	gěi	nà	zhī	lànwūhuò
already forgot	you	already	is	give	that	le	slut

迷昏	了	啦!	也	是	轻声	说,
míhūn	le	la	Yě	shì	qīngshēng	shuō
weak-headed	part.	fin. part.	Also	is	softly	to say

露出	一口	好像	连铁梗	都	咬	得
lùchū	yīkǒu	hǎo xiàng	liántiěgěng	dōu	yǎo	de
to expose	a mouthful	apparently	strong	all	definitely	part.

此时	汽车	戛然而止,	老关	忙	即	跳
cǐshí	qìchē	jiárán érzhǐ	Lǎo Guān	tiào	jí	tiào
then	car	stopped abruptly	name	hurriedly	promptly	jump

车	去,	摸摸	腰间的	勃郎宁,	又	向
chē	qù	mōmo	yāojiānde	Bólángníng	yòu	xiàng
car	to go	feel	waist	Browning*	and	toward

下四里	瞥了	一眼,	就	过去	开了	车门,
sìxiàli	piēle	yīyǎn	jiù	guòqu	kāile	chēmén
all around	glance	an eye	then	went	opened	car door

威风凛凛	地	站	在	旁边。
wēifēnglǐnlǐn	de	zhàn	zài	pángbiān
menacingly	-ly	stand	at	beside

* Browning, an automatic handgun

Extract 5 from Chapter 1

车厢里先探出一个头来，紫酱色的一张方脸，浓眉毛，圆眼睛，脸上有许多小疱。看见迎面那所小洋房的大门上正有“戴生昌轮船局”六个大字，这人也就跳下车来，一直走进去。老关紧跟在后面。

“云飞轮船快到了么？”

紫酱脸的人傲然问，声音宏亮而清晰。他大概有四十岁了，身材魁梧，举止威严，一望而知是颐指气使惯了的“大亨”。他的话还没完，坐在那里的轮船局办事员霍地一齐站了起来，内中有一个瘦长子堆起满脸的笑容抢上一步，恭恭敬敬回答：

Translation 1.

A head stuck out cautiously; a square, pimple, purplish face with thick eyebrows and round eyes. Spotting the signboard over the gate with the name “The Tai Sheng Chang Shipping Company”, the man emerged completely and quickly made for the building with his bodyguard close behind him.

‘Is the Flying Cloud arriving soon?’ the puplish-faced man asked in a loud and arrogant voice. About forty, powerfully built and imposing, he struck you at once s a solid and prosperous businessman, accustomed to giving orders. Before the words were out of his mouth, the clerks sitting there in the office jumped up as one man, and a tall young man, smiling broadly, stepped forward.

Synthesis

车厢	里	先	探出	一	个	头	来，
Chēxiāng	lǐ	xiān	tànchū	yī	gè	tóu	lái
Car	inside	first	lean out	a	class.	head	come

紫酱色的	一张方脸	浓	眉毛，	圆眼睛，	脸
zǐjiàngsède	yī zhāng fāng liǎn	nóng	méimao	yuán yǎnjing	liǎn
purplish	a long square face	thick	eyebrows	round eyes	face

上	有	许多	小	疱。	看见	迎面	那
shàng	yǒu	xǔduō	xiǎo	pào	Kànjiàn	yíng miàn	nà
on	to have	a lot	small	pimples	Seeing	facing	this

所	小	洋房的	大门	上正	有	“戴生昌
suǒ	xiǎo	yángfángde	dàmén	shàngzhèng	yǒu	Dài Shēng Chāng
class.	small	foreign style	entrance	exactly	to have	company name

轮船	局”	六个大字	这	人	也就	跳下
Lúnchuán	Jú	liù gè dà zì	zhè	rén	yě jiù	tiào xià
Steamship	Bureau	si big letters	this	man	then	jumped out

车	来，	一直	走进	去。	老关	紧跟
chē	qù	yīzhí	zǒujìn	qù	Lǎo Guān	jǐngēn
car	to go	directly	to enter	to go	name	follow close

在后面。	云飞	轮船	快到了	么？	紫酱脸的
Zàihòumiàn	Yúnfēi	lúnchuán	kuàidàole	ma	Zǐjiàng liǎn de
behind	name	steamer	arriving soon	interog.	Purple faced

人	傲然	问，	声音	宏亮	而	清晰。
rén	àorán	wèn	shēngyīn	hóng liàng	ér	qīngxī
man	grandly	to ask	voice	loud	and	clear

他	大概	有	四十	岁	了，	身材	魁梧，
Tā	dàgài	yǒu	40	suì	le	shēncái	kuíwú
He	about	have		class. years	part.	stature	tall, sturdy

举止	威严，	一望而知	是	颐指气使	惯
jǔzhǐ	wēiyán	yīwàngérzhī	shì	yízhǐqìshǐ	guàn
manner	imposing	idiom – evident	is	idiom – ordering	used to

了	的	“大亨”。	他	的	话	还	没	完
le	de	dàhēng	Tā	de	huà	hái	méi	wán
part.	part.	big shot	He	part.	words	yet	not	finish

坐	在	那里	的	轮船局	办事员	霍地
zuò	zài	nàli	de	lúnchuán jú	bànshìyuán	huòde
sit	at	there	part.	steamship office	personel	suddenly

一齐	站了	起来,	内中	有	一	个	瘦长	子
yīqí	zhànle	qǐlai	nèizhòng	yǒu	yī	gè	shòucháng	zǐ
together	stood	up	inside	have	one	class.	slim	youth

堆起	满脸	的	笑容	抢	上一步,	恭恭敬敬
duīqǐ	mǎnliǎn	de	xiàoróng	qiǎng	shàngyībù	gōnggōngjìngjìng
a mass	whole face	part.	smile	hurry	stepped over	respectfully

回答:
huídá
to reply

Extract 6 from Chapter 1

“快了，快了！三老爷，请坐一会儿罢。——倒茶来。”

瘦长子一面说，一面就拉过一把椅子来放在三老爷的背后。三老爷脸上的肌肉一动，似乎是微笑，对那个瘦长子瞥了一眼，就望着门外。这时三老爷的车子已经开过去了，第二辆汽车补了缺，从车厢里下来一男一女，也进来了。

Translation 1.

‘Yes, Mr Wu, very soon,’ he answered respectfully. ‘Please take a seat.’ He turned to a boy: ‘Go and get some tea.’

While he was speaking he drew up a chair and placed it

behind the visitor, whose fleshy face twitched in what could have been a smile as he glanced at the young man, and then looked out towards the street. By now the visitor's car had moved on to make room for the second, out of which a man and a woman appeared and came into the hall.

Synthesis

快了,	快了!	三老爷	请	坐	一会儿	罢。
Kuàile	kuàile	sānlǎoye	qǐng	zuò	yīhuier	ba
Quick	quick	Sir (Mr Wu)	please	to sit	a moment	fin. part.

倒	茶	来。	瘦长	子	一面	说,	一面	就
Dào	chá	lái	Dhòucháng	zǐ	yīmiàn	shuō	yīmiàn	jiù
pour	tea	to come	Slim	lad	on one side	said	on one side	then

拉过	一	把	椅子	来	放	在	三老爷
lāguò	yī	bǎ	yǐzi	lái	fàng	zài	sānlǎoye
pulled	a, one	class.	chair	come	to put	at	Sir (Mr Wu)

的	背后。	三老爷	脸	上	的	肌肉
de	bèihòu	sānlǎoye	liǎn	shàng	de	jīròu
part.	behind	Sir (Mr Wu)	face	on	part.	flesh

一动,	似乎	是	微笑,	对	那个	瘦长
yī dòng	sìhū	shì	wēixiào	duì	nàge	shòucháng
twitched,	apparently	to be	smile	towards	the	slim

子	瞥	了	一眼,	就	望着	门外。
zǐ	piē	le	yīyǎn	jiù	wàngzhe	ménwài
lad	glance	part.	a look	the	looked	outside

这时	三老爷	的	车子	已经	开	过去了,
Zhèshí	sānlǎoye	de	chēzi	yǐjīng	kāi	guòqule,
At this time	Sir (Mr Wu)	part.	car	already	start	to leave

第二	辆	汽车	补	了	缺,	从	车	厢里
dièr	liàng	qìchē	bǔ	le	quē	cóng	chē	xiānglǐ
second	class.	car	fill	part.	opening	from	car	inside

下来	一男	一女，	也	进来了。
xiàlai	yī nán	yī rǔ,	yě	jìnláile
got out	a man	a woman	and	entered

Extract 7 from Chapter 1

男的是五短身材，微胖，满面和气的一张白脸。女的却高得多，也是方脸，和三老爷有几分相像，但颇白嫩光泽。两个都是四十开外的年纪了，但女的因为装饰入时，看来至多不过三十左右。男的先开口：

“荪甫，就在这里等候么？”

紫酱色脸的荪甫还没回答，轮船局的那个瘦长子早又陪笑说：

“不错，不错，姑老爷。已经听得拉过回声。我派了人在那里看着，专等船靠了码头，就进来报告。顶多再等五分钟，五分钟！”

Translation 1.

The man was short and stoutish with a bland and pallid face, while the woman was much taller, and bore a certain resemblance to the other man with her square face, although her skin was smooth and fair. Both she and her husband were in their forties, but in her fashionable dress she did not look more than thirty. The husband greeted the first arrival:

‘Why, hello, Sun-fu! Are we all waiting here?’

Before the purplish-faced man could answer the spindly youth quickly chimed in with a broad smile:

'Yes, here, Mr Tu. I've just heard her hooter and sent some one to keep a look-out at the landing-stage. He'll run back as soon as the boat arrives. I don't think we'll have to wait more than five minutes. Only five more minutes.'

Synthesis

男的	是	五短	身材,	微胖,	满面	和气的
Nánde	shì	wǔduǎn	shēncái	wēipàng	mǎnmiàn	héqide
Man	was	short	stature	stout	face	friendly

一	张	白脸。	女的	却	高得多,	也是
yī	zhāng	báiliǎn	Nǚde	què	gāodeduō	yěshì
a	class.	pale faced	Woman	however	much taller	though

方脸,	和	三老爷	有	几分	相像,	但
fāngliǎn	hé	sānlǎoye	yǒu	jǐfēn	xiāngxiàng	dàn
square faced	with	Mr Wu	was	somewhat	similar	but

颇	白	嫩	光泽。	两个	都	是	四十
pō	bái	nèn	guāngzé	Liǎng	dōu	shì	sìshí
rather	white	delicate	sheen	Both	all	were	forty

开外	的	年纪	了,	但	女的	因为
kāiwài	de	niánjì	le	dàn	nǚde	yīnwèi
over	part.	age	part.	but	woman	because

装饰	入时,	看来	至多	不过	三十	左右。
zhuāngshì	rùshí	kànlai	zhìduō	bùguò	sānshí	zuǒyòu
adorned	fashionably	looked	not more than	only	thirty	about

男的	先	开口:	荪甫,	就	在	这里	等候
Nánde	xiān	kāikǒu	Sūnfǔ	jiù	zài	zhèlǐ	děnghòu
Man	first	spoke	name	then	at	here	waiting

么?	紫酱色	脸的	荪甫	还	没	回答,
má	Zǐjiàngsè	liǎnde	Sūnfǔ	hái	méi	huídá
part.	Purple coloured	face	name	still	not	reply

轮船	局	的	那	个	瘦长	子	早又	陪
lúnchuán	jú	de	nà	ge	shòucháng	zǐ	zǎoyòu	péi
steamship	office	part.	that	class.	slim	lad	already	with

笑	说:	不错,	不错,	姑老爷。	已经	听得
xiào	shuō	bùcuò	bùcuò	Tū lǎoye	Yǐjīng	tīngde
smile	said	correct	correct	HonorableTu	Already	heard

拉过	回声。	我	派了	人	在	那里	看着
lāguò	huíshēng	Wǒ	pàile	rén	zài	nàli	kànzhe
play	echo	I	sent	man	at	there	to see

专	等	船	靠了	码头,	就	进来	报告。
zhuān	děng	chuán	kàole	mǎtóu	jiù	jìnlái	bàogào
purpose	wait	boat	accost	dock	at once	come in	to inform

顶多	再	等	五	分钟,	五	分钟!
Dǐngduō	zài	děng	wǔ	fēnzhōng	wǔ	fēnzhōng
At most	another	wait	five	minutes	five	minutes

<u>Extract 8 from Chapter 1</u>

“呀，福生，你还在这里么？好！做生意要有长性。老太爷向来就说你肯学好。你有几年不见老太爷罢？”

“上月回乡去，还到老太爷那里请安。——姑太太请坐罢。”

叫做福生的那个瘦长男子听得姑太太称赞他，快活得什么似的，一面急口回答，一面转身又拖了两把椅子来放在姑老爷和姑太太的背后，又是献茶，又是敬烟。

Translation 1.

'Ah, Fu-sheng! I'm very glad to see you're still here. Yes, the best way to learn a trade is to stick to it. Father has often said you're very keen. How long is it since you saw the old man last?'

'I paid a visit to Old Mr Wu only a month ago while I was home on leave,' babbled the spindly youth Fu-sheng in reply, dazzled by Mrs Tu's compliments; then, placing a chair behind her and another behind the husband, he begged her to take a seat.

Then he bustled about serving tea and offering cigarettes all round.

Synthesis

呀,	福生,	你	还	在	这里	么?	好!
Ya	Fúshēng	nǐ	hái	zài	zhèlǐ	má	Hǎo
Ah!	name	you	still	at	here	interrog.	Good!

做生意	要有	长	性。	老太爷	向来	就
zuòshēngyì	yàoyǒu	zhǎng	xìng	Lǎotàiyé	xiànglái	jiù
to do business	need	develop	character	Father (respect.)	always	justly

说	还	肯	学好。	你	有	几年	不见
shuō	hái	kěn	xuéhǎo	Nǐ	yǒu	jǐnián	bùjiàn
said	in addition	willing	to learn	You	have	a few years	not seen

老太爷	罢?	上月	回	乡	去,	还	到
lǎotàiyé	ba	shàngyuè	huí	xiāng	qù	huán	dào
father	fin. part.	last month	returned	country	went	in addition	to

老太爷	那里	请安。	姑太太	请	坐	罢。
lǎotàiyé	nàli	qǐngān	Gūtàitai	qǐng	zuò	ba
hon. father	there	to pay respects	Mrs Tu	please	sit	fin. part.

叫做	福生	的	那个	瘦长	男子	听得
Jiàozuò	Fúshēng	de	nàge	shòucháng	nánzǐ	tīngde
called	name	part.	this	slim	lad	heard

姑太太	称赞	他,	快活得	什么	似的,	一面
gūtàitai	chēngzàn	tā	kuàihuo	shénme	shìde	yīmiàn
Mrs Tu	praise	him	cheerfully	somewhat	possessed	one side

急口	回答,	一面	转身	又	拖了	两把
jíkǒu	huídá	yīmiàn	zhuǎnshēn	yòu	tuōle	liǎngbǎ
blurted	reply	one side	turn around	and	pulled	both

椅子	来	放	在	姑老爷	和	姑太太
yǐzi	lái	fàng	zài	gūlǎoye	hé	tàitai
chair	came	placed	at	Mr Tu	and	Mrs Tu

的	背后	又是	献茶,	又是	敬烟。
de	bèihòu	yòushì	xiànchá	yòushì	jìngyān
part.	behind	and	serving tea	and	offering cigarettes

Extract 9 from Chapter 1

他是荪甫三老爷家里一个老仆的儿子，从小就伶俐所以荪甫的父亲——吴老太爷特嘱荪甫安插他到这戴生昌轮船局。但是荪甫他们三位且不先坐下，眼睛都看着门外。门口马路上也有一个彪形大汉站着，背向着门，不住地左顾右盼；这是姑老爷杜竹斋随身带的保镖。

Translation

This young man was the son of an old servant of the Wu family. He had always been a nimble witted lad, so Old Mr Wu had asked his son Sun-fu to put him in this shipping office as an employee. The two men and the woman remained standing, looking every now and then towards the entrance. There at the gate another hefty fellow was standing with his back to the door, looking vigilantly right and left; Mr Tu's bodyguard.

Synthesis

他	是	苏甫,	三老爷	家里	一	个	老仆
Tā	shì	Sūnfǔ	sānlǎoye	jiālǐ	yī	gè	lǎopú
He	was	name	grandfather Wu	family	a	class.	old servant

的	儿子,	从小	就	伶俐,	所以	苏甫的
de	érzi	cóngxiǎo	jiù	língli	suǒyǐ	Sūnfǔde
part.	son	from childhood	already	bright	so	Sunfu's

父亲	吴	老太爷	特	嘱	苏甫,	安插
fùqīn	wú	lǎotàiyé	tè	zhǔ	Sūnfǔ	ānchā
father	Wu (surname)	Honorable	specially	entrusted	name	find a job

他	到	这	戴生昌	轮船	局。	但是	苏甫
tā	dào	zhè	Dàishēngchāng	lúnchuán	jú	Dànshì	Sūnfǔ
him	in	this	Tai Sheng Chang	steamship	office	However	name

他们	三	位	且	不	先	坐下,	眼睛
tāmen	sān	wèi	qiě	bù	xiān	zuòxia	yǎnjing
they	three	class.persons	as yet	not	start	sit down	eyes

都	看着	门外。	门口	马路	上	也	有
dōu	kànzhe	ménwài	Ménkǒu	mǎlù	shàng	yě	yǒu
all	looking	out the door	Doorway	street	on	also	was

一	个	彪形大汉	站着,	背	向着	门,
yī	gè	biāoxíngdàhàn	zhànzhe	bèi	xiàngzhe	mén
a	class.	well built guy	standing	back	towards	door

不住地	左顾右盼;	这	是	姑老爷
bùzhùde	zuǒgùyòupàn	zhè	shì	Tū lǎoye
continually	looking left and right (id.)	this	was	Mr (Honourable)Tu

杜竹斋 随身带的 保镖。
Dù Zhúzhāi suíshēndàide bǎobiāo
Du Zhuzhai armed bodyguard

Extract 10 from Chapter 1

杜姑太太轻声松一口气，先坐了，拿一块印花小丝巾，在嘴唇上抹了几下，回头对荪甫说：

“三弟，去年我和竹斋回乡去扫墓，也坐这云飞船。是一条快船。单趟直放，不过半天多，就到了；就是颠得厉害。骨头痛。这次爸爸一定很辛苦的。他那半肢疯，半个身子简直不能动。竹斋，去年我们看见爸爸坐久了就说头晕——”

Translation

Mrs Tu sat down first with a sigh of relief. She dabbed her lips with a print silk handkerchief, the said over her shoulder to Mr Wu:

‘When I went home with Chu-chai last year to visit the ancestral graves, we travelled on this same Flying Cloud. It’s a fast boat and didn’t stop on the way, and we did the journey in half a day, but it did roll terribly, and made my joints ache. I’m sure father must be having an awful time of it today. Of course, being paralysed like that, he can hardly move a muscle.’ She turned to her husband: ‘Chu-chai, do you remember how father complained of feeling giddy last year when he had been sitting down too long...?’

Synthesis

杜姑太太	轻声	松一口气，	先	坐下，	拿
Dù gūtàitai	qīngshēng	sōngyīkǒuqì	xiān	zuòxia	ná
Mrs Tu (Du)	quietly	heaved a sigh of relief	start	sit down	taking

一	块	印花	小	丝巾，	在	嘴唇	上	抹了
yī	kuài	yìnhuā	xiǎo	sījīn	zài	zuǐchún	shàng	mǒle
a	class.	printed	small	handkerchief	at	lips	on	wiped

几下，	回头	对	苏甫	说：	三弟，	去年
jǐxià	huítóu	duì	Sūnfǔ	shuō	sāndì	qùnián
a little	turned	towards	name	said	third brother	last year

我	和	竹斋	回	乡	去	扫墓，	也	坐
wǒ	hé	Zhúzhāi	huí	xiāng	qù	sǎomù	yě	zuò
I	and	name	returned	country	go	sweep tombs	also	travelled

这	云飞	船。	是	一	条	快	船。	单趟
zhè	yúnfēi	chuán	Shì	yī	tiáo	kuài	chuán	Dāntàng
this	Flying Cloud	boat	Is	a	classifier	fast	boat	One way

直放，	不过	半天	多，	就到了；	就是	颠得
zhí fàng	bùguò	bàntiān	duō	jiùdàole	jiùshi	diānde
direct	only	half a day	in all	to arrive	but	shook

厉害。	骨头	痛。	这	次	爸爸	一定	很
lìhai	gǔtou	tòng	zhè	cì	bàba	yīdìng	hěn
terribly	Head	ached	This	time	daddy	already	very

辛苦的。	他	那	半肢疯，	半个	身子	简直
xīnkǔde	tā	nà	bànzhīfēng	bànge	shēnzi	jiǎnzhí
exhausting	His	this	paralysis	half	body	simply

不能	动。	竹斋，	去年	我们	看见	爸爸
bùnéng	dòng	Zhúzhāi	qùnián	wǒmen	kànjiàn	bàba
could not	move	name	last year	we	saw	daddy

坐	久	了	就	说	头晕....
zuò	jiǔ	le	jiù	shuō	tóuyūn
sitting	long time	part.	then	said	dizzy

Extract 11 from Chapter 1

姑太太说到这里一顿，轻轻吁了一口气，眼圈儿也像有点红了。她正想接下去说，猛的一声汽笛从外面飞来。接着一个人跑进来喊道：

“云飞靠了码头了！”

姑太太也立刻站了起来，手扶着杜竹斋的肩膀。那时福生已经飞步抢出去，一面走，一面扭转脖子，朝后面说：

“三老爷，姑老爷，姑太太；不忙，等我先去招呼好了，再出来！”

Translation

Mrs Tu paused and sighed slightly, her eyes reddening at the edges. She was going to say something more when a steam-whistle screeched, and a boy dashed in announcing excitedly:

‘The boat’s drawing level with the landing-stage!’

Mrs Tu instantly rose, laying one hand on Mr Tu’s shoulder. Fu-sheng dashed out, at the same time looking back to say:

‘Mr Wu, Mr Tu, Mrs Tu, there’s no need to hurry. Wait till I’ve seen to things before you come out.’

Synthesis

姑太太	说到	这里	一顿,	轻轻	吁了	一口气,
gūtàitai	shuōdào	zhèlǐ	yīdùn	qīngqīng	yùle	yīkǒuqì
Mrs Tu	said	here	pause	softly	implored	sigh

眼圈儿	也	像	有点	红	了。	她	正想
yǎnquāner	yě	xiàng	yǒudiǎn	hóng	le	Tā	zhèngxiǎng
eye rims	too	seemed	a little	red	part.	She	wanted to

接下	去	说,	猛的	一声	汽笛	从
jiēxià	qù	shuō	měngde	yīshēng	qìdí	cóng
to continue	to go on	speaking	suddenly	a sound	steam whistle	from

外面	飞来。	接着	一个人	跑进来	喊道:
wàimian	fēilái	Jiēzhe	yīgèrén	pǎojìnlái	hǎndào
outside	blew	Then	somebody	ran in	shouting

云飞	靠了	码头	了!	姑太太	也	立刻
yúnfēi	kàole	mǎtóu	le	Gūtàitai	yě	likè
Flying Cloud	alongside	dock	part.	Mrs Tu	also	at once

站了起来,	手	扶着	杜竹斋	的	肩膀。	那时
zhànleqǐlai	shǒu	fúzhe	Dù Zhúzhāi	de	jiānbǎng	Nàshí
stood up	hand	leaning on	name	part.	shoulder	Then

福生	已经	飞步	抢出去,	一面走,	一面
Fúshēng	yǐjīng	fēibù	qiǎngchūqù	yīmiànzǒu	yīmiàn
name	already	flying	out in a rush	ahead	at the same time

扭转	脖子	朝	后面	说:	三老爷,	姑老爷,
cháohòu	bózi	cháo	hòumiàn	shuō	Sānlǎoye	Tūlǎoye
backwards	neck	facing	behind	saying	Mr Wu	Honorable Tu

姑太太:	不忙,	等	我	先	去	招呼	好了,
Gūtàitai	Bùmáng	děng	wǒ	xiān	qù	zhāohu	hàole
Mrs Tu	there's no hurry	wait	me	first	go	to call out	it's OK

再	出来!
zài	chūlái
then	come

Extract 12 from Chapter 1

轮船局里其他的办事人也开始忙乱；一片声唤脚夫。就有一架预先准备好的大藤椅由两个精壮的脚夫抬了出去。苏甫眼睛望着外边，嘴里说：

“二姊，回头你和老太爷同坐一八八九号，让四妹和我同车，竹斋带阿萱。”

姑太太点头，眼睛也望着外边，嘴唇翕翕地动：

Translation

All the clerks in the office began to bustle about. Somebody summoned two stout porters who had been standing by, and who immediately ran in, took up a cane-chair, and carried it off. Wu Sun-fu, looking out on the street, said to Mrs Tu:

‘On our way home you’ll sit with father in the first car N° 1889. I’ll keep Huei-fang company in the second, and Chu-chai will have Ah-hsuan in the third.’

Mrs Wu nodded and looked towards the entrance, moving her lips as she silently recited Buddhist sutras.

Synthesis

轮船	局	里	其他	的	办事	人	也
Lúnchuán	jú	lǐ	qítā	de	bànshì	rén	yě
Steamship	office	in	the others	part.	staff	people	also

开始	忙乱;	一	片	声	唤	脚夫。	就
kāishǐ	mángluàn	yī	piàn	shēng	huàn	jiǎofū	Jiù
started	hurry about	a	classifier	voice	called	porters	Then

有	一	架	预先	准备	好的	大	藤
yǒu	yī	jià	yùxiān	zhǔnbèi	hàode	dà	téng
there was	a	class.	in advance	prepared	well	large	wicker

椅	由	两	个	精壮	的	脚夫	抬了
yǐ	yóu	liǎng	gè	jīng zhuàng	de	jiǎofū	táile
chair	followed by	a couple	class.	strong	part.	porters	carry

出去。	苏甫	眼睛	望着	外边,	嘴里说:
chūqù	Sūnfǔ	yǎnjing	wàngzhc	wàibian	zuǐlǐshuō
out	name	eyes	looked	outside	said

二姊,	回头	你	和	老太爷	同	坐
èrzǐ	huítóu	nǐ	hé	lǎotàiyé	tóng	zuò
2nd older sister	going back	you	and	father	together	ride in

一八八九	号,	让	四妹	和	我	同	车,
yībābājiǔ	hào	ràng	sìmèi	hé	wǒ	tóng	chē
1889	number	let	4th younger sister	and	me	same	car

竹斋	带	阿萱。	姑太太	点头,	眼睛	也
Zhúzhāi	dài	A Xuān	Gūtàitai	diǎntóu	yǎnjing	yě
name	take	name	Mrs Tu	nodded	eyes	also

望着	外边,	嘴唇	翕翕地	动:	在那里	念佛!
wàngzhe	wàibian	zuǐchún	xīxīde	dòng	zàinàli	niànfó
looked	outside	lips	whispering	moving	there	praying*

*Buddhist sutras

Extract 13 from Chapter 1

在那里念佛！竹斋含着雪茄，微微地笑着，看了荪甫一眼，似乎说“我们走罢”。恰好福生也进来了，十分为难似的皱着眉头：

“真不巧。有一只苏州班的拖船停在里挡——

“不要紧。我们到码头上去看罢！”

荪甫截断了福生的话，就走出去了。保镖的老关赶快也跟上去。后面是杜竹斋和他的夫人，还有福生。本来站在门口的杜竹斋的保镖就作了最后的“殿军”。

Translation

A cigar in his mouth and a smile on his face, Chu-chai glanced at Wu Sun-fu as much as to say: Let’s go now.

Just then Fu-sheng came back frowning with annoyance.

'What a nuisance!' he said. 'There's a Soochow Line tug occupying the landing-stage.'

'That doesn't matter: let's go and see,' Wu Sun-fu interrupted and made off with his bodyguard. Tu Chu-chai and his wife followed; Fu-sheng and the other bodyguard,

<u>Synthesis</u>

竹斋	含着	雪茄，	微微地	笑着，	看了
Zhúzhāi	hánzhe	xuějiā	wēiwēide	xiàozhe	kànle
name	sucking	cigar	somewhat	smiled	looked

荪甫	一眼，	似乎	说：	我们	走
Sūnfǔ	yīyǎn	sìhū	shuō	Wǒmen	zǒu
name	a glance	as if	to say	we	go

罢。	恰好	福生	也	进来了，	十分
ba!	Qiàhǎo	Fúshēng	yě	jìnláile	shífēn
final part.	Precisely	name	also	came in	extremely

为难	似的	皱着	眉头：	真不巧。	有	一
wéinán	shìde	zhòuzhe	méitóu	zhēnbùqiǎo	Yǒu	yī
embarrassed	annoyed	wrinkling	brows	sorry!	There is	a

只	苏州	班的	拖船	停	在	里挡
zhī	Sūzhōu	bān	tuōchuán	tíng	zài	lǐdǎng
classifier	a city	line	tugboat	stopped	at	warfside

不要紧。	我们	到	码头	上去	看	罢！
búyàojǐn	Wǒmen	dào	mǎtóu	shàngqù	kàn	ba
don't worry	We	to	dock	to go up	look	fin.part.

荪甫	截断了	福生	的	话，	就	走出去了。
Sūnfǔ	jiéduànle	Fúshēng	de	huà	jiù	zǒuchūqùle
name	interrupted	name	part.	words	then	went out

保镖	的	老关	赶快	也	跟上去。	后面
Bǎobiāo	de	Lǎo Guān	gǎnkuài	yě	gēnshàngqù	Hòumian
Bodyguard	part.	name	at once	also	followed	Behind

是	杜竹斋	和	他	的	夫人，	还有	福生。
shì	Dù Zhúzhāi	hé	tā	de	fūren	háiyǒu	Fúshēng
was	name	and	his	part.	wife	and also	name

本来	站	在	门口	的	杜竹斋	的	保镖
Běnlái	zhàn	zài	ménkǒu	de	Dù Zhúzhāi	de	bǎobiāo
initially	standing	in	doorway	part.	name	part.	bodyguard

就	作了	最后的	“殿军”。
jiù	zuòle	zuìhòude	diànjūn
then	acting	finally	runner-up

Extract 14 from Chapter 1

云飞轮船果然泊在一条大拖船——所谓“公司船”的外边。那只大藤椅已经放在云飞船头，两个精壮的脚夫站在旁边。码头上冷静静地，没有什么闲杂人：轮船局里的两三个职员正在那里高声吆喝，轰走那些围近来的黄包车夫和小贩。荪甫他们三位走上了那“公司船”的甲板时，吴老太爷已经由云飞的茶房扶出来坐上藤椅子了。

Translation

The Flying Cloud was moored alongside a tug, commonly known as a “company boat”. The large cane-chair was placed in readiness on the foredeck, the two bearers waiting on either side. Along the warf there was not the usual bustle and din. On the landing-stage several men from the shipping company were shouting and trying to shoo off the rickshaw-men and hawkers, who kept pushing forward. While Wu Sun-fu and the Tu couple were picking their way across the deck of the tug, a cabin boy helped Old Mr Wu out on deck and sat him down in the cane chair.

Synthesis

云飞	轮船	果然	泊	在	一	条	大	拖船
Yúnfēi	lúnchuán	guǒrán	bó	zài	yī	tiáo	dà	tuōchuán
name	steamer	sure enough	anchored	by	a	class.	big	tugboat

所谓	“公司船”	的	外边。	那	只	大	藤
suǒwèi	gōngsīchuán	de	wàibian	Nà	zhī	dà	téng
known as	company boat	part.	aside	This	class.	large	wicker

椅	已经	放	在	云飞	船头，	两	个
yǐ	yǐjīng	fàng	zài	Yúnfēi	chuán tóu	liǎng	gè
chair	already	put	by	name	ship's bow	two	class.

精壮	的	脚夫	站	在	旁边。	码头	上
jīngzhuàng	de	jiǎofū	zhàn	zài	pángbiān	Mǎtóu	shàng
strong	part.	porters	stood	by	side	Dock	on

冷静静地，	没有什么	闲杂人：	轮船局	里
lěngjìngjìngde	méiyǒushénme	xiánzárén	lúnchuán	lǐ
calmly	waiting	employees	steamer office	in

的	两三	个	职员	正在	那里	高声
de	liǎng sān	gè	zhíyuán	zhèngzài	nàli	gāoshēng
part.	two or three	class.	office workers	occupied	there	loudly

吆喝，	轰走	那些	围	近来的	黄包车夫
yāohe	hōngzǒu	nàxiē	wéi	jìnláide	huángbāochēfu
shouting	pushing back	those	encircling	recently arrived	rickshaw drivers

和	小贩。	苏甫	他们	三	位	走上了
hé	xiǎofàn	Sūnfǔ	tāmen	sān	wèi	zǒushàngle
and	hawkers	name	they	three	class.	walked on

那	“公司船”	的	甲板	时，	吴老太爷
nǎ	gōngsīchuán	de	jiǎbǎn	shí	Wú lǎotàiyé
this	company boat	part.	deck	when	old Mr Wu

已经	由	云飞	的	茶房	扶	出来
yǐjīng	yóu	Yúnfēi	de	cháfáng	fú	chūlái
already	followed	name	part.	steward	supporting	came out

坐	上	藤	椅子	了。
zuò	shàng	téng	yǐzi	le
sat	on	wicker	chair	part.

Extract 15 from Chapter 1

福生赶快跳过去，做手势，命令那两个脚夫抬起吴老太爷，慢慢地走到“公司船”上。于是儿子，女儿，女婿，都上前相见。虽然路上辛苦，老太爷的脸色并不难看，两圈红晕停在他的额角。可是他不作声，看看儿子，女儿，女婿，只点了一下头，便把眼睛闭上了。

这时候，和老太爷同来的四小姐蕙芳和七少爷阿萱也挤上那“公司船”。

“爸爸在路上好么？”杜姑太太——吴二小姐，拉住了四小姐，轻声问。

Translation

Fu-sheng ran up and made signs to the bearers to hoist up the old man and carry him carefully onto the “company boat”. The old man was met by his son and his daughter, and son-in-law, who were relieved to find him none the worse for the voyage, except for the red blotches on his temples. But he did not speak; he merely glanced at them, nodded his head slightly, and closed his eyes. Huei-fang, the old man’s fourth daughter, and Ah-hsuan, his seventh son, also came aboard the tug from the Flying Cloud.

'How did father feel on the journey, Huei-fang?' Mrs Tu asked her younger sister in a whisper.

Synthesis

福生	赶快	跳过去，	做	手势，	命令	那
Fúshēng	gǎnkuài	tiàoguòqu	zuò	shǒu shì	mìnglìng	nà
name	at once	jumped	making	gesture	ordering	those

两	个	脚夫	抬起	吴老太爷，	慢慢地
liǎng	gè	jiǎofū	táiqǐ	Wú lǎotàiyé	mànmànde
two	class.	porters	lifted	old Mr Wu	slowly

走到	"公司船"	上。	于是	儿子，	女儿，
zǒudào	gōngsīchuán	shàng	Yúshì	érzi	nǚér
to	company boat	on	With that	son	daughter

女婿，	都	上前	相见。	虽然	路上	辛苦，
nǚxu	dōu	shàngqián	xiāngjiàn	Suīrán	lùshang	xīnkǔ
son-in-law	all	followed	to meet	Then	on the road	with effort

老太爷，	的	脸色	并不	难看，	两	圈	红
lǎotàiyé	de	liǎnsè	bìngbù	nánkàn	liǎng	quān	hóng
old man	part.	complexion	not at all	bad	two	class.	red

晕	停	在	他	的	额角。	可是	他
yùn	tíng	zài	tā	de	éjiǎo	Kěshì	tā
aureoles	remain	at (on)	his	part.	temples	However	he

不	作	声，	看看	儿子，	女儿，	女婿，	只
bù	zuò	shēng	kànkan	érzi	nǚér	nǚxu	zhǐ
not	make	sound	looked at	son	daughter	son-in-law	only

点了一下头，	便	把	眼睛	闭上了。	这
diǎn le yīxià tóu	biàn	bǎ	yǎnjing	bìshangle	Zhè
nodded	then	part.	eyes	closed	This

时候，	和	老太爷	同来的	四小姐	蕙芳	和
shíhòu	hé	lǎotàiyé	tóngláide	sì xiǎojie	Huìfāng	hé
time	and	old man	along with	4th daughter	name	and

七少爷	阿萱	也	挤	上	那	“公司船”。
qī shàoye	Ā xuān	yě	jǐ	shàng	nà	gōngsīchuán
7th son	name	also	crowded	on	this	company boat

爸爸	在	路上	好么？	杜姑太太	吴二小姐，
Bàba	zài	lùshang	hǎomá	Dù gūtàitai	Wú èrxiǎojie
Daddy	at (on)	on the road	alright?	Auntie Gu	Wu 2nd younger sister

拉住了	四小姐，	轻声	问。
lā zhù le	sìxiǎojie	qīng shēng	wèn
stopping	4th daughter	quietly	asked

Extract 16 from Chapter 1

“没有什么。只是老说头眩。”

“赶快上汽车罢！福生，你去招呼一八八九号的新车子先开来。”

苏甫不耐烦似的说。让两位小姐围在老太爷旁边，苏甫和竹斋，阿萱就先走到码头上。

一八八九号的车子开到了，藤椅子也上了岸，吴老太爷也被扶进汽车里坐定了，二小姐——杜姑太太跟着便坐在老太爷旁边。

Translation

‘Pretty well, though he kept saying he felt giddy.’

‘Let’s hurry up and get to the cars,’ said Wu Sun-fu impatiently. ‘Fu-sheng go and tell the chauffeur to bring the new car round first.’

Leaving the old gentleman in the care of the ladies, Wu Sun-fu, Tu Chu-chai, and the lad Ah-hsuan went ashore first. The new car drove up, while the bearers landed the cane-chair with its occupant. They got the old man settled in the car, and Mrs Tu took her place beside him.

<u>Synthesis</u>

没有什么	只是	老	说	头眩。	赶快	上
Méiyǒushénme	zhǐshì	lǎo	shuō	tóuxuàn	Gǎnkuài	shàng
It's nothing	only	old (father)	said	dizzy	Quickly	on (in)

汽车	罢!	福生,	你	去	招呼	一八八九	号
qìchē	ba	Fúshēng	nǐ	qù	zhāohu	yībābājiǔ	hào
car	fin.part.	name	you	go	call	1889	number

的	新	车子	先	开	来。	荪甫	不耐烦
de	xīn	chēzi	xiān	kāi	lái	Sūnfǔ	bùnàifán
part.	new	car	first	start	to come	name	impatiently

似的	说。	让	两	位	小姐	围	在
shìde	shuō	Ràng	liǎng	wèi	xiǎojie	wéi	zài
it seemed	said	Let	both	classifier	girls	around	at

老太爷	旁边,	荪甫	和	竹斋,	阿萱	就
lǎotàiyé	pángbiān	Sūnfǔ	hé	Zhúzhāi	Ā xuān	jiù
father	lateral	name	and	name	name	then

先	走	到	码头	上。	一八八九	号
xiān	zǒu	dào	mǎtóu	shàng	Yībābājiǔ	hào
first	went	to	dock	on	1889	number

的	车子	开	到了,	藤	椅子	也	上
de	chēzi	kāi	dàole	téng	yǐzi	yě	shàng
part.	car	start	to	wicker	chair	also	on

了	岸,	吴老太爷	也	被	扶	进	汽车
le	àn	Wú lǎotàiyé	yě	bèi	fúzhe	jìn	qìchē
part.	shore	old Mr Wu	also	by	lean on	in	car

里	坐定了,	二小姐,	杜姑太太	跟着	便
lǐ	zuòdìngle	èrxiǎojie	Dù gūtàitai	gēnzhe	biàn
in	seated	2th sister	Auntie Gu	followed after	then

坐	在	老太爷	旁边。
zuò	zài	lǎotàiyé	pángbiān
sat	at	the oldman	beside

Extract 17 from Chapter 1

本来还是闭着眼睛的吴老太爷被二小姐身上的香气一刺激，便睁开眼来看一下，颤着声音慢慢地说：

“芙芳，是你么？要蕙芳来！蕙芳！还有阿萱！”

荪甫在后面的车子里听得了，略皱一下眉头，但也不说什么。老太爷的脾气古怪而且执拗，荪甫和竹斋都知道。于是四小姐蕙芳和七少爷阿萱都进了老太爷的车子。

Translation

Her perfume seemed to wake him, and he opened his eyes to see who it was and said in a slow and wavering voice:

'Is that you, Fu-fang? I want Huei-fang to come with me...and Ah-hsuan as well.'

Wu Sun-fu, who was in the second car, heard this and frowned slightly, but said nothing. He knew how eccentric and obstinate his father was...so did Chu-chai. So Huei-fang and Ah-hsuan squeezed into the car beside their father.

Synthesis

本来	还是	闭着	眼睛	的	吴老太爷	被
Běnlái	háishì	bìzhe	yǎnjing	de	Wú lǎotàiyé	bèi
At first	still	closed	eyes	part.	old Mr Wu	by

二小姐，身 上 的 香气 一 刺激，便
èrxiǎojie shēn shang de xiāngqì yī cìjī biàn
2nd sister body on part. fragrance a stimulate then

睁开 眼 来看 一下，颤着 声音 慢慢地
zhēngkāi yǎn láikàn yīxià chànzhe shēngyīn mànmàn
opened eye to see slightly trembling voice slowly

说：芙芳，是你么？要 蕙芳 来！蕙芳！
shuō Fúfāng shì nǐ má? Yāo Huìfāng lái Huìfāng
said name Is it you Want name to come name

还有 阿萱！荪甫 在 后面 的 车子 里
háiyǒu Ā xuān Sūnfǔ zài hòumiàn de chēzi lǐ
and also name name at (in) behind part. car in

听得了，略皱 一下 眉头，但 也 不说
tīngdele lüè yīxià méitóu dàn yě bùshuō
heard wrinkled a little brows but also not say

什么。老太爷 的 脾气古怪 而且 执拗，
shénme Lǎotàiyé de píqìgǔguài érqiě zhíniù
anything The oldman part. eccentric but also stubborn

荪甫 和 竹斋 都 知道。于是 四小姐，
Sūnfǔ hé Zhúzhāi dōu zhīdào Yúshì sìxiǎojie
name and name both knew Then 4th sister

蕙芳 和 七少爷 阿萱 都 进了 老太爷
Huìfāng hé qī shàoye Ā xuān dōu jìnle lǎotàiyé
name and 7th son name both got in the oldman

的 车子。
de chēzi
part. car

Extract 18 from Chapter 1

二小姐芙芳舍不得离开父亲，便也挤在那里。两位小姐把老太爷夹在中间。马达声音响了，一八八九号

汽车开路，已经动了，忽然吴老太爷又锐声叫了起来：

“《太上感应篇》！”

这是裂帛似的一声怪叫。在这一声叫喊中，吴老太爷的残余生命力似乎又复旺炽了；他的老眼闪闪地放光，额角上的淡红色转为深朱，虽然他的嘴唇簌簌地抖着。

Translation

Fu-fang, who couldn’t bear to leave her father, remained where she was, so that the old man was now sandwiched between his two daughters. The engine started up but as the car moved forward the old man suddenly cried in a shrill voice:

‘The Supreme scriptures of Rewards and Punishments!’

It was a strange, strident cry. His eyes gleamed, the faint reddish patches on his temples turned a deep red, and his lips trembled.

Synthesis

二小姐	芙芳，	舍不得	离开	父亲，	便	也
èrxiǎojie	Fúfāng	shěbude	líkāi	fùqīn	biàn	yě
2nd sister	name	reluctant	leave	father	then	also

挤	在	那里。	两	位	小姐	把	老太爷
jǐ	zài	nàli	Liǎng	wèi	xiǎojie	bǎ	lǎotàiyé
squeezed	at (in)	there	Both	class., pol.	girls	part.	the oldman

夹	在	中间。	马达	声音	响了，	一八八九
jiá	zài	zhōngjiān	Mǎdá	shēngyīn	xiǎngle	yībābājiǔ
between	at (in)	between	Motor	noise	echoed	1889

号	车子	开路,	已经	动了,	忽然	吴老太爷
hào	chēzi	kāilù	yǐjīng	dòngle	hūrán	Wú lǎotàiyé
number	car	start	already	moving	suddenly	old Mr Wu

又	锐	声	叫了起来:	太上感应篇!	这
yòu	ruì	shēng	jiàole qǐlai	Tàishànggǎnyìngpiān	Zhè
then	shrill	voice	cried out	Taoist book	This

是	裂	帛	似的	一声	怪	叫。	在	这
shì	liè	bó	shìde	yīshēng	guài	jiào	Zài	zhè
is	tearing	silk	seemed as if	sound	strange	cry	At (in)	this

一声	叫喊	中,	吴老太爷	的	残余	生命力
yīshēng	jiàohǎn	zhōng	Wú lǎotàiyé	de	cányú	shēngmìnglì
sound	cry	middle	old Mr Wu	part.	remaining	vitality

似乎	又复	旺炽了;	他	的	老	眼	闪闪地
sìhū	yòu fù	wàngchìle	tā	de	lǎo	yǎn	shǎnshǎnde
seemed	once more	flamed	his	part.	old	eyes	flickered

放光,	额角	上	的	淡红色	转为	深朱,
fàngguāng	éjiǎo	shàng	de	dànhóngsè	zhuǎnwéi	shēnzhū
brightly	temples	on	part.	rose	turning into	deep crimson

虽然	他	的	嘴唇	簌簌地	抖着。
suīrán	tā	de	zuǐchún	sùsù	dǒuzhe
though	his	part.	lips	quivered	trembling

Notes

太上感应篇! Tàishànggǎnyìngpiān – Taoist Book of Rewards and Punishments

Extract 19 from Chapter 1

一八八九号的汽车夫立刻把车煞住，惊惶地回过脸来。荪甫和竹斋的车子也跟着停止。

大家都怔住了。四小姐却明白老太爷要的是什么。她看见福生站在近旁，就唤他道：“福生，赶快到云飞的大餐间里拿那部《太上感应篇》来！

是黄绫子的书套！”

吴老太爷自从骑马跌伤了腿，终至成为半肢疯以来，就虔奉《太上感应篇》，

Translation

The driver immediately braked and cast a startled glance over his shoulder. The other two cars also stopped. Nobody knew what had happened. Only Huei-fang understood what it was her father wanted. Fu-sheng had come up, and she told him:

‘Fu-sheng, run back to the boat and look in the dining room for a book in a yellow damask-covered case.’

Twenty-five years before Old Mr Wu hd had a fall from a horse, and an injury to his leg had led to partial paralysis. He had since developed a strong faith in the religious book on virtue rewarded and vice punished.

Synthesis

一八八九	号	的	汽车夫	立刻	把	车
Yībābājiǔ	hào	de	qìchēfū	lìkè	bǎ	chē
1889	number	part.	chauffeur	promptly	part.	car

煞住，	惶地惊	回过脸来。	荪甫	和	竹斋
shāzhù	jīnghuángde	huíguò liǎnlái	Sūnfǔ	hé	Zhúzhāi
braked	anxiously	turned around	name	and	name

的	车子	也	跟着	停止。	大家	都	怔住了。
de	chēzi	yě	gēnzhe	tíngzhǐ	Dàjiā	dōu	zhèngzhùle
part.	car	also	following	stopped	Everyone	all	puzzled

四小姐,	却	明白	老太爷	要的	是	什么。
Sixiǎojie	què	míngbai	lǎotàiyé	yāode	shì	shénme
4th sister	however	explained	the oldman	want	was	what

她	看见	福生	站	在	近旁,	就	唤	他	道:
tā	kànjiàn	Fúshēng	zhàn	zài	jìnpáng	jiù	huàn	tā	dào
She	saw	name	standing	at	close	then	called	him	to

福生,	赶快	到	云飞	的	大餐间	里	拿
Fúshēng	gǎnkuài	dào	yúnfēi	de	dàcānjiān	lǐ	ná
name	at once	to	Flying Cloud	part.	dinning room	in	take

那	部	太上感应篇	来!	是	黄	绫子	的
nà	bù	Tàishànggǎnyìngpiān	lái	Shì	huáng	língzi	de
this	classifier	Taoist book	go on!	Is	yellow	damask	part.

书	套!	吴老太爷	自从	骑马	跌	伤了
shū	tào	Wú lǎotàiyé	zìcóng	qímǎ	diē	shānġle
book	pocket	Old Mr Wu	since	horse riding	fall	injured

腿,	终至	成为	半肢疯	以来,	就	虔奉
tuǐ	zhōngzhì	chéngwéi	bànzhīfēng	yǐlái	jiù	qiánfèng
leg	ended up	becoming	half paralysed	since	then	devoted to

太上感应篇,
Tàishànggǎnyìngpiān
Taoist book

Extract 20 from Chapter 1

二十余年如一日；除了每年印赠而外，又曾恭楷手抄一部，是他坐卧不离的。

一会儿，福生捧着黄绫子书套的《感应篇》来了。吴老太爷接过来恭恭敬敬摆在膝头，就闭了眼睛，干瘪的嘴唇上浮出一丝放心了的微笑。

“开车！”

二小姐轻声喝，松了一口气，一仰脸把后颈靠在弹簧背垫上，也忍不住微笑。

Translation

Every year he had given free copies of the book to fellow-believers as a practice of virtue. He had also copied the whole book in his own neat and pious hand, and this transcript had become for him a talisman against vice, with which he could never part for a moment.

Very soon Fu-sheng was back, holding the book with both hands. Old Mr Wu took it and laid it reverently on his lap. He closed his eyes again, a faint smile of peace on his shrivelled lips.

'Carry on now, driver,' Mrs Tu ordered quietly. With a sigh of relief, she sank back into her seat and rested her head against the cushioned back, smiling with satisfaction.

Synthesis

二十余年如一日;	除了	每年	印	赠	而外,
èrshí yúnián rú yī rì	chú le	měinián	yìn	zèng	érwài
For twenty years	besides	every year	printing	to offer	in addition

又	曾	恭	楷手	抄	一部,	是	他	坐卧
yòu	céng	gōng	kǎishǒu	chāo	yī bù	shì	tā	zuòwò
also	once	reverently	handwritten	copy	a volume	was	his	lasting

不离的。	一会儿,	福生	捧着	黄	绫	子
bùlíde	Yīhuìer	Fúshēng	pěngzhe	huáng	líng	zi
never parted from	A while	name	holding	yellow	damask	suffix

书	套	的	《感应篇》	来了。	吴老太爷
shū	tào	de	(Tàishàng)gǎnyingpiān	láile	Wú lǎotàiyé
book	cover	part.	Taoist book (abbr.)	arrived	Old Mr Wu

接过	来	恭恭敬敬	摆	在	膝头，	就
jiēguò	lái	gōnggōng-jìngjìng	bǎi	zài	xītóu	jiù
took	next	very respectfully	arranged	on	knees	at once

闭了	眼睛，	干瘪	的	嘴唇	上浮出	一丝
bìle	yǎnjing	gānbiě	de	zuǐchún	shàngfúchū	yīsī
closed	eyes	wizened	part.	lips	appeared	a trace

放心了	的	微笑。	开车！	二小姐	轻声	喝，
fàngxīn	de	wēixiào	Kāichē	Erxiǎojie	qīngshēng	hè
relieved	part.	smile	Start	2nd sister	softly	shouted

松了	一口气，	一仰脸	把	后颈	靠	在
sōngle	yīkǒuqì	yīyǎngliǎn	bǎ	hòujǐng	kào	zài
letting out	a sigh	face up	part.	nape of neck	against	at (on)

弹簧背垫	上，	也	忍不住	微笑。
tánhuángbèidiàn	shàng	yě	rěnbuzhù	wēixiào
spring back cushion	on	and	cannot help	smiling

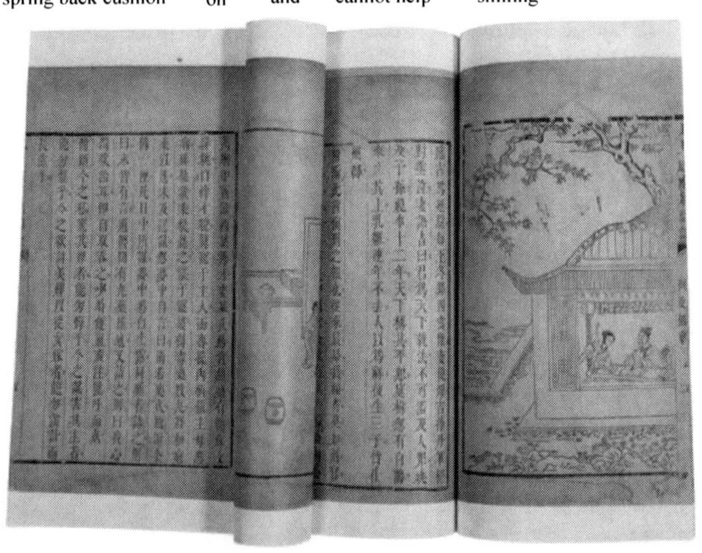

全名《太上感应篇》
A Taoist book (p.216)

Midnight

子夜

一

太阳刚刚下了地平线。软风一阵一阵地吹上人面，怪痒痒的。苏州河的浊水幻成了金绿色，轻轻地，悄悄地，向西流去。黄浦的夕潮不知怎的已经涨上了，现在沿这苏州河两岸的各色船只都浮得高高地，舱面比码头还高了约莫半尺。风吹来外滩公园里的音乐，却只有那炒豆似的铜鼓声最分明，也最叫人兴奋。暮霭挟着薄雾笼罩了外白渡桥的高耸的钢架，电车驶过时，这钢架下横空架挂的电车线时时爆发出几朵碧绿的火花。从桥上向东望，可以看见浦东的洋栈像巨大的怪兽，蹲在暝色中，闪着千百只小眼睛似的灯火。向西望，叫人猛一惊的，是高高地装在一所洋房顶上而且异常庞大的霓虹电管广告，射出火一样的赤光和青燐似的绿焰：Light，Heat，Power！

这时候——这天堂般五月的傍晚，有三辆一九三〇年式的雪铁笼汽车像闪电一般驶过了外白渡桥，向西转弯，一直沿北苏州路去了。

过了北河南路口的上海总商会以西的一段，俗名唤作“铁马路”，是行驶内河的小火轮的汇集处。那三辆汽车到这里就减低了速率。第一辆车的汽车夫轻声地对坐在他旁边的穿一身黑拷绸衣裤的彪形大汉说：

“老关！是戴生昌罢？”

“可不是！怎么你倒忘了？您准是给那只烂污货迷昏了啦！”

老关也是轻声说，露出一口好像连铁梗都咬得断似的大牙齿。他是保镖的。此时汽车戛然而止，老关忙即跳下车去，摸摸腰间的勃郎宁，又向四下里瞥了一眼，就过去开了车门，威风凛凛地站在旁边。车厢里先探出一个头来，紫酱色的一张方脸，浓眉毛，圆眼睛，脸上有许多小疱。看见迎面那所小洋房的大门上正有“戴生昌轮船局”六个大字，这人也就跳下车来，一直走进去。老关紧跟在后面。

“云飞轮船快到了么？”

紫酱脸的人傲然问，声音宏亮而清晰。他大概有四十岁了，身材魁梧，举止威严，一望而知是颐指气使惯了的“大亨”。他的话还没完，坐在那里的轮船局办事员霍地一齐站了起来，内中有一个瘦长子堆起满脸的笑容抢上一步，恭恭敬敬回答：

“快了，快了！三老爷，请坐一会儿罢。——倒茶来。”

瘦长子一面说，一面就拉过一把椅子来放在三老爷的背后。三老爷脸上的肌肉一动，似乎是微笑，对那个瘦长子瞥了一眼，就望着门外。这时三老爷的车子已经开过去了，第二辆汽车补了缺，从车厢里下来一男一女，也进来了。男的是五短身材，微胖，满面和气的一张白脸。女的却高得多，也是方脸，和三老爷有几分相像，但颇白嫩光泽。两个都是四十开外的年纪了，但女的因为装饰入时，看来至多不过三十左右。男的先开口：

“荪甫，就在这里等候么？”

紫酱色脸的荪甫还没回答，轮船局的那个瘦长子早又陪笑说：

“不错，不错，姑老爷。已经听得拉过回声。我派了人在那里看着，专等船靠了码头，就进来报告。顶多再等五分钟，五分钟！”

“呀，福生，你还在这里么？好！做生意要有长性。老太爷向来就说你肯学好。你有几年不见老太爷罢？”

“上月回乡去，还到老太爷那里请安。——姑太太请坐罢。”

叫做福生的那个瘦长男子听得姑太太称赞他，快活得什么似的，一面急口回答，一面转身又拖了两把椅子来放在姑老爷和姑太太的背后，又是献茶，又是敬烟。他是荪甫三老爷家里一个老仆的儿子，从小就伶俐，所以荪甫的父亲——吴老太爷特嘱荪甫安插他到这戴生昌轮船局。但是荪甫他们三位且不先坐下，眼睛都看着门外。门口马路上也有一个彪形大汉站着，背向着门，不住地左顾右盼；这是姑老爷杜竹斋随身带的保镖。

杜姑太太轻声松一口气，先坐了，拿一块印花小丝巾，在嘴唇上抹了几下，回头对荪甫说：

“三弟，去年我和竹斋回乡去扫墓，也坐这云飞船。是一条快船。单趟直放，不过半天多，就到了；就是颠得厉害。骨头痛。这次爸爸一定很辛苦的。他那半肢疯，半个身子简直不能动。竹斋，去年我们看见爸爸坐久了就说头晕——”

姑太太说到这里一顿，轻轻吁了一口气，眼圈儿也像有点红了。她正想接下去说，猛的一声汽笛从外面飞来。接着一个人跑进来喊道：

“云飞靠了码头了！”

姑太太也立刻站了起来，手扶着杜竹斋的肩膀。那时福生已经飞步抢出去，一面走，一面扭转脖子，朝后面说：

“三老爷，姑老爷，姑太太；不忙，等我先去招呼好了，再出来！”

轮船局里其他的办事人也开始忙乱；一片声唤脚夫。就有一架预先准备好的大藤椅由两个精壮的脚夫抬了出去。荪甫眼睛望着外边，嘴里说：

“二姊，回头你和老太爷同坐一八八九号，让四妹和我同车，竹斋带阿萱。”

姑太太点头，眼睛也望着外边，嘴唇翕翕地动：在那里念佛！竹斋含着雪茄，微微地笑着，看了荪甫一眼，似乎说“我们走罢”。恰好福生也进来了，十分为难似的皱着眉头：

“真不巧。有一只苏州班的拖船停在里挡——”

“不要紧。我们到码头上去看罢！”

荪甫截断了福生的话，就走出去了。保镖的老关赶快也跟上去。后面是杜竹斋和他的夫人，还有福生。本来站在门口的杜竹斋的保镖就作了最后的“殿军”。

云飞轮船果然泊在一条大拖船——所谓“公司船”的外边。那只大藤椅已经放在云飞船头，两个精壮的脚夫站在旁边。码头上冷静静地，没有什么闲杂人：轮船局里的两三个职员正在那里高声吆喝，轰走那些围近来的黄包车夫和小贩。荪甫他们三位走上了那“公司船”的甲板时，吴老太爷已经由云飞的茶房扶出来坐上藤椅子了。福生赶快跳过去，做手势，命令那两个脚夫抬起吴老太爷，慢慢地走到“公司船”上。于是儿子，女儿，女婿，都上前相见。虽然路上辛苦，老太爷的脸色并不难看，两圈红晕停在他的额角。可是他不作声，看看儿子，女儿，女婿，只点了一下头，便把眼睛闭上了。

这时候，和老太爷同来的四小姐蕙芳和七少爷阿萱也挤上那“公司船”。

“爸爸在路上好么？”

杜姑太太——吴二小姐，拉住了四小姐，轻声问。

“没有什么。只是老说头眩。”

“赶快上汽车罢！福生，你去招呼一八八九号的新车子先开来。”

荪甫不耐烦似的说。让两位小姐围在老太爷旁边，荪甫和竹斋，阿萱就先走到码头上。

一八八九号的车子开到了，藤椅子也上了岸，吴老太爷也被扶进汽车里坐定了，二小姐——杜姑太太跟着便坐在老太爷旁边。本来还是闭着眼睛的吴老太爷被二小姐身上的香气一刺激，便睁开眼来看一下，颤着声音慢慢地说：

“芙芳，是你么？要蕙芳来！蕙芳！还有阿萱！”

荪甫在后面的车子里听得了，略皱一下眉头，但也不说什么。老太爷的脾气古怪而且执拗，荪甫和竹斋都知道。于是四小姐蕙芳和七少爷阿萱都进了老太爷的车子。二小姐芙芳舍不得离开父亲，便也挤在里两位小姐把老太爷夹在中间。马达声音响了，一八八九号汽车开路，已经动了，忽然吴老太爷又锐声叫了起来：

“《太上感应篇》！”

这是裂帛似的一声怪叫。在这一声叫喊中，吴老太爷的残余生命力似乎又复旺炽了；他的老眼闪闪地放光，额角上的淡红色转为深朱，虽然他的嘴唇簌簌地抖着。

一八八九号的汽车夫立刻把车煞住，惊惶地回过脸来。荪甫和竹斋的车子也跟着停止。

大家都怔住了。四小姐却明白老太爷要的是什么。她看见福生站在近旁，就唤他道：“福生，赶快到云飞的大餐间里拿那部《太上感应篇》来！

是黄绫子的书套！”

吴老太爷自从骑马跌伤了腿，终至成为半肢疯以来，就虔奉《太上感应篇》，二十余年如一日；除了每年印赠而外，又曾恭楷手抄一部，是他坐卧不离的。

一会儿，福生捧着黄绫子书套的《感应篇》来了。吴老太爷接过来恭恭敬敬摆在膝头，就闭了眼睛，干瘪的嘴唇上浮出一丝放心了的微笑。

Ba Jin

FAMILY

FAMILY

Since it first appeared in 1931, *Family* has undergone many modifications. As Ba Jin explains in the preface to the 1978 edition of this novel: 'I was an author in semi-feudal, semi-colonial China,' before going on to praise the then Chairman of the Central Committee of the Chinese Communist Party, Hua Guofeng.

Family is an autobiographical novel by Li Feigan, whose pen name was Ba Jin (1904-2005). The novel tells the story of conflict between tradition and modernism, and between generations, in a well-to-do bourgeois family. It is situated in the city of Chengdu, a prosperous but provincial city in Sichuan Province, in the early nineteen-twenties at the time of the *New Culture Movement*. The novel was a great success among China's youth and established Ba Jin as a leading proponent of reform.

Family recounts the story of three brothers Juexin, Juemin and Juehui, and their struggles with the ways of their fiercely traditionalist family, the Gaos. The idealistic, if reckless Juehui, the youngest of the brothers, is the main protagonist, and he is frequently portrayed in opposition to his weaker elder brother Juexin, who gives in to the demands of his grandfather, living a life he does not want.

The novel was serialized in 1931-32, then released in a single volume in 1933. Its original title *Turbulent Stream* was changed after a Ba Jin released it as a single volume.

There have been several modifications since the first version was published. This extract is drawn from an earlier version and is different from that currently published.

Extract 1 from Chapter 1

风刮得很紧，雪片像扯破了的棉絮一样在空中飞舞，没有目的地四处飘落。左右两边墙脚各有一条白色的路，好像给中间满是水泥的石板路镶了两道宽边。街上有行人和两人抬的轿子。他们斗不过风雪，显出了畏缩的样子。雪片愈落愈多，白茫茫地布满在天空中，向四处落下，落在伞上，落在轿顶上，落在轿夫的笠上，落在行人的脸上。

Translation 1.

The wind was blowing hard; snowflakes, floating like cotton from a ripped quilt, drifted down aimlessly. Layers of white were building up at the foot of the walls on both sides of the streets, providing broad borders for their dark muddy centres.

Pedestrians and sedan chair porters struggled against the wind and snow, but to no avail. They looked weary, and the snowfall was becoming heavier. Snow filled the sky, falling everywhere; on umbrellas, on the sedan chairs, on the reed capes of the chair carriers, on the faces of the pedestrians.

Translation 2.

The wind blew hard, snowflakes fluttered in the sky, drifting aimlessly down like pieces of cotton wool. A layer of snow had formed under the walls that lined both sides of the street, framing the edges flagstone surface and its mud filled middle.

Passers-by and sedan chairs porters struggled vainly against the wind and snow. They looked tired and weary as the snow fell more and more. The sky was a vast expanse of white. Everything was covered in snow, umbrellas, sedan chairs, the porters hats, the faces of the passers-by.

Synthesis

风	刮	得	很	紧，	雪片	像	扯破	了
Fēng	guā	de	hěn	jǐn	xuěpiàn	xiàng	chěpò	le
Wind	blow	part.	very	hard	snow flake	resemble	tear apart	part.

的	棉絮	一样	在	空中	飞舞，	没有
de	miánxù	yīyàng	zài	kōngzhōng	fēiwǔ	méiyǒu
part.	cotton-wool	same; like	at	in the sky	to flutter	without

目的地	四处	飘落。	左右	两边	墙	脚
mùdìdì	sì chù	piāoluò	Zuǒyòu	liǎngbian	qiáng	jiǎo
destination	all around	float down	Left and right	either side	wall	foot

各	有	一	条	白色	的	路，	好像	给
gè	yǒu	yī	tiáo	báisè	de	lù	hǎoxiàng	gěi
each	to have	a, one	strip	white	part.	road	as if	give

中间	满	是	水泥	的	石板	路镶	了
zhōngjiān	mǎn	shì	shuǐní	de	shíbǎn	lùxiāng	le
middle	full	is	muddy	part.	flagstone	edge	part.

两	道	宽	边。	街上	有	行人	和	两
liǎng	dào	kuān	biān	Jiēshang	yǒu	xíngrén	hé	liǎng
both	street	broad	side	On the street	to have	pedestrian	and	two

人	抬	的	轿子。	他们	斗不过	风
rén	tái	de	jiàozi	Tāmen	dòu	fēng
man	carry	part.	a sedan chair	They	struggle against	wind

雪，	显出	了	畏缩	的	样子。	雪片	愈落愈多，
xuě	xiǎnchū	le	wèisuō	de	yàngzi	Xuěpiàn	yùluòyùduō
snow	show	part.	flinch	part.	air	Snow	more and more

白茫茫地	布满	在	天空中，	向	四处
báimángmáng	bùmǎn	zài	tiānkōngzhòng	xiàng	sìchù
vast white expanse	strewn	at	sky	direction	everywhere

落下，	落	在	伞	上，	落	在	轿	顶上
luòxià	luò	zài	sǎn	shàng	luò	zài	jiào	dǐngshàng
fall	fall	at (on)	umbrella	on	fall	at (on)	sedan	on top of

落	在	轿夫	的	笠	上，	落	行人
luò	zài	jiàofū	de	lì	shàng	luò	xíngrén
fall	at (on)	a porter	part.	bamboo hat	on	fall	pedestrian

的	脸	上。
de	liǎn	shàng
part.	face	on

Notes

白茫茫 báimángmáng (of mist, snow, floodwater etc) a vast expanse of whiteness

Extract 2 from Chapter 1

风玩弄着伞，把它吹得向四面偏倒，有一两次甚至吹得它离开了行人的手。风在空中怒吼，声音凄厉，跟雪地上的脚步声混合在一起，成了一种古怪的音乐，这音乐刺痛行人的耳朵，好像在警告他们：风雪会长久地管治着世界，明媚的春天不会回来了。已经到了傍晚，路旁的灯火还没有燃起来。街上的一切逐渐消失在灰暗的暮色里。路上尽是水和泥。空气寒冷。一个希望鼓舞着在僻静的街上走得很吃力的行人——那就是温暖、明亮的家。

Translation 1.

The wind buffeted the umbrellas in all directions; it blew one or two out of their owners hands. Howling mournfully, the wind joined with the sound of footsteps to form a strange, irritating music. This snowstorm will rule the world, a long, long time, it seemed to warn the people on the streets, the bright warm sun of spring will never return again....

It was nearly evening, the street lamps had not yet been lit. Everything was gradually disappearing into a pall of grey. Water and mud filled the streets. The air was icy cold. Only one thought sustained the walker struggling through these dismal surroundings; they would soon be back in the warmth and brightness of their homes.

Translation 2.

The wind tore at the umbrellas, blowing them in every direction, even blowing them out of the hands of one or two people. It howled angrily, the snow underfoot squelched, like the sound of strange music, the kind of music that hurt one's ears, as if to say the wind and snow was there to stay; the bright days of spring gone forever.

Already night was falling, the street lamps were not yet

been lit. In the twilight the murky streets, full of water and mud, slowly emptied. The air was bitterly cold. The only encouraging thought for those struggling along the lonely streets was the thought of the warmth that awaited them at home.

<u>Synthesis</u>

风	玩弄	着	伞，	把	它	吹	得	向	四面
Fēng	wánnòng	zhe	sǎn	bǎ	tā	chuī	de	xiàng	sìmiàn
Wind	play with	part.	umbrella	hold	it	blow	part.	direction	all sides

偏	倒，	有	一两次	甚至	吹	得	它
piān	dào	yǒu	yī liǎng cì	shènzhì	chuī	de	tā
lean	upside down	have	once or twice	even	to blow	part.	it

离开	了	行人	的	手。	风	在	空中	怒吼，
líkāi	le	xíngrén	de	shǒu	Fēng	zài	kōngzhōng	nù hǒu
from	part.	pedestrians	part.	hand	Wind	at	in the sky	howled

声音	凄厉，	跟	雪	地上	的	脚步	声
shēngyīn	qīlì	gēn	xuě	dìshang	de	jiǎobù	shēng
sound	mournfull	with	snow	on ground	part.	footstep	sound

混合	在一起，	成了	一种	古怪	的	音乐，
hùnhé	zàiyīqǐ	chéngle	yīzhǒng	gǔguài	de	yīnyuè
mix	together	become	a kind of	strange	part.	music

这	音乐	刺痛	行人	的	耳朵，	好像
zhè	yīnyuè	cìtòng	xíngrén	de	ěrduo	hǎoxiàng
this	music	hurt	pedestrians	part.	ear	as if

在	警告	他们:	风	雪	会长久	地	管治
zài	jǐnggào	tāmen	fēng	xuě	huìzhǎngjiǔ	de	guǎnzhì
at	to warn	them	wind	snow	long time	part.	rule

着	世界，	明媚	的	春天	不会	回来	了。
zhe	shìjiè	míngmèi	de	chūntiān	bùhuì	huílai	le
part.	world	bright	part.	spring	would never	return	part.

已经	到了	傍晚，	路旁	的	灯火	还
Yǐjīng	dàole	bàngwǎn	lùpáng	le	dēnghuǒ	hái
Already	arrive	evening	roadside	part.	lamps	still

没有	燃	起来。	街	上	的	一切
méiyǒu	rán	qǐlái	Jiē	shàng	de	yīqiè
not	lit	action complem.	Street	on	part.	everything

逐渐	消失	在	灰暗	的	暮色	里。
zhújiàn	xiāoshī	zài	huīàn	de	mùsè	lǐ
gradually	disappear	at	gray and dark	part.	twilight	inside

路上	尽是	水	和	泥。	空气	寒冷。
Lùshang	jìnshì	shuǐ	hé	ní	Kōngqì	hánlěng
On the road	full of	water	and	mud	Air	cold

一	个	希望	鼓舞	着	在	僻静	的
Yī	gè	xīwàng	gǔwǔ	zhe	zài	pìjìng	de
One	class.	hope	encourage	part.	at	lonely	part.

街上	走	得	很	吃力	的	行人	那
jiēshang	zǒu	de	hěn	chīlì	de	xíngrén	nà
on the street	walk	part.	very	strenuous	part.	pedestrians	that

就是	温暖、	明亮	的	家。
jiùshì	wēnnuǎn	míngliàng	de	jiā
very	warm	brightness	part.	home

<u>Extract 2 from Chapter 1</u>

“三弟，走快点，”说话的是一个十八岁的青年，一手拿伞，一手提着棉袍的下幅，还掉过头看后面，圆圆的脸冻得通红，鼻子上架着一副金丝眼镜。在后面走的弟弟是一个有同样身材、穿同样服装的青年。他的年纪稍微轻一点，脸也瘦些，但是一双眼睛非常明亮。

<u>Translation 1.</u>

'Walk faster, Juehui, or we'll be late for dinner,' said a youth of eighteen. He carried an umbrella in one hand and held the skirt of his padded gown with the other. His round face was red with cold as he turned to speak to his brother; a pair of gold spectacles rested on the bridge of his nose. Juehui, the boy walking behind him, although the same size and wearing the same kind of clothes, was a bit younger. His face was thinner, his eyes were very bright.

<u>Translation 2.</u>

'Juehui, hurry up,' said Juemin, an eighteen year old youth. He was holding an umbrella in one hand and the skirt of his long gown in the other. He turned his head as he spoke to his brother, his round face was red with the cold, a pair of gold rimmed glasses were perched on his nose. Walking behind him was his younger brother, Juemin, who was dressed in the same way and was about the same build. His face was somewhat thinner, but his eyes much brighter.

<u>Synthesis</u>

三弟，	走	快点，	说话	的	是	一	个	十八
Sāndì	zǒu	kuàidiǎn	shuōhuà	de	shì	yī	gè	shíbā
3rd brother	walk	faster	speaking	part.	was	a	class.	eighteen

岁	的	青年，	一	手	拿	伞，	一	手
suì	de	qīngnián	yī	shǒu	ná	sǎn	yī	shǒu
class.years	part.	youth	one	hand	held	umbrella	one	hand

提着	棉袍	的	下幅,	还	掉过	头	看
tizhe	miánpáo	de	xiàfú	hái	diàoguò	tóu	kàn
holding	padded robe	part.	hem	as	turned	head	look

后面,	圆圆	的	脸	冻得	通红,	鼻子
hòumian	yuányuán	de	liǎn	dòngde	tōnghóng	bízi
behind	round	part.	face	frozen	very red	nose

上	架着	一	副	金丝	眼镜。	在	后面	走
shàng	jiàzhe	yī	fù	jīn sī	yǎnjìng	Zài	hòumiàn	zǒu
on	sat	a	class. pairs	gold wire	spectacles	At	behind	walked

的	弟弟	是	一	个	有	同样	身材、
de	dìdi	shì	yī	gè	yǒu	tóngyàng	shēncái
part.	younger brother	was	a	class.	have	same	stature

穿	同样	服装	的	青年。	他	的	年纪
chuān	tóngyàng	fúzhuāng	de	qīngnián	Tā	de	niánjì
wore	same	clothing	part.	youth	His	part.	age

稍微	轻	一点,	脸	也	瘦	些,	但是
shāowēi	qīng	yīdiǎn	liǎn	yě	shòu	xiē	dànshì
a little	younger	a bit	face	also	thin	little	however

一	双	眼睛	非常	明亮。
yī	shuāng	yǎnjīng	fēicháng	míngliàng
a	pair	eyes	extremely	bright

Notes

棉 mián – generic term for cotton or kapok / cotton / padded or quilted with cotton

袍 páo – Chinese gown (lined)

Extract 3 from Chapter 1

“不要紧，就快到了。……二哥，今天练习的成绩算你最好，英文说得自然，流利。你扮李医生，很不错，”他用热烈的语调说，马上加快了脚步，水泥又溅到他的裤脚上面。“这没有什么，不过我的胆子大一点，”哥哥高觉民带笑地说，便停了脚步，让弟弟高觉慧走到他旁边。

Translation 1.

No, it’s alright, we’re nearly there.... Brother you were best in today’s rehearsal, your English comes naturally, fluently. You play the part of the doctor just right, you’ve got the lines and everything quite well now,’ Juehui said with enthusiasm, quickening his pace at the same time. Mud was sent splashing, more clots were collected on the legs of his trousers.

‘There is nothing to it, it’s only that I am bolder,’ the older brother Juehui said with pride and satisfaction while halting to wait for his brother to come abreast.

Translation 2.

‘Don’t worry, we’re nearly there,’ said Juehui. ‘You know you were very good at today’s rehearsal, your English is very natural, fluent. You played the Doctor Livesey very well,’ he added enthusiastically, suddenly accelerating his pace, the mud splashing the leg of his trousers.

‘No, anyway I wasn’t that nervous,’ said Juemin laughing, stopping to let Juehui catch up with him.

Family

Synthesis

不要紧,	就	快	到	了。	二哥,	今天
Bùyàojǐn	jiù	kuài	dào	le	Ergē	jīntiān
never mind	soon	almost	arrive	part.	2nd brother	today

练习	的	成绩	算	你	最好,	英文	说
liànxí	de	chéngjì	suàn	nǐ	zuìhǎo	yīngwén	shuō
practice	part.	achievement	regarding	you	best	English	speech

得	自然,	流利。	你	扮	李医生,	很
de	zìrán	liúlì	Nǐ	bàn	Lǐ yīshēng	hěn
part.	natural	fluent	You	role	Doctor Livesy	very

不错,	他	用	热烈	的	语调	说,	马上
bùcuò	tā	yòng	rèliè	de	yǔdiào	shuō	mǎshàng
good	he	to use	enthusiastic	part.	tone	speech	at once

加快	了	脚步,	水泥	又	溅	到	他的
jiākuài	le	jiǎobù	shuǐní	yòu	jiàn	dào	tāde
accelerate	part.	step	mud	again	to splash	to	his

裤脚	上面。	这	没有什么,	不过	我的	胆子
kùjiǎo	shàngmian	Zhè	méiyǒushénme	bùguò	wǒde	dǎnzi
trouser leg	on	This	is nothing	only	my	courage

大一点,	哥哥	高觉民	带	笑	地	说,
dàyīdiǎn	gēge	Gāo Juémín	dài	xiào	de	shuō
a little bigger	older brother	name	wear	smile	part.	said

便停	了	脚步,	让	弟弟	高觉慧	走
biàntíng	le	jiǎobù	ràng	dìdi	Gāo Juéhuì	zǒu
pause	part.	step	permit	younger brother	name	walk

到	他	旁边。
dào	tā	pángbiān
to	his	side

Notes

李医生 Doctor David Livesey (Treasure Island)

Extract 4 from Chapter 1

"你的胆子太小了，你扮'黑狗'简直不像。你昨天不是把那几句话背得很熟吗？怎么上台去就背不出来了。要不是朱先生提醒你，恐怕你还背不完嘞！"哥哥温和地说着，没有一点责备的口气。

Translation 1.

'You are too timid, your Black Dog is not right at all. Didn't you learn your lines so well yesterday? Why can't you deliver them at the rehearsal? If it were not for Teacher Chu's prompting, you couldn't have finished the scene!' Thus the elder brother spoke with great tenderness, without a hint of reproach.

Translation 2.

'You're too frightened, your Black Dog is not convincing. Didn't you learn your lines yesterday? How can you go on the stage and forget your lines? If it wasn't for your teacher prompting you, I'm sorry to say you wouldn't have finished your lines,' said his brother softly, without any tone of reproach in his voice.

Synthesis

你的	胆子	太	小	了,	你	扮	‘黑狗’	简直
Nǐde	dǎnzi	tài	xiǎo	le	nǐ	bàn	Hēi Gǒu	jiǎnzhí
Your	courage	too	small	part.	you	role	Black Dog	simply

不	像。	你	昨天	不	是	把	那	几	句	话
bu	xiàng	Nǐ	zuótiān	bu	shì	bǎ	nà	jǐ	jù	huà
neg.	seem	You	yesterday	neg.	is	part.	these	few	sentence	words

背	得	很	熟	吗?	怎么	上台	去	就	背
bèi	de	hěn	shú	ma?	Zěnme	shàngtái	qù	jiù	bèi
recite	part.	very	familiar	part.	How	on stage	go	then	recite

不	出来	了。	要不是	朱先生	提醒	你,
bu	chūlái	le	Yàobushì	Zhū xiānsheng	tíxǐng	nǐ
neg.	come out	part.	But for	Mr Zhu	prompt	you

恐怕	你	还	背	不	完	嘞!	哥哥
kǒngpà	nǐ	hái	bèi	bu	wán	part.	Gēge
fear	you	yet	recite	neg.	finish	了	old bros.

温和	地	说	着,	没有	一点	责备	的
wēnhé	de	shuō	de	méiyǒu	yīdiǎn	zébèi	de
gentle	part.	said	part.	have not	a little	reproach	part.

口气。
kǒuqì
tone

Extract 5 from Chapter 1

觉慧脸红了。他着急地说：“不晓得什么缘故，我一上讲台心就慌了。好像有好多人的眼光在看我，我恨不得把所有的话一字不遗漏地说出来……”一阵风把他手里的伞吹得旋转起来，他连忙闭上嘴，用力捏紧伞柄。这一阵风马上就过去了。路中间已经堆积了落下来未融化的雪，望过去，白皑皑的，上面留着重重叠叠的新旧脚迹，常常是一步踏在一步上面，新的掩盖了旧的。

Translation 1.

Juehui was embarrassed, and the blood rushed to his face as he spoke with perplexity as well as for self-retrieval. 'I don't know why, once I was on the stage I got frightened; I felt like I was in front of a great many people with all their eyes on me. I tried to do my very best, I wanted to render my lines without a single slip....' A gust of wind turned his umbrella awhirl, cutting short his speech while he geld on to the handle without much avail. But the gust was over sooner than it came. The road was covered with unmelted snow, a patch of white all the way, spattered with footsteps one on top of the other, the newly made covering up the old.

Translation 2.

Juehui blushed, then said uneasily: 'I don't know why, when I go on the stage I just panic. It seems like everybody is watching me. I hate being unable to speak without missing my lines....' A sudden gust of wind almost blew the umbrella out of his hand, prompting him to tighten his grip on the handle; then it was gone as soon as it had come. The middle of the road already was already covered with layers of fresh white snow, and with footprints, the new on top of the old.

Family

Synthesis

觉慧	脸红	了。	他	着急	地	说:
Juéhuì	liǎnhóng	le	Tā	zháojí	tā	shuō
Juehui	blush	part.	He	to worry	he	said

不	晓得	什么	缘故,	我	一上	讲台	心
Bù	xiǎode	shénme	yuángù	wǒ	yīshàng	jiǎngtái	xīn
neg.	to know	what	reason	I	on	stage	mind

就	慌	了。	好像	有	好多	人	的	眼光
jiù	huāng	le	Hǎoxiàng	yǒu	hǎoduō	rén	de	yǎnguāng
at once	panicky	part.	Seem	to have	many	people	part.	look

在	看	我,	我	恨不得	把	所有	的
zài	kàn	wǒ	wǒ	hènbudé	bǎ	suǒyǒu	de
at	see	I	I	wish	part.	all	part.

话	一字	不	遗漏	地	说出来...	一阵风
huà	yīzì	bù	yílòu	de	shuō chū lái	yī zhèn fēng
speak	in a row	neg.	to overlook	part.	speak out	a gust

把	他	手	里	的	伞	吹	得	旋转
bǎ	tā	shǒu	lǐ	de	sǎn	chuī	de	xuánzhuǎn
take/handle	he	hand	in	part	umbrella	to blow	part.	to rotate

起来,	他	连忙	闭上	嘴,	用力,	捏紧
qǐlai	tā	liánmáng	bìshang	zuǐ	yònglì	niējǐn
	he	promptly	to close	mouth	exert	clench

伞柄。	这	一阵风	马上	就	过去了。	路
sǎnbǐng	Zhè	yī zhèn fēng	mǎshàng	jiù	guòqule	Lù
handle	This	a gust	suddenly	then	âssed	Road

中间	已经	堆积	了	落下	来未	融化
zhōngjiān	yǐjīng	duījī	le	luòxià	láiwèi	rónghuà
middle	already	to pile up	part.	to fall	not yet	to melt

的	雪,	望过去,	白皑皑的,	上面	留着
de	xuě	wàngguò qu	báiáiáide	shàngmian	liúzhe
part.	snow,	looked	snowwhite	on top of	leaving

重重叠叠	的	新旧	脚迹,	常常	是
chóngchóngdiédié	de	xīnjiù	jiǎojì	chángcháng	shì
layer after layer	part.	old and new	footprints	usually	to be

一步踏	在一步	上面,	新的	掩盖	了	旧的。
yī bù tà	zài yī bù	shàngmian	xīnde	yǎngài	le	jiù
footprint	step	on top of	new	hide	part.	old

Extract 6 from Chapter 1

“我恨不得把全篇的话一字不遗漏地背了出来，”觉慧用刚才中断了的话接着说下去；“可是一开口，什么话都忘掉了，连平日记得最熟的几句，这时候也记不起来。一定要等朱先生提一两个字，我才可以说下去。不晓得将来正式上演的时候是不是还是这样。要是那时候也是跟现在一样地说不出，那才丢脸嘞！”

Translation 1.

‘I wanted to deliver the whole thing without a single slip,’ Juehui went on with his interrupted words, ‘but once I opened my lips everything was wrong was gone, even the best learned lines were lost by that time. Only after teacher Chu prompted a word or two did they come back so that I could go on. If it’s like this at the rehearsals now, I wonder what it would be like at the opening. If it’s going to be the same, what a disgrace it will be!’

Translation 2.

'I wanted to speak my lines without making a single mistake,' Juehui continued, 'but once I opened my mouth, I forgot everything, I practised my lines everyday, but this time they didn't come back. Mr Chu had to prompt me with a couple of words so I could continue. I don't know what it would be like if I can't speak a word when the real show comes, I'd really be ashamed.

Synthesis

我	恨不得	把	全篇	的	话	一	字	不
Wǒ	hènbude	bǎ	quánpiān	de	huà	yī	zì	bù
I	wish	manage	complete	part.	speak	a, one	word	neg.

遗漏	地	背了	出来,	觉慧	用	刚才
yílòu	de	bēile	chūlái	Juéhuì	yòng	gāng cái
overlook	ârt.	learned	come out	name	always	just

中断	了	的	话接	着	说	下去;	可是
zhōngduàn	le	de	huàjiē	zhe	shuō	xiàqù	kěshì
cut short	part.	part.	pickup	part.	speak	continue	but

一	开口,	什么	话	都	忘掉	了,	连	平日
yī	kāikǒu	shénme	huà	dōu	wàngdiào	le	lián	píngrì
once	open,	any	words	all	forget	part.	even	usually

记	得	最熟	的	几句,	这	时候	也	记
jì	de	zuìshóu	de	jǐjù	zhè	shíhòu	yě	jì
remember	part.	familiar	part.	sentences	this	time	also	remember

不	起来。	一定	要	等	朱先生	提	一两
bù	qǐlai	Yīdìng	yāo	děng	zhū xiānsheng	tí	yī liǎng
neg.	succeed	Surely	want	wait	Mr Zhu	for	a couple

个	字，	我	才	可以	说	下去。	不	晓得
gè	zì	wǒ	cái	kě yǐ	shuō	xiàqù	Bù	xiǎode
class.	words	I	only	could	speak	continue	neg.	to know

将来	正式	上演	的	时候	是不是	还是
jiānglái	zhèngshì	shàngyǎn	de	shíhòu	shì bù shì	hái shi
future	official	performance	part.	time	to question	still

这样。	要是	那	时候	也	是	跟	现在
zhèyàng	Yàoshi	nà	shíhòu	yě	shì	gēn	xiànzài
like this	If	that	time	and	is	with	now

一样	地	说	不	出，	那	才	丢	脸嘞!
yīyàng	de	shuō	bù	chū	nǎ	cái	diū	liǎnlei
same	part.	speak	neg.	out	then	then	lose	face

Extract 7 from Chapter 1

孩子似的天真的脸上现出了严肃的表情。脚步踏在雪地上，软软的，发出轻松的叫声。“三弟，你不要怕，”觉民安慰道，“再练习两三次，你就会记得很熟的。你只管放胆地去做。……老实说，朱先生把《宝岛》改编成剧本，就编得不好，演出来恐怕不会有什么好成绩。”

Translation 1.

On his childlike and naive face there were expressions of gravity and gloom, and in his words a tone of self-reproach. His footsteps were making rhythmic squeaky sounds on the soft snow surface, each step a sound, marking his pace.

'Juehui, don't be scared,' Juemin said to comfort him. 'Two or three rehearsals more and you will be alright, just brace up your courage.... To tell the truth, Teacher Chu's rendering of Treasure Island into a play is not really successful, the staging probably won't be much of a success anyway.'

<u>*Translation 2.*</u>

His young, naïve, face wore a solemn expression. Their footsteps on the fresh snow produced a soft noise.

'Juehui, you needn't be afraid, after a few rehearsals you'll gradually become familiar with it and be able to remember everything, be positive. Anyway, Mr Chu's adaptation of Treasure Island is not so great, the play probably won't be that much of a success.'

<u>Synthesis</u>

孩子	似	的	天真	的	脸	上	现出了
Háizi	shì	de	tiānzhēn	de	liǎn	shǎng	xiàn chū le
Child	like	part.	naive	part.	face	on	appeared

严肃	的	表情。	脚步	踏	在	雪	地上,
yánsù	de	biǎoqíng	Jiǎobù	tà	zài	xuě	dìshang
solemn	part.	expression	Footsteps	step on	on	snow	ground

软软的,	发出	轻松	的	叫声。	三弟,	你
ruǎn ruǎn de	fā chū	qīngsōng	de	jiàoshēng	Sāndì	nǐ
soft	produce	light	part.	sound	3rd brother	you

不	要	怕,	觉民	安慰	道,	再	练习	两
bù	yào	pà	Juémin	ānwèi	dào	zài	liànxí	liǎng
neg.	need	fear	name	comfort	said.	at	exercise	two

三	次,	你	就	会	记	得	很	熟	的。
sān	cì	nǐ	jiù	hui	jì	de	hěn	shóu	de
three	times	you	then	can	remember	part.	very	familiar	part.

你	只管	放	胆	地	去做。	老实	说,
Nǐ	zhǐguǎn	fàng	dǎn	de	qù zuò	Lǎoshi	shuō
You	by all means	put	courage	part.	do it	Honestly	said

朱先生	把	《宝岛》,	改编	成	剧本,
zhū xiānsheng	bǎ	bǎo dǎo	gǎibiān	chéng	jùběn
Teacher Zhu	adv	Treasure Island	adapt	into	play

就	编	得	不	好,	演出	来	恐怕	不
jiù	biān	de	bù	hǎo	yǎnchū	lái	kǒngpà	bù
then	adapt	part.	neg.	good	performance	come	afraid	

会	有	什么	好	成绩。
huì	yǒu	shénme	hǎo	chéngjì
can	have	any	good	success

Extract 8 from Chapter 1

觉慧不作声了。他感激哥哥的友爱。他在想要怎样才能够把那一幕戏演得好，博得来宾和同学们的称赞，讨得哥哥的欢喜。他这样想着，过了好些时候，他觉得自己渐渐地进入了一个奇异的境界。忽然他眼前的一切全改变了。在前面就是那个称为“彭保大将”的旅馆，他的老朋友毕尔就住在那里。他，有着江湖气质的“黑狗”，在失去了两根手指、经历了许多变故以后，

Translation 1.

Juehui did not say anything, and was grateful for his brother's loving care or him. His mind turned intensely on how he could do that scene to its perfection, to win the applause of his school mates, and the appreciation of his brother. As he so thought, over quite a long while, he began to feel that he was in a dream land; all of a sudden everything in front of his eyes underwent a transformation. There was the inn where his old pal Bill lived. He, the Black Dog, a figure of the seaman's world, after losing his two fingers and undergoing a number of other incidents,

Translation 2.

Juehui said nothing, he was grateful for his brother's kindness and warm-heartedness. He thought of how he could improve his ability and win the praise of his classmates and guests, and kindle the appreciation of his older brother. He drifted into a kind of trance. Suddenly, before his eyes everything changed; in front of him stood the Admiral Benbow Inn where his old friend Bill lived. He, in the role of Black Dog, who had lost two fingers, who had gone through so many adventures...

Synthesis

觉慧	不作	声了。	他	感激	的	友爱。
Juéhuì	bù zuò	shēngle	Tā	gǎnjī	de	yǒuài
name	not make	sound	he	grateful	part.	affection

他	在	想要	怎样	才能	够	把	那	一
Tā	zài	xiǎngyào	zěnyàng	cáinéng	gòu	bǎ	nà	yī
he	at	want to	how	talent	enough	particle	this	a

幕戏	演得	好，	博得	来宾	和	同学们
mùxì	yǎnzhe	hào	bódé	láibīn	hé	tóngxuémen
scene	act	well	to win	guests	and	classmates

的	称赞，	讨得	哥哥	的	欢喜。	他	这样
de	chēngzàn	tǎode	gēge	de	huānxǐ	Tā	zhèyàng
part.	praise	to elicit	older brother	part.	happiness	He	this way

想着，	过了	好些	时候，	他	觉得	自己
xiǎngzhe	guòle	hǎoxiē	shíhou	tā	juéde	zìjǐ
thought	after	some	time	he	felt	(him) oneself

渐渐地	进入了	一	个	奇异	的	境界。
jiànjiànde	jìnrùle	yī	gè	qíyì	de	jìngjiè
gradually	entering into	a	class.	strange	part.	trance

忽然	他	眼前	的	一切	全	改变了。
Hūrán	tā	yǎnqián	de	yīqiè	quán	gǎibiànle
Suddenly	he	before (his) eyes	part.	everything	all	changed

在	前面	就是	那个	称为	《彭保大将》
Zài	qiánmiàn	jiùshì	nàge	chēngwéi	Péngbǎo Dàjiàng
At	before	there was	the	called	Admiral Benbow

的	旅馆，	他	的	老朋友	毕尔	就	住在
de	lǚguǎn	tā	de	lǎopéngyou	Bìěr	jiù	zhùzài
part.	inn	his	part.	old friend	Bill (translit.)	then	lived

那里。	他，	有着	江湖气质	的	"黑狗"，	在
nàli	Tā	yǒuzhe	jiānghúqìzhì	de	Hēi Gǒu	zài
there	It	was	character	part.	Black Dog	at

失去了	两	根	手指、	经历了	许多
shīqù	liǎng	gēn	shǒuzhǐ	jīnglì	xǔduō
lost	two	classifier	fingers	experienced	many

变故	以后，
biàngù	yǐhòu
adventures	after

Notes

彭保大将"的旅馆　The Admiral Benbow Inn from Treasure Island

The Admiral Benbow Inn from Treasure Island (p.246)
“彭保大将”的旅馆

Extract 9 from Chapter 1

终于找到了毕尔的踪迹，他心里交织着复仇的欢喜和莫名的恐怖。他盘算着，怎样去见毕尔，对他说些什么话，又如何责备他弃信背盟隐匿宝藏，失了江湖上的信义。这样想着，平时记熟了的剧本中的英语便自然地涌到脑子里来了。他醒悟似地欢叫起来：“二哥，我懂得了！”觉民惊讶地看他一眼，问道：“什么事情？你这样高兴！”

Translation 1.

...finally was able to locate the whereabouts of Bill. The joy of revenge and the threatening imminence of the showdown criss-crossed his heart. He began to figure how he was going to approach Bill, how to upbraid him, condemning him for breaking his vow and hiding the treasure chart, selling out the good name of the fraternity of the high seas. All these visions passed, the English lines he had learned so well popped up one by one from his head, without the lightest effort. He shouted with joy as if suddenly, 'Brother, I have got it!' Surprised, Juemin looked at him. 'What's the matter? You look so happy.'

Translation 2.

...had finally been able to track-down Bill. His heart was twisted with vengeance, joy and indescribable fear. He planned how he would confront Bill, accuse him of abusing his trust, hiding the treasure, and breaking the pirate's code of honour. His script flooded back and he snapped out of his daydream with a joyous cry: 'I've got it!' Surprised, Juemin looked at him. 'What's the matter? You look so pleased with yourself all of a sudden.'

Synthesis

终于	找到了	毕尔	的	踪迹,	他	心里
zhōngyú	zhǎodào	Bièr	de	zōngjì	tā	xīnli
finally	found	Bill (translit.)	part.	trail	his	heart

交织着	复仇	的	欢喜	和	莫名	的
jiāozhīle	fùchóu	de	huānxǐ	hé	mòmíng	de
twisted	vengeance	part.	happiness	and	indescribable	part.

恐怖。	他	盘算着,	怎样	去见	毕尔,	对
kǒngbù	tā	pánsuànzhe	zěnyàng	qùjiàn	Bièr	duì
fear	He	planned	how	go to see	Bill (translit.)	to

他	说	些	什么	话,	又	如何	责备	他
tā	shuō	xiē	shénme	huà	yòu	rúhé	zébèi	tā
him	say	a few	things	words	also	how	blame	him

弃	信	背盟	隐匿	宝藏,	失了	江湖上
qì	xìn	bèiméng	yǐnnì	bǎozàng	shīle	jiānghúshàng
abandon	trust	break promise	hide	treasure	lose	high seas

的	信义。	这样	想着,	平时	记熟了	的
de	xìnyì	Zhèyàng	xiǎngzhe	píngshí	jìshúle	de
part.	trust	these	ideas	usually	memorized	part.

剧本	中的	英语	便	自然地	涌到	脑子
jùběn	zhòngde	yīngyǔ	biàn	zìrán	yǒngdào	nǎozi
script	precisely	English	then	automatically	flooded back	mind

里	来了。	他	醒悟	似地	欢	叫起来:
lǐ	láile	Tā	xǐngwù	sìde	huān	jiàoqǐlai
in	back	He	woke up	seemingly	joyous	shout out

二哥,	我	懂得了!	觉民	惊讶地	看	他
Ergē	wǒ	Dǒngdele	Juémín	jīngyàde	kàn	tā
2nd brother	I	understand	name	amazed	looked	him

一眼,	问道;	什么事	情?	你	这样	高兴!
yīyǎn	wèndào	shénmeshì	qíng	nǐ	zhèyàng	gāoxìng
a glance	asked	what	feeling	you	so	happy

Extract 10 from Chapter 1

“二哥，我现在才晓得演戏的奥妙了，”觉慧带着幼稚的得意的笑容说。“我想着，仿佛我自己就是‘黑狗’一样，于是话自然地流露了出来，并不要我费力思索。”

“对的，演戏正是要这样，”觉民微笑地说。“你既然明白了这一层，你一定会成功的。……现在雪很小了，把伞收起来罢。刮着这样的风，打伞很吃力。”他便抖落了伞上的雪，收了伞。

Translation 1.

'Brother I have found the secret of of play acting,' Juehui said with smiles of boyish pride. 'If I could bring myself to feel as if I myself were Black Dog, the lines would come out spontaneously, without any effort of searching or recollecting.'

'That's right, that is the way to perform,' Juemin smiled. 'Now that you have mastered this, you will surely succeed.... It looks like the snow is over, let's shut our umbrellas. The gust make open umbrellas hard to hold on to.' So saying he jerked his umbrella to get rid of the snow collected on it, and shut it.

Translation 2.

'Juemin, I've just found the secret of acting,' said Juehui with a childish smile of pride on his face. 'I was thinking, if I really was Black Dog, the words would come out naturally, without any effort.'

'Right, that's acting. Like that you'll surely be a success, said Juemin, '...it's snowing less now, we can close our umbrellas. The wind is making it hard to hold onto them.' He then shook the snow off his umbrella and closed it.

Synthesis

二哥，	我	现在	才	晓得	演戏的	奥妙了，
Ergē	wǒ	xiànzài	cái	xiǎode	yǎnxìde	àomiàole
2nd brother	I	now	just	know	acting	subtle

觉慧	带着	幼稚	的	得意	的	笑容	说。
Juéhuì	dàizhe	yòuzhì	de	déyì	de	xiàoróng	shuō
name	wearing	childish	part.	pride	part.	smile	said

我	想着，	仿佛	我	自己	就是	‘黑狗’
Wǒ	xiǎngzhe	fǎngfú	wǒ	zìjǐ	jiùshì	Hēigǒu
I	thinking	if	I	myself	(emphatic)	Black Dog

一样，	于是	话	自然地	流露了	出来，
yīyàng	yúshì	huà	zìrán	liúlùle	chūlái
like	thus	words	naturally	express	come out

并不	要	我	费力	思索。	对	的，	演戏
bìngbù	yāo	wǒ	fèilì	sīsuǒ	Duì	de	yǎnxì
not at all	require	me	great effort	think	Right	part.	acting

正是	要	这样，	觉民	微笑地	说。	你
zhèngshì	yāo	zhèyàng	Juémín	wēixiàode	shuō	Nǐ
(emphatic)	want	like this	name	smiling	said	You

既然	明白了	这	一	层，	一定	会	成功
jìrán	míngbaile	zhè	yī	céng	yīdìng	huì	chénggōng
as	clearly	this	a	class.	surely	be able to	succeed

的。	现在	雪	很	小	了，	把	伞
de	xiànzài	xuě	hěn	xiǎo	me	bǎ	sǎn
part.	Now	snow	very	little	part.	take	umbrella

收起来	罢。	刮着	这样	的	风，	打	伞
shōuqǐlai	ba	Guāzhe	zhèyàng	de	fēng	dǎ	sǎn
fold up	fin.part	Blowing	like this	part.	wind	hit	umbrella

很	吃力。	他	便	抖落了	伞	上	的
hěn	chīlì	Tā	biàn	dǒuluòle	sǎn	shàng	de
very	strenuous	He	then	shook out	umbrella	on	part.

雪，	收了	伞。
xuě	shōule	sǎn
snow	closed	umbrella

Extract 11 from Chapter 1

觉慧也把伞收起了。两个人并排走着，伞架在肩上身子靠得很近。　　雪已经住了，风也渐渐地减轻了它的威势。墙头和屋顶上都积了很厚的雪，在灰暗的暮色里闪闪地发亮。几家灯烛辉煌的店铺夹杂在黑漆大门的公馆中间，点缀了这条寂寞的街道，在这寒冷的冬日的傍晚，多少散布了一点温暖与光明。"三弟，你觉得冷吗？"觉民忽然关心地问。"不，我很暖和，在路上谈着话，一点也不觉得冷。"

Translation 1.

Juehui did the same thing, and they walked side by side, with their umbrellas on their shoulders, very close to each other.

The snow was indeed over, and the ferocious wind was gradually abating. Over the walls and house tops much snow was collected. Reflecting gleams of brightness in the darkening dusk. Shop fronts brightly lit, interspersed between residential houses with huge gates of black lacquer, decorated the quiet street, giving it a spattering of warmth and light in this cold winter evening.

'Juehui are you cold?' Juemin asked suddenly with fond care.

'No, I feel quite warm; as we walk along while talking. I don't feel cold at all.'

Translation 2.

Juehui closed his to. They continued side by side with their umbrellas on their shoulders. The snow had already stopped and the wind was gradually easing. The wall tops and roofs were covered with thick snow. It was twilight; in the shops that stood between the houses and their large black doors, candles flickered brightly decorating the lonely street on the cold winter's evening, diffusing a glow of light and warmth.

'Juehui, are you cold?' Juemin gently asked.

'No, I'm very warm, walking along and talking, not the least bit cold.'

Synthesis

觉慧	也	把	伞	收起了。	两	个	人	并排
Juéhuì	yě	bà	sǎn	shōuqǐle	Liǎng	gè	rén	bìngpái
name	also	part.	umbrella	put away	Both	class.	person	side by side

走着，	伞	架	在	肩	上，	身子	靠	得
zǒuzhe	sǎn	jià	zài	jiān	shàng	shēnzi	kàokào	de
walked	umbrella	support	at (on)	shoulder	on	body	lean	part.

很	近。	雪	已经	住了，	风	也	渐渐	地
hěn	jìn	Xuě	yǐjīng	zhùle	fēng	yě	jiànjiàn	de
very	close	Snow	Already	stopped	wind	also	gradually	part.

减轻了	它	的	威势。	墙头	和	屋顶	上
jiǎnqīngle	tā	de	wēishì	Qiángtóu	hé	wūdǐng	shàng
lessening	it	part	force	Wall tops	and	roofs	on

都	积	了	很	厚	的	雪，	在	灰暗	的
dōu	jī	le	hěn	hòu	de	xuě	zài	huīàn	de
all	amass	part.	very	thick	part.	snow	at (on)	gray and dark	part.

暮色	里	闪闪	地	发亮。	几	家	灯	烛
mùsè	lǐ	shǎnshǎn	de	fāliàng	Jǐ	jiā	dēng	zhú
twilight	inside	flickering	part.	to shine	Many	homes	light	candle

辉煌	的	店铺	夹杂在	黑	漆	大门	的
huīhuáng	de	diànpù	jiāzá zài	hēi	qī	dàmén	de
brilliant	part.	shops	mixed with	black	paint	doors	part.

公馆	中间,	点缀	了	这	条	寂寞	的
gōngguǎn	zhōngjiān	diǎnzhuì	le	zhè	tiáo	jìmò	de
residences	in between	to decorate	part.	this	class;	lonely	part.

街道,	在	这	寒冷	的	冬	日	的	傍晚,
jiēdào	zài	zhè	hánlěng	de	dōng	rì	de	bàngwǎn
street	at (on)	this	cold	part.	winter	day	part.	evening

多少	散布	了	一点	温暖	与	光明。
duō shǎo	sànbù	le	yīdiǎn	wēnnuǎn	yǔ	guāngmíng
somewhat	diffusing	part.	a little	warmth	and	light

三弟,	你	觉得	冷	吗?	觉民	忽然	关心地
Sāndì	nǐ	juéde	lěng	ma	Juémin	hūrán	guānxīnde
3rd brother	you	feel	cold	interrog.	name	suddenly	caringly

问。	不,	我	很	暖和,	在	路	上	谈着话,
wèn	Bù	wǒ	hěn	nuǎnhuo	zài	lù	shang	tánzhehuà
asked	No	I	very	warm	at (on)	road	on	talking

一点也不	觉得	冷。
yīdiǎn yěbù	juéde	lěng
not in the least	feel	cold

Extract 12 from Chapter 1

"那么，你为什么发抖？"

"因为我很激动。我激动的时候都是这样，我总是发抖，我的心跳得厉害。我想到演戏的事情，我就紧张。老实说，我很希望成功。二哥，你不笑我幼稚吗？”觉慧说着，掉过头去望了觉民一眼。

“三弟，”觉民同情地对觉慧说。“不，一点也不。我也是这样。我也很希望成功。我们都是一样。所以在课堂上先生的称赞，即使是一句简单的话，不论哪一个听到也会高兴。”

<u>Translation 1.</u>

‘Then why are you trembling?’

‘It’s because I am excited. I am like this whenever I’m excited, always trembling with my heart beating very fast. As I have been thinking of our play, I have the urge to do it right away. To tell you the truth I very much want success, I am after the admiration and praise of everybody. Brother, won’t you be laughing at me for being too vain, too childish?’ So said Juehui as he turned his head to cast a glance at his brother, showing embarrassment, as if anticipating with dismay his brother’s disapproving ridicule.

‘Juehui,’ said Juemin tenderly and full of sympathy, ‘no, not at all. I am just like that. I also want success, want the applause of everybody, just like you. We are all the same. Didn’t you notice, in class, any approval from the teacher, no matter how simple it is, is always taken with great pleasure by the one it is intended for.’

<u>Translation 2.</u>

‘Then why are you trembling?’

‘Because I’m so excited. I’m always excited at times like this. When I think of the play I immediately get uptight, my heart beats madly and I tremble. Honestly, I

really want to be a success. Juehui you won't laugh at my childishness?' he asked with a shy glance at his brother.

'No, not in the least. I'm like that too. I also want to succeed. We're all the same. In class when the teacher praises someone, even if its just a few words, they are always happy.'

Synthesis

那么,	你	为什么	发抖?	因为	我	很	激动。
Nàme	nǐ	wèishénme	fādǒu	Yīnwèi	wǒ	hěn	jīdòng
Then	you	why	tremble?	Because	I	very	excited

我	激动	的	时候	都	是	这样	我	总是
Wǒ	jīdòng	de	shíhou	dōu	shì	zhèyàng	wǒ	zǒngshì
I	excited	part.	moment	all	are	this	my	always

发抖,	我	的	心跳	得	厉害。	我	想到
fādǒu	wǒ	de	xīntiào	de	lìhai	Wǒ	xiǎngdào
tremble	my	part.	heartbeat	part.	terrible	I	think of

演戏	的	事情,	我	就	紧张。	老实说,
yǎnxì	de	shìqíng	wǒ	jiù	jǐnzhāng	Lǎoshíshuō
play	part.	matters	I	at once	uptight	Honestly speaking

我	很	希望	成功。	二哥,	你	不	笑	我
wǒ	hěn	xīwàng	chénggōng	Ergē	nǐ	bù	xiào	wǒ
I	very	wish	to succeed	2nd brother	you	won't	laugh	my

幼稚	吗?	觉慧	说着,	掉过	头	去望了
yòuzhì	ma	Juéhuì	shuōzhe	diàoguò	tóu	qùwàngle
childishness	interrog.	name	said	turning	head	towards

觉民	一眼。	三弟,	觉民	同情地	对	觉慧
Juémin	yīyǎn	Sāndì	Juémin	tóngqíngde	duì	Juéhuì
name	a glance	3rd brother	name	longingly	towards	name

说。	不,	一点也不。	我	也	是	这样。	我	也
shuō	Bù	yīdiǎnyěbù	Wǒ	yě	shì	zhèyàng	Wǒ	yě
said	No	not in the least	I	also	am	like this	I	also

我	也	很	希望	成功。	我们	都	是	一样。
wǒ	yě	hěn	xīwàng	chénggōng	Wǒmen	dōu	shì	yīyàng
I	also	very	wish	to succeed	We	all	are	same

所以	在	课堂上	先生	的	称赞,	即使
Suǒyǐ	zài	kètángshàng	xiānsheng	de	chēngzàn	jíshǐ
Therefore	in	classroom	teacher	part.	praise	even if

是	一句	简单	的	话,	不论	哪一个	听到
shì	yījù	jiǎndān	de	huà	bùlùn	nǎyīge	tīngdào
is	a line	simple	part.	words	no matter	anyone	hear

也	会	高兴。
yě	huì	gāoxìng
also	will	happy

Extract 13 from Chapter 1

“对，你说得不错，”弟弟的身子更挨近了哥哥的，两个人一块儿向前走着，忘却了寒冷，忘却了风雪，忘却了夜。

“二哥，你真好，”觉慧望着觉民的脸，露出天真的微笑。觉民也掉过头看觉慧的发光的眼睛，微笑一下，然后慢慢地说：“你也好。”过后，他又向四周一望，知道就要到家了，便说：“三弟，快走，转弯就到家了。”

觉慧点了点头，于是两个人加速了脚步，一转眼就走入了一条更清静的街道。

Translation 1.

'Yes, you have said it,' said Juehui, edging closer to his brother. The two of them walked on side by side, forgetting the cold, forgetting the wind and darkness.

'Brother, you are my beloved, good older brother.' Juehui looked at his brother's face and said this with a childlike smile. Juemin also turned to look at his brother's shining eyes, smiled, and said very slowly, 'You are too...my beloved, good younger brother.' He then glanced around, and was aware of their approaching home. Thus in a happy mood he said to his brother: 'Juehui, hurry up, our home is just around the corner.'

Juehui nodded his consent. The two of them quickened their steps, and in a wink they turned into a still quieter street.

Translation 2.

'Yes, you're right,' said Juehui drawing closer to his brother. They continued their way, side by side, forgetting the cold, the wind and the night.

'Juemin, you really are a great brother,' said Juehui looking at Juemin with a timid smile.

Juemin turned to his brother, grinned, and looking into his bright eyes slowly said: 'You too.' Suddenly, looking around, he saw they were almost home. 'Juehui, hurry up, we're almost there.'

Juehui nodded. They quickened their pace and a moment later they turned into a quieter street.

Family

Synthesis

对,	你	说	得	不错,	弟弟	的	身子
Duì	nǐ	shuō	de	bùcuò	dìdi	de	shēnzi
right	you	said	part.	correct	younger brother	part.	body

更	挨近了	哥哥	的,	两	个	人	一块儿
gèng	āijìn	gēge	de	liǎng	gè	rén	yīkuàier
evenmore	approached	older brother	part.	both	class	person	together

向前	走	着,	忘却	了	寒冷,	忘却	了
xiàngqián	zǒu	zhe	wàngquè	le	hánlěng	wàngquè	le
forward	walk	part.	forget	part.	cold	forget	part.

风	雪	忘却	了	夜。	二哥,	你	真	好,
fēng	xuě	wàngquè	le	yè	Ergē	nǐ	zhēn	hào
wind	snow	forget	part.	night	2nd brother	you	really	good

觉慧	望着	觉民	的	脸,	露出	天真	的
Juéhuì	wàngzhe	Juémin	de	liǎn	lòuchū	tiānzhēn	de
name	looked at	name	part.	face	showing	innocent	part.

微笑。	觉民	也	掉过	头	看	觉慧	的	发光
wēixiào	Juémin	yě	diàoguò	tóu	kàn	Juéhuì	de	fāguāng
smile	name	also	turned	head	to see	name	part.	shine

的	眼睛,	微笑一下,	然后	慢慢地	说:
de	yǎnjing	wēixiào yīxià	ránhòu	mànmàndi	shuō
part.	eye	smile	then	slowly	said

你	也	好。	过后,	他	又	向	四周	一望,
Nǐ	yě	hào	Guòhòu	tā	yòu	xiàng	sìzhōu	yī wàng
you	to	good	Then	he	again	towards	all around	looked

知道	就要	到	家	了,	便	说:	三弟,	快走,
zhīdào	jiùyào	dào	jiā	le	biàn	shuō	Sāndì	kuàizǒu
know	about to	arrive	home	part.	then	said	3rd brother	walk quick

转弯	就	到	家	了。	觉慧	点了点头,
zhuǎnwān	jiù	dào	jiā	le	Juéhuì	diǎnlediǎntóu
around corner	just	to	home	part.	name	nodded

于是	两	个	人	加速了	脚步，	一转眼
yúshì	liǎng	gè	rén	jiāsùle	jiǎobù	yīzhuǎnyǎn
thereupon	both	class	person	accelerated	pace	in a wink

就	走入了	一	条	更	清静	的	街道。
jiù	zǒurùle	yī	tiáo	gèng	qīngjìng	de	jiēdào
at once	went into	a	class.	even	quiet	part.	street

Extract 14 from Chapter 1

街灯已经燃起来了，方形的玻璃罩里，清油灯的光在寒风中显得更孤寂，灯柱的影子淡淡地躺在雪地上。街中寥寥的几个行人匆忙地走着：留了一些脚印在雪上，就默默地消失了。深深的脚迹疲倦地睡在那里，也不想动一动，直到新的脚来压在它们的身上，它们才发出一阵低微的叹声，被压碎成了奇怪的形状，于是在这一白无际的长街上，不再有清清楚楚的脚印了，在那里只有大的和小的黑洞。

Translation 1.

Here the oil lamps had been lit, and their dull gleam, casting pale shadows of the lamp posts on the snow, looked particularly lonely in the frigid windy atmosphere. Few persons were abroad, and these walked quickly, leaving their footprints in the snow and silently vanishing. The deep imprints rested exhausted, without even a thought of moving, until new feet pressed down upon them. The uttered low sighs and were transformed into queer shape; on the interminably long, white-mantled street the regular patterns of footprints became only large and small dark shapeless holes.

Translation 2.

The street lamps had already been lit. The glow from the glass covers of the oil lamps cast an insipid light, creating stark shadows on the snow with the cold wind. The few passers-bye abroad hurried past in silence leaving footprints in the snow, which lay there until another foot squashed them out of existence with a soft squelch, transforming them into strange forms; black holes, in the middle of a vast white expanse of the street.

Synthesis

街灯	已经	燃	起来	了,	方形	的	玻璃
Jiēdēng	yǐjīng	rán	qǐlái	le	fāngxíng	de	bōli
Streetlamp	already	light	suff.	part.	square	part.	glass

罩子	里,	清油灯	的	光	在	寒风
zhàozǐ	lǐ	qīngyóudēng	de	guāng	zài	hánfēng
cover	inside	oil lamp	part.	light	at	cold wind

中	显	得	更	孤寂,	灯柱	的	影子
zhōng	xiǎn	de	gèng	gūjì	dēngzhù	de	yǐngzi
in	seem	part.	even	desolate	lamppost	part.	shadow

淡淡	地	躺	在	雪	地	上。	街	显
dēngzhù	de	tǎng	zài	zài	de	shang	Jiē	xiǎn
insipid	part.	incline	at	snow	part.	on	Street	appear

中	寥寥	的	几个	行人	匆忙	地	走	着:
zhōng	liáoliáo	de	jǐge	xíngrén	cōngmáng	de	zǒu	zhe
in	very few	part.	a few	pedestrian	hurried	part.	walk	part.

留	了	一些	脚印	在	雪	上,	就	默默
liú	le	yīxiē	jiǎoyìn	zài	zài	shang	jiù	mòmò
to leave	part.	a few	footprint	at	snow	on	then	in silence

地	消失	了。	深深	的	脚迹	疲倦
de	xiāoshī	le	Shēnshēn	de	jiǎoji	píjuàn
part.	to disappear	part.	Deep	part.	tracks	tired

地	睡	在	那里，	也不	想	动一动，
de	shuì	zài	nàli	yěbù	xiǎng	dòngyīdòng
part.	laying	at	there	not even	think	move

直到	新	的	脚	来	压	在	它们	的
zhídào	xīn	de	jiǎo	lái	yà	zài	tāmen	de
until	new	part.	foot	come	squash	at (on)	them	part.

身	上，	它们	才	发出	一阵	低微	的
shēn	shang	tāmen	cái	fāchū	yīzhèn	dīwēi	de
existence	on	they	just	sent out	a fit	low	part.

叹声，	被	压碎	成了	奇怪	的	形状，	于是
tànshēng	bèi	yāsuì	chéngle	qíguài	de	xíngzhuàng	yúshì
sighs	by	squashing	becoming	strange	part.	shapes	hence

在	这	一	白	无际	的	长	街	上，
zài	zhè	yī	bái	wú jì	de	cháng	jiē	shang
at (on)	this	entire	white	limitless	part.	long	street	on

不再	有	清清楚楚	的	脚印	了，	在那里
bùzài	yǒu	qīngqīng chǔchǔ	de	jiǎoyìn	le	zài nàli
no longer	have	very distinct	part.	footprints	part.	there

只有	大的	和	小的	黑洞。
zhǐyǒu	dàide	hé	xiǎode	hēidòng
only	large	and	small	black holes

Extract 15 from Chapter 1

有着黑漆大门的公馆静寂地并排立在寒风里。两个永远沉默的石狮子蹲在门口。门开着，好像一只怪兽的大口。里面是一个黑洞，这里面有什么东西，谁也望不见。每个公馆都经过了相当长的年代，或是更换了几个姓。每一个公馆都有它自己的秘密。大门上的黑漆脱落了，又涂上新的，虽然经过了这些改变，可是它们的秘密依旧不让外面的人知道。走到了这条街的中段，在一所更大的公馆的门前，弟兄两个站住了。

Translation 1.

A row of residential compounds, with large solid wood gates painted black, stood motionless in the icy gale. Pairs of eternally mute stone lions crouched outside their entrances, one on each side. Opened gates gave the appearance of fantastic beasts. Within were dark caverns; what was inside them, no one could see.

Each of these residences had a long history; some had changed owners several times. Each had its secrets. When the black veneer peeled off the big gates, they were painted again. But no matter what changes took place, the secrets were kept. No outsider was ever permitted to know them.

In the middle of this street, before the gates of an especially large compound, the two brothers halted.

Translation 2.

A row of courtyard houses with their large black doors stood silently in the wind. Pairs of eternally silent lions crouched before their doorways. Once open, the doors were black holes, the gaping mouths of strange beasts, concealing all that was within from outsiders. Each house had undergone many changes over the course of time, when paint peeled off the doors they were repainted, families changed and secrets were hidden from those outside. Walking down the middle of this street the two brothers stopped before the door of a very large house.

A courtyard house in Beijing 公馆 (p.262)

Synthesis

有	着	黑	漆	大门	的	公馆	静寂
Yǒu	zhe	hēi	qī	dàmén	de	gōngguǎn	jìngjì
to have	part.	black	paint	gate	part.	residence	silent

地	并排	立	在	寒风	里。	两	个
de	bìngpái	lì	zài	hánfēng	lǐ	Liǎng	gè
part.	side by side	to stand	at	cold wind	in	Two	class.

Family

永远	沉默	的	石狮子	蹲	在	门口。
yǒngyuǎn	chénmò	de	shíshīzi	dūn	zài	ménkǒu
Forever	silent	part.	stone lions	to crouch	at	doorway

门	开	着，	好像	一	只	怪兽	的	大口。
Mén	kāi	zhe	hǎoxiàng	yī	zhī	guàishòu	de	dàkǒu
Door	open	part.	like	a	class.	strange beast	part.	mouth

里面	是	一	个	黑洞，	这里面	有
Lǐmiàn	shì	yī	gè	hēidòng	zhèlǐmiàn	yǒu
Inside	is	a	class.	dark hole	here inside	to have

什么	东西，	谁	也	望	不	见。
shénme	dōngxi	shéi	yě	wàng	bù	jiàn
what	things	who	also	to look	not	see

每	个	公馆	都	经过	了	相当	长	的
Měi	gè	gōngguǎn	dōu	jīngguò	le	xiāngdāng	cháng	de
Each	class.	residence	all	undergone	part.	considerable	long	part.

年代，	或是	更换	了	几个	姓。	每一
niándài	huòshì	gēnghuàn	le	jǐge	xìng	Měiyī
decades	perhaps	replace	part.	several	family name	Every

个	公馆	都	有	它	自己	的	秘密。
gè	gōngguǎn	dōu	yǒu	tā	zìjǐ	de	mìmì
class.	residence	each	to have	it	oneself	part.	secret

大门	上	的	黑	漆	脱落	了，	又	涂
Dàmén	shàng	de	hēi	qī	tuōluò	le	yòu	tú
Entrance door	on	part.	black	paint	to drop off	part.	again	apply

上	新	的，	虽然	经过	了	这些	改变，
shàng	xīn	de	suīrán	jīngguò	le	zhèxiē	gǎibiàn
on	new	part.	although	undergone	part.	these	changes

可是	它们	的	秘密	依旧	不	让	外面
kěshì	tāmen	de	mìmì	yījiù	bù	ràng	wàimian
however	they	part.	secret	still	not	let	outside

的	人	知道。	走	到	了	这	条	街	的
de	rén	zhīdào	zǒu	dào	le	zhè	tiáo	jiē	de
part.	people	know	Walking	down	part.	this	class.	street	part.

中段，	在	一	所	更	大	的	公馆	的
zhōngduàn	zài	yī	suǒ	gèng	dà	de	gōngguǎn	de
middle	at	a	class.	even	big	part.	residence	part.

门	前，	弟兄	两	个	站住了。
mén	qián	dìxiong	liǎng	gè	zhànzhùle
door	in front	brothers	two	class.	stopped

Extract 16 from Chapter 1

他们把皮鞋在石阶上擦了几下，抖了抖身上的雪水，便提着伞大步走了进去。他们的脚步声很快地消失在黑洞里面。门前又恢复了先前的静寂。这所公馆和别的公馆一样，门口也有一对石狮子，屋檐下也挂着一对大的红纸灯笼，只是门前台阶下多一对长方形大石缸，门墙上挂着一副木对联，红漆底子上现出八个隶书黑字："国恩家庆，人寿年丰。"两扇大门开在里面，门上各站了一位手执大刀的顶天立地的彩色门神。

Translation 1.

They scuffed their leather shoes on the stone flagging, shook the snow from their clothing, and let their robes fall straight. Holding their umbrellas, they strode in, the sound of their footsteps being quickly swallowed up in the dark cavern of the long entrance-way. Silence again descended on the street.

The outside of this compound resembled the others in that a pair of crouching stone lions flanked its entrance and two big red paper lanterns also hung from the eaves of its gate. What made it distinctive was the pair of rectangular stone vats placed before the gate.

On the walls on either side of the entrance, hung vertically, were red veneered plaques inscribed with black ideographs. Reading from top to bottom, first the right board then the left, the wishful motto was set forth: “Benevolent rulers, happy family; long life, good harvests”.

<u>*Translation 2.*</u>

They scraped their shoes on the stone steps, shook off the melting snow, then still carrying their umbrellas walked inside. Their footsteps echoed as they hurriedly disappeared into the dark entrance and the silence returned. Like the other homes a pair of stone lions guarded the doorway, from the eaves hung a pair of paper lanterns. Before the door stood a pair of large rectangular stone pots and hanging on either side of the doorway was a red painted wood panel calligraphied in black characters: “benevolent ruler, happy family”; “long life, good harvest”. In addition a pair of colourful door gods, each clasping a broadsword, watched over the house.

<u>Synthesis</u>

他们	把	皮鞋	在	石阶	上	擦	了	几下，
Tāmen	bǎ	píxié	zài	shíjiē	shàng	cā	le	jǐxià
They	part.	leather shoes	at, on	stone step	on	to wipe	part.	several

抖了抖	身上	的	雪水	便	提	着	伞
dǒuledǒu	shēnshang	de	xuěshuǐ	biàn	tí	zhe	sǎn
shaking	on body	part.	wet snow	then	carry	part.	umbrella

大步走	了	进去。	他们	的	脚步	声	很
dàbùzǒu	le	jìnqù	Tāmen	de	jiǎobù	shēng	hěn
stride	part.	to go in	They	part.	footstep	sound	very

快	地	消失	在	黑洞	里面。	门	前
kuài	de	xiāoshī	zài	hēidòng	lǐmiàn	Mén	qián
rapid	part.	disappear	at, on	dark hole	inside	Gate	before, at

又	恢复	了	先前	的	静寂。	这	所
yòu	huīfù	le	xiānqián	de	jìngjì	Zhè	suǒ
again	return	part.	previous	part.	silence	This	class.

公馆	和	别的	公馆	一样,	门口	也	有
gōngguǎn	hé	biéde	gōngguǎn	yīyàng	ménkǒu	yě	yǒu
residence	and	other	residence	same	doorway	also	have

一对	石狮子,	屋檐	下	也	挂	着	一对
yīduì	shíshīzi	wūyán	xià	yě	guà	zhe	yīduì
a pair	stone lions	eaves	down	also	to hang	part.	a pair

大的	红纸	灯笼,	只是	门前	台阶	下多
dàde	hóngzhǐ	dēnglóng	zhǐshì	ménqián	táijiē	xiàduō
big	red paper	lantern	but	before door	steps	under

一对	长方形	大	石	缸,	门	墙	上
yīduì	chángfāngxíng	dà	shí	gāng	mén	qiáng	shàng
a pair	rectanglular	big	stone	jars	gate	wall	on

挂	着	一	副	木	对联,	红漆
guà	zhe	yī	fù	mù	duìlián	hóng qī
to hang	part.	a	class.	wood	scrolls	red lacquer

底子	上	现出	八	个	隶书	黑字:
dǐzi	shàng	xiànchū	bā	gè	lìshū	hēizì
base	on	display	eight, 8	class.	calligraphy	black characters

"国恩家庆,	人寿年丰"。	两	扇	大门
Guó ēn jiā qìng	Rén shòu nián fēng	Liǎng	shàn	dàmén
Benevolent ruler, happy family	Long life, good harvest	Both	class.	door

开 在 里面，门 上 各 站 了 一
kāi zài lǐmiàn mén shàng gè wèi le yī
open to inside door on each part. on

位 手 执 大刀 的 顶天立地 的
wèi shǒu zhí dàdāo de dǐng tiān lì dì de
class. hand grasp broadsword part. a powerful part.

彩色 门神。
cǎisè ménshén
colorful door god

A courtyard house entrance door

Extract 17 from Chapter 1

风止了，空气还是跟先前一样地冷。夜来了，它却没有带来黑暗。上面是灰色的天空，下面是堆着雪的石板地。一个大天井里铺满了雪。中间是一段垫高的方形石板的过道，过道两旁各放了几盆梅花，枝上积了雪。

觉民在前面走，刚刚走上左边厢房的一级石阶，正要跨过门槛进去，一个少女的声音在左上房窗下叫起来：“二少爷，二少爷，你们回来得正好。刚刚在吃饭。请你们快点去，里头还有客人。”

Translation 1.

Although the wind now died down completely, the air was still as cold as before. Night came, but did not bring darkness. The sky remained grey, the ground was paved with snow. In the large snow-covered courtyard, pots of golden plum blossoms were ranged on either side of a raised stone-flagged path. Coated with frosty white, the branches were like lovely jade.

Advancing along this path, Juemin, the elder of the two brothers, had reached the steps of the one-storey wing on the left side of the courtyard, and was about to cross the threshold, when a girl’s voice called:

‘Second Young Master, Third Young Master, you've come back just in time. Dinner has just started. Hurry. We have guests.’

<u>*Translation 2.*</u>

Although the wind had stopped, the air was just as cold as before. Night had fallen, but had not brought darkness. Above the sky was grey and below snow had piled up on the flagstones. The large courtyard was carpeted with snow. In the middle was an elevated pathway, on both sides were several potted plum blossoms with snow accumulated on their branches. Juemin walked in front, just as he was about to go up the steps on the left wing of the house, at the point of entering a doorway, a young girl's voice called out from the window of the main room: 'Second young master, third young master, you have just come back in time. We have started eating, please be quick, there are guests.'

A courtyard looking towards the street door

Synthesis

风	止	了，	空气	还是	跟	先前	一样
Fēng	zhǐ	le	kōngqì	háishì	gēn	xiānqián	yīyàng
Wind	stop	part.	air	still	as	before	same

地	冷。	夜	来	了，	它	却	没有	带来
de	lěng	Yè	lái	le	tā	què	méiyǒu	dàilái
part.	cold	Night	come	part.	it	however	has not	brought

黑暗。	上面	是	灰色	的	天空，	下面
hēiàn	Shàngmian	shì	huīsè	de	tiānkōng	xiàmian
dark	above	is	grey	part.	sky	beneath

是	堆	着	雪	的	石板地。	一	个	大
shì	duī	zhe	xuě	de	shíbǎndì	Yī	gè	dà
is	pile up	part.	snow	part.	flagstone area	a	class.	big

天井	里	铺满	了	雪。	中间	是	一
tiānjǐng	lǐ	pūmǎn	le	xuě	Zhōngjiān	shì	yī
courtyard	inside	carpeted	part.	snow	In the middle	was	a

段	垫高	的	方	形	石板	的
duàn	diàngāo	de	fāng	xíng	shíbǎn	de
class.	elevated	part.	square	shaped	flagstone	part.

过道，	过道	两旁	各	放	了	几	盆
guòdào	guòdào	liǎngpáng	gè	fàng	le	jǐ	pén
passageway	passageway	both sides	each	place	part.	several	pots

梅花，	枝	上	积了	雪。	觉慧
méihuā	zhī	shàng	jīle	xuě	Juémín
plum blossom	branch	on	accumulated	snow	name

在	前面	走，	刚刚	走	上	左边
zài	qiánmiàn	zǒu	gānggang	zǒu	shàng	zuǒbian
at	in front	walk	just	walk	on	left

厢房	的	一	级	石阶，	正要	跨过
xiāngfáng	de	yī	jí	shíjiē	zhèngyào	kuàguò
house wing	part.	a	stair	stone step	on the point of	stepping

门槛	进去,	一	个	少女	的	声音	在
mén kǎn	jìnqu	yī	gè	shàonǚ	de	shēngyīn	zài
doorway	to go in	a	class.	young girl	part.	voice	at

左	上房	窗	下	叫	起来:	二少爷,
zuǒ	shàng fáng	chuāng	xià	jiào	qǐlai	Ershàoye
left	main room	window	down	call	coming	second young master

你们	回来	得	正好。	刚刚	在	吃饭
nǐmen	huílai	de	zhènghǎo	Gānggang	zài	chīfàn
you	to return	part.	just (in time)	Right now	at	eating

请	你们	快点	去,	里头	还有	客人。
qǐng	nǐmen	kuàidiǎn	qù	lǐtou	háiyǒu	kèrén
please	you	quick	go	inside	in addition	visitors

Extract 18 from Chapter 1

说话的婢女鸣凤，是一个十六岁的少女，脑后垂着一根发辫，一件蓝布棉袄裹着她的苗条的身子。瓜子形的脸庞也还丰润，在她带笑说话的时候，脸颊上现出两个酒窝。她闪动着两只明亮的眼睛天真地看他们。觉慧在后面对她笑了一笑。

“好，我们放了伞就来，”觉民高声答道，并不看她一眼就大步跨进门槛去了。

“鸣凤，什么客？”觉慧也踏上了石阶站在门槛上问。

“姑太太和琴小姐。快点去罢，”她说了便转身向上房走去。

<u>Translation 1.</u>

The speaker was the bondsmaid Mingfeng, a girl of sixteen. She wore her hair in along single braid down her back. Her trim young frame was encased in a padded jacket of blue cloth. When she smiled, dimples appeared in the firm healthy flesh of her oval face. She regarded the brothers innocently with bright sparkling eyes, quite free of any timidity or hesitation.

Standing behind Juemin, Juehui smiled at her. 'Right. We'll get rid of these umbrellas and be there directly,' Juemin retorted. Without giving her another glance, he entered the door. 'Mingfeng, who are the guests?' Juehui called from the steps.

'Mrs Chang and Miss Chin. Hurry up.' Mingfeng turned and went into the main building.

<u>Translation 2.</u>

It was Mingfeng, the bonds-maid servant, a sixteen year old girl, she wore a single plait hanging from the back of her head, and a blue cotton coat wrapped around her slender body. She had a soft oval face, she smiled as she spoke with dimples appearing on her cheeks and her innocent eyes sparkled as she looked at them. Juemin smiled back. 'Good, we'll put our umbrellas away, then come,' he replied in a loud voice. Without further a glance at her he strode in.

'Mingfeng, what guests?' asked Juehui as he stopped in the doorway.

'Mrs Gu and Miss Qin. Hurry up,' she said as she turned and walked out.

A courtyard view towards the living room door

Synthesis

说话	的	婢女	鸣凤,	是	一	个	十六
Shuōhuà	de	binǚ	Míngfèng	shì	yī	gè	shíliù
Speak	part.	servant	name	was	a	class.	sixteen

岁	的	少女,	脑后	垂	着	一	根
suì	de	shàonǚ	nǎohòu	chuí	zhe	yī	gēn
age class.	part.	girl	back of head	hang	part.	a	class.

发辫,	一	件	蓝	布棉	袄	裹	着
fàbiàn	yī	jiàn	lán	miánǎo	ǎo	guǒ	zhuó
plait	a	class.	blue	cotton	coat	wrap	to wear

她的	苗条	的	身子。	瓜子	形	的
tāde	miáotiáo	de	shēnzi	Guāzǐ	xíng	de
her	slender	part.	body	melon seed	Shape	class.

脸庞	也	还	丰润,	在	她	带笑	说话
liǎnpáng	yě	hái	fēngrùn	zài	tā	dàixiào	shuōhuà
face	and	also	soft	as	she	smile	spoke

的	时候,	脸颊	上	现出	两	个	酒窝。
de	shíhou	liǎnjiá	shàng	xiànchū	liǎng	gè	jiǔwō
part.	moment	cheek	on	appear	two	class.	dimple

她	闪动	着	两	只	明亮	的	眼睛
Tā	shǎndòng	zhe	liǎng	zhī	míngliàng	de	yǎnjing
She	sparkling	part.	two	class.	brightness	part.	eye

天真	地	看	他们。	觉慧	在	后面	对
tiānzhēn	de -ly	kàn	tāmen	Juéhuì	zài	hòumiàn	duì
innocent	part.	look	them	name	at	behind	to

她	笑了一笑。	好,	我们	放	了	伞	就	来,
tā	xiàoleyīxiào	Hào	wǒmen	fàng	le	sǎn	jiù	lái
she	smiled	Good	we	put	part.	umbrella	then	come

觉民	高声	答道,	并不	看	她	一眼	就
juémin	gāoshēng	dādào	bìngbù	kàn	tā	yīyǎn	jiù
name	loudly	replied,	without	look	her	a glance	then

大步	跨	进	门槛	去了。	鸣凤,	什么
dàbù	kuà	jìn	ménkǎn	qùle	Míngfèng	shénme
large strides	stepped	enter	doorway	went	name	what

客?	觉慧	也	踏上	了	石阶	站	在	门槛
kè	Juéhuì	yě	tàshàng	le	shíjiē	zhàn	zài	mén kǎn
guest	name	also	stepping	part.	stone step	stand	at	doorway

上	问。	姑太太	和	琴小姐。	快点	去
shàng	wèn	Gū tàitai	hé	Qín xiǎojie	Kuàidiǎn	qù
in	to ask	Mrs Gu	and	Miss Qin	quickly	go

罢,	她	说	了	便	转身	向上	房	走去。
ba	tā	shuō	le	biàn	zhuǎnshēn	xiàngshàng	fáng	zǒuqù
part.	she	said	part.	then	turned	towards	room	walked out

Extract 19 from Chapter 1

觉慧望着她的背影笑了一笑，他看见她的背影在上房门里消失了，才走进自己的房间。觉民正从房里走出来，便说："你在跟鸣凤说些什么？快点去吃饭，再晏点恐怕饭都吃完了。"觉民说毕就往外面走。"好，我就这样跟你去罢，好在我的衣服还没有打湿，不必换它了，"觉慧回答道，他就把伞丢在地板上，马上走了出来。

"你总是这样不爱收拾，屡次说你，你总不听。真是江山易改，本性难移！"

Translation 1.

Juehui smiled after her retreating figure until the door closed behind her. Then he entered his own room, bumping into his brother, who was coming out.

'What were you and Mingfeng talking about that kept you so long?' Juemin demanded. 'Get a move on! The food will all be gone if you delay much longer.'

'I'll go with you now. I don't have to change my clothes. They're not very wet.' Juehui tossed his umbrella on the floor.

'Sloppy! Why can't you do things right? The old saying is certainly true; It's easier to move a mountain than change a man's character!'

Translation 2.

Juehui looked at her as she disappeared. He smiled and went into the room.

'What were you saying to Mingfeng? asked Juemin. Come on, hurry up now, there won't be any food left.'

'Alright then, I'm coming, luckily my clothes are not wet, I don't have to change them,' Juehui said as he threw his umbrella on the floor and walked out.

'I keep telling you, you're always so untidy, it's true what they say, old habits habits die hard!'

Synthesis

觉慧	望	着	她	的	背影	笑了一笑,
Juéhuì	wàng	zhe	tā	de	bèiyǐng	xiàoleyīxiào
name	looked	part.	she	part.	rear view	smiled

他	看见	她	的	背影	在上	房门	消失
tā	kànjiàn	tā	de	bèiyǐng	zài shàng	fángmén	xiāoshī
he	to see	she	part	rear view	in	door	disappear

了,	才	走进	自己	的	房间。	觉民	正
le	cái	zǒujìn	zìjǐ	de	fángjiān	Juémin	zhèng
part.	then	to enter	oneself	part.	room	name	just

从	房	走出来,	便	说:	你	在	跟	鸣凤
cóng	fáng	zǒuchūlái	biàn (就)	shuō	Nǐ	zài	gēn	míngfèng
from	room	coming out	then	said	You	at	with	name

说些	什么?	快点	去	吃饭,	再	晏	点
shuōxiē	shénme	Kuàidiǎn	qù	chīfàn	zài	yàn	diǎn
said	what?	quickly	to go	eat a meal	more	late	a bit

恐怕	饭	都	吃	完了。	觉民	说毕	就
kǒngpà	fàn	dōu	chī	wánle	Juémin	shuō	jiù
fear	food	all	food	finished.	name	said	then

往	外面	走。	好,	我	就	这	样	跟	你
wǎng	wàimiàn	zǒu	Hǎo	wǒ	jiù	zhè	yàng	gēn	nǐ
to	outside	to walk	Good,	I	then	this	kind	with	you

去	罢,	好在	我的	衣服	还	没有	打湿,
qù	ba	hǎozài	wǒde	yīfu	hái	méiyǒu	dǎshī
to go;	part. (吧)	luckily	my	clothes	also	not	wet

不必	换	它	了,	觉慧	回答	道,	他	就
bùbì	huàn	tā	le	Juéhuì	huídá	dào	tā	jiù
need not	to change	it	part.	name	answer	said,	he	then

把	伞	丢	在	地板	上,	马上	走了
bǎ	sǎn	diū	zài	dìbǎn	shàng	mǎshàng	zǒule
took	umbrella	throw	action	floor	on	suddenly	walked

出来。	你	总是	这样	不爱收拾,	屡次	说
chūlái	Nǐ	zǒngshì	zhèyàng	bùàishōushi	lǚcì	shuō
out	you	always	this kind	disorderly	repeatedly	tell

你,	你总不听。	真	是	江山易改, 本性难移!
nǐ	nǐ zǒng bù tīng	Zhēn	shì	jiāngshānyìgǎi, běnxìngnányí
you	you never listen	really	are	old habits die hard!!

Notes

江山易改, 本性难移! Chinese idiom – It's easier to move a mountain than change a man's character!'

Extract 20 from Chapter 1

他又回转身走进房去拾起了伞，把它张开，小心地放在地板上。

“这又有什么办法呢？”觉慧在门口看着他做这一切，带笑地说，“我的性情永远是这样。可笑你催我快，结果反而是你耽搁时间。”

“你总是嘴硬，我说不过你！”觉民笑了笑，就往前走了。觉慧依旧带笑地跟着他的哥哥走。他的脑海里现出来一个少女的影子，但是马上又消失了，因为他走进了上房，在他的眼前又换了新的景象。

<u>Translation 1.</u>

Though he spoke critically, Juemin still wore a pleasant expression. He picked up the dripping umbrella, opened it an carefully placed it on the floor again.

‘What can I do?’ said Juehui, watching with a grin. ‘That’s the way I am. But I thought you were in a hurry. You’re the one who’s holding us up.’

‘You’ve got a sharp tongue. Nobody can out-talk you!’ Juemin walked out as if in a great huff.

Juehui knew his brother as well as Juehui knew him, so he wasn't alarmed. Smiling, he followed behind Juemin, his mind filled with the pretty bondsmaid. But his thoughts of her vanished at the scene which met his eyes as he entered the main building.

<u>Translation 2.</u>

He then went back into the room and picked up the umbrella, opened it and carefully placed it on the floor.

‘So that’s how to do it?’ said Juehui with a grin as he watched from the door. ‘I’m like that. It’s funny you telling me to hurry up and now you’re wasting our time.’

‘You’re always so stubborn, I can’t tell you anything,’ he said with a smile as he followed his brother out. In his mind the image of Mingfeng appeared, then vanished just as quickly as he entered the dining room.

Family

Synthesis

他 又 回转 身 走进 房 去 拾起 伞，
Tā yòu huízhuǎn shēn zǒujìn fáng qù shíqǐ sǎn
he again turn body to enter room to go pick up umbrella

把 它 张开，小心 地 放 在 地板 上。
bǎ tā zhāngkāi xiǎoxīn de fàng zài dìbǎn shàng
take it to open, careful -ly put on floor on

这又 有 什么 办法 呢？ 觉慧 在 门口
Zhèyòu yǒu shénme bànfǎ ne Juéhuì zài ménkǒu
That is what way part. name at doorway

看 着 他 做 这 一切，带 笑 地
kàn zhe tā zuò zhè Yīqiè dài xiào de
watch -ing him to do this all wear smile part.

说，我的 性情 永远 是 这样。 可笑 你
shuō wǒde xìngqíng yǒngyuǎn shì zhèyàng Kěxiào nǐ
speak my temperament always is like this Funny you

催 我 快，结果 反而 是 你 耽搁
cuī wǒ kuài jiéguǒ fǎnér shì nǐ dānge
urge me hurry result instead is you tarry

时间。 你 总是 嘴硬， 我 说不过 你！
shíjiān Nǐ zǒngshì zuǐyìng wǒ shuō bù guò nǐ
time you always stubborn I can't tell you

觉民 笑了笑，就 往前 走了。 觉慧 依旧
Juémín xiàolexiào jiù wǎngqián zǒu Juéhuì yījiù
name smiled then advance walked name still

带 笑 地 跟着 他的 哥哥 走。 他的
dài xiào de gēnzhe tāde gēge zǒu Tā
wear smile part. follow his brother to walk His

脑海 里 现出来 一 个 少女 的 影子，
nǎohǎi lǐ xiànchūlái yī gè shàonǚ de yǐngzi
mind in appeared a, one class. girl part. image

但是	马上	又	消失了,	因为	他	走进了
dànshì	mǎshàng	yòu	xiāoshīle	yīnwèi	tā	zǒujìnle
but	at once	again	disappeared	because	he	entered

上房,	在	他的	眼前	又	换了	新的
shàngfáng	zài	tāde	yǎnqián	yòu	huàn	xīn
room	at	his	before one's eyes	again	changed	anew

景象。
jǐngxiàng
scene

Notes

又有什么办法呢? but what can I (we, one) do?

Extract 21 from Chapter 1

围着一张方桌坐了六个人，上面坐着他的继母周氏和姑母张太太，左边坐着张家的琴表姐和嫂嫂李瑞珏，下面坐着大哥觉新和妹妹淑华，右边的两个位子空着。他和觉民向姑母行了礼，又招呼了琴，便在那两个空位子上坐下。女佣张嫂连忙盛了两碗饭来。

“你们今天怎么回来得这样晏？要不是姑妈来玩，我们早吃过饭了，”周氏端着碗温和地说。

Translation 1.

Seated around a square table were six people. On the side farthest from the door, the seats of honour, sat his stepmother Mrs Zhou and his aunt, his father's sister, Mrs Zhang. On the left sat his cousin Qin, Mrs Zhang's daughter, and Jui-chueh, wife of his eldest brother Juexin. On the near side sat Juexin and their young sister Shuhua. The two seats on the right side were vacant.

Juehui and his brother bowed to Mrs. Zhang and greeted Qin, the slipped into the two empty seats. A maid quickly served them bowls of rice.

'Why are you so late today?' Madam Zhou, holding her rice bowl, asked them kindly. 'If your aunt hadn't come for a visit we would have finished eating long ago.'

Translation 2.

Seated at a square table were six people, at the head was his stepmother Zhoushi and his aunt Mrs Zhang, on the left side was seated cousin Qin, from the Zhang side of the family, and aunt Li Ruijue, next was his brother Juexin and his sister Shuhua, on the right side were two empty chairs. Juemin and his brother bowed to their aunt and greeted Qin, then took the empty seats. The maid Zhang Sao promptly served them with bowls of food.

'Why have you come back so late? If your aunt had not come to visit us we would have already finished eating,' said Mrs Zhou softly as she took her bowl.

Synthesis

围着	一	张	方	桌	坐了	六	个	人,
Wéizhe	yī	zhāng	fāng	zhuō	zuò	liù	gè	rén
Around	a	class.	square	table	seated	six	class.	persons

上面	坐着	他的	继母	周氏	和	姑母
shàngmian	zuòzhe	tāde	jìmǔ	Zhōu shì	hé	gūmǔ
on top of	seated	his	stepmother	name	and	father's sister

张太太，	左边	坐着	张家	的	琴
Zhāng tàitai	zuǒbian	zuòzhe	Zhāng jiā	de	Qín
Mrs Zhang	left side	seated	Zhang family	part.	name

表姐	和	嫂嫂	李瑞珏，	下面	坐着	大哥
biǎojiě	hé	sǎosao	Lǐ Ruìjué	xiàmian	zuò	dàgē
female cousin	and	aunt	name	next	sitting	brother

觉新	和	妹妹	淑华，	右边	的	两	个
Juéxīn	hé	mèimei	Shūhuá	yòubian	de	liǎng	gè
name	and	sister	name	right side	part.	two	class.

位子	空	着。	他	和	觉民	向	姑母
wèizi	kòng	zhe	Tā	hé	Juémín	xiàng	gūmǔ
seat	empty	particle	He	and	name	toward	aunt

行	了	礼，	又	招呼	了	琴，	便
xíng	le	lǐ	yòu	zhāohu	le	Qín	biàn
perform	part.	pay respect	and	greeted	part.	name	then

在	那	两	个	空	位子	上坐下。	女佣
zài	nà	liǎng	gè	kòng	wèizi	shàngzuòxia	Nǚyōng
at	those	two	class.	empty	seat	sit down	Maid

张嫂	连忙	盛	了	两	碗	饭	来。
Zhāng Sǎo	liánmáng	chéng	le	liǎng	wǎn	fàn	lái
name	promptly	ladle	part.	two	bowl	food	arrive

你们	今天	怎么	回来	得	这样	晏?
Nǐmen	jīntiān	zěnme	huílai	de	zhèyàng	yàn
You	today	why	return	part.	so	late

要不是	姑妈	来	玩，	我们	早	吃	过
Yàobushì	gūmā	lái	wán	wǒmen	zǎo	chī	guò
if	aunt	come	social visit	we	early	eat	part.

饭	了，	周氏	端	着	碗	温和	地	说。
fàn	le	Zhōu shì	duān	zhe	wǎn	wēnhé	de	shuō
food	part.	name	end	part.	bowl	gently	part.	said

<u>Notes</u>

姑妈 gūmā – father's married sister
嫂嫂 sǎosao – aunt
大哥 dàgē – eldest brother
妹妹 mèimei – younger sister

Ba Jin

家

I

风刮得很紧，雪片像扯破了的棉絮一样在空中飞舞，没有目的地四处飘落。左右两边墙脚各有一条白色的路，好像给中间满是水泥的石板路镶了两道宽边。街上有行人和两人抬的轿子。他们斗不过风雪，显出了畏缩的样子。雪片愈落愈多，白茫茫地布满在天空中，向四处落下，落在伞上，落在轿顶上，落在轿夫的笠上，落在行人的脸上。

风玩弄着伞，把它吹得向四面偏倒，有一两次甚至吹得它离开了行人的手。风在空中怒吼，声音凄厉，跟雪地上的脚步声混合在一起，成了一种古怪的音乐，这音乐刺痛行人的耳朵，好像在警告他们：风雪会长久地管治着世界，明媚的春天不会回来了。

已经到了傍晚，路旁的灯火还没有燃起来。街上的一切逐渐消失在灰暗的暮色里。路上尽是水和泥。空气寒冷。一个希望鼓舞着在僻静的街上走得很吃力的行人——那就是温暖、明亮的家。

"三弟，走快点，"说话的是一个十八岁的青年，一手拿伞，一手提着棉袍的下幅，还掉过头看后面，圆圆的脸冻得通红，鼻子上架着一副金丝眼镜。

在后面走的弟弟是一个有同样身材、穿同样服装的青年。他的年纪稍微轻一点，脸也瘦些，但是一双眼睛非常明亮。“不要紧，就快到了。……二哥，今天练习的成绩算你最好，英文说得自然，流利。你扮李医生，很不错，”他用热烈的语调说，马上加快了脚步，水泥又溅到他的裤脚上面。“这没有什么，不过我的胆子大一点，”

哥哥高觉民带笑地说，便停了脚步，让弟弟高觉慧走到他旁边。“你的胆子太小了，你扮‘黑狗’简直不像。你昨天不是把那几句话背得很熟吗？怎么上台去就背不出来了。要不是朱先生提醒你，恐怕你还背不完嘞！”哥哥温和地说着，没有一点责备的口气。觉慧脸红了。他着急地说：“不晓得什么缘故，我一上讲台心就慌了。

好像有好多人的眼光在看我，我恨不得把所有的话一字不遗漏地说出来……”一阵风把他手里的伞吹得旋转起来，他连忙闭上嘴，用力捏紧伞柄。这一阵风马上就过去了。路中间已经堆积了落下来未融化的雪，望过去，白皑皑的，上面留着重重叠叠的新旧脚迹，常常是一步踏在一步上面，新的掩盖了旧的。

“我恨不得把全篇的话一字不遗漏地背了出来，”觉慧用刚才中断了的话接着说下去；“可是一开口，什么话都忘掉了，连平日记得最熟的几句，这时候也记不起来。一定要等朱先生提一两个字，我才可以说下去。不晓得将来正式上演的时候是不是还是这样。要是那时候也是跟现在一样地说不出，那才丢脸嘞！”

孩子似的天真的脸上现出了严肃的表情。脚步踏在雪地上，软软的，发出轻松的叫声。

“三弟，你不要怕，”觉民安慰道，“再练习两三次，你就会记得很熟的。你只管放胆地去做。……老实说，朱先生把《宝岛》改编成剧本，就编得不好，演出来恐怕不会有什么好成绩。”

觉慧不作声了。他感激哥哥的友爱。他在想要怎样才能够把那一幕戏演得好，博得来宾和同学们的称赞，讨得哥哥的欢喜。他这样想着，过了好些时候，他觉得自己渐渐地进入了一个奇异的境界。忽然他眼前的一切全改变了。在前面就是那个称为“彭保大将”的旅馆，他的老朋友毕尔就住在那里。他，有着江湖气质的“黑狗”，在失去了两根手指、经历了许多变故以后，终于找到了毕尔的踪迹，他心里交织着复仇的欢喜和莫名的恐怖。他盘算着，怎样去见毕尔，对他说些什么话，又如何责备他弃信背盟隐匿宝藏，失了江湖上的信义。这样想着，平时记熟了的剧本中的英语便自然地涌到脑子里来了。他醒悟似地欢叫起来：“二哥，我懂得了！”

觉民惊讶地看他一眼，问道：“什么事情？你这样高兴！”

“二哥，我现在才晓得演戏的奥妙了，”觉慧带着幼稚的得意的笑容说。“我想着，仿佛我自己就是‘黑狗’一样，于是话自然地流露了出来，并不要我费力思索。”

“对的，演戏正是要这样，”觉民微笑地说。“你既然明白了这一层，你一定会成功的。……现在雪很小了，把伞收起来罢。刮着这样的风，打伞很吃力。”他便抖落了伞上的雪，收了伞。觉慧也把伞收起了。

两个人并排走着，伞架在肩上，身子靠得很近。

雪已经住了，风也渐渐地减轻了它的威势。墙头和屋顶上都积了很厚的雪，在灰暗的暮色里闪闪地发亮。几家灯烛辉煌的店铺夹杂在黑漆大门的公馆中间，点缀了这条寂寞的街道，在这寒冷的冬日的傍晚，多少散布了一点温暖与光明。

“三弟，你觉得冷吗？”觉民忽然关心地问。

“不，我很暖和，在路上谈着话，一点也不觉得冷。”

“那么，你为什么发抖？”

“因为我很激动。我激动的时候都是这样，我总是发抖，我的心跳得厉害。我想到演戏的事情，我就紧张。老实说，我很希望成功。二哥，你不笑我幼稚吗？”

觉慧说着，掉过头去望了觉民一眼。

“三弟，”觉民同情地对觉慧说。“不，一点也不。我也是这样。我也很希望成功。我们都是一样。所以在课堂上先生的称赞，即使是一句简单的话，不论哪一个听到也会高兴。”

“对，你说得不错，”弟弟的身子更挨近了哥哥的，两个人一块儿向前走着，忘却了寒冷，忘却了风雪，忘却了夜。

“二哥，你真好，”觉慧望着觉民的脸，露出天真的微笑。

觉民也掉过头看觉慧的发光的眼睛，微笑一下，然后慢慢地说：“你也好。”过后，他又向四周一望，知道就要到家了，便说：“三弟，快走，转弯就到家了。”

觉慧点了点头，于是两个人加速了脚步，一转眼就走入了一条更清静的街道。

街灯已经燃起来了，方形的玻璃罩子里，清油灯的光在寒风中显得更孤寂，灯柱的影子淡淡地躺在雪地上。街中寥寥的几个行人匆忙地走着：留了一些脚印在雪上，就默默地消失了。深深的脚迹疲倦地睡在那里，也不想动一动，直到新的脚来压在它们的身上，它们才发出一阵低微的叹声，被压碎成了奇怪的形状，于是在这一白无际的长街上，不再有清清楚楚的脚印了，在那里只有大的和小的黑洞。

有着黑漆大门的公馆静寂地并排立在寒风里。两个永远沉默的石狮子蹲在门口。门开着，好像一只怪兽的大口。里面是一个黑洞，这里面有什么东西，谁也望不见。每个公馆都经过了相当长的年代，或是更换了几个姓。每一个公馆都有它自己的秘密。大门上的黑漆脱落了，又涂上新的，虽然经过了这些改变，可是它们的秘密依旧不让外面的人知道。走到了这条街的中段，在一所更大的公馆的门前，弟兄两个站住了。他们把皮鞋在石阶上擦了几下，抖了抖身上的雪水，便提着伞大步走了进去。他们的脚步声很快地消失在黑洞里面。门前又恢复了先前的静寂。这所公馆和别的公馆一样，门口也有一对石狮子，屋檐下也挂着一对大的红纸灯笼，只是门前台阶下多一对长方形大石缸，门墙上挂着一副木对联，红漆底子上现出八个隶书黑字：“国恩家庆，人寿年丰。”两扇大门开在里面，门上各站了一位手执大刀的顶天立地的彩色门神。

II

风止了，空气还是跟先前一样地冷。夜来了，它却没有带来黑暗。上面是灰色的天空，下面是堆着雪的石板地。一个大天井里铺满了雪。中间是一段垫高的方形石板的过道，过道两旁各放了几盆梅花，枝上积了雪。

觉民在前面走，刚刚走上左边厢房的一级石阶，正要跨过门槛进去，一个少女的声音在左上房窗下叫起来：“二少爷，二少爷，你们回来得正好。刚刚在吃饭。请你们快点去，里头还有客人。”说话的婢女鸣凤，是一个十六岁的少女，脑后垂着一根发辫，一件蓝布棉袄裹着她的苗条的身子。瓜子形的脸庞也还丰润，在她带笑说话的时候，脸颊上现出两个酒窝。她闪动着两只明亮的眼睛天真地看他们。觉慧在后面对她笑了一笑。

“好，我们放了伞就来，”觉民高声答道，并不看她一眼就大步跨进门槛去了。

“鸣凤，什么客？”觉慧也踏上了石阶站在门槛上问。“姑太太和琴小姐。快点去罢，”她说了便转身向上房走去。

觉慧望着她的背影笑了一笑，他看见她的背影在上房门里消失了，才走进自己的房间。觉民正从房里走出来，便说：“你在跟鸣凤说些什么？快点去吃饭，再晏点恐怕饭都吃完了。”觉民说毕就往外面走。

“好，我就这样跟你去罢，好在我的衣服还没有打湿，不必换它了，”觉慧回答道，他就把伞丢在地板上，马上走了出来。

“你总是这样不爱收拾，屡次说你，你总不听。真是江山易改，本性难移！”觉民抱怨道，但是他的脸上还带着笑容。他又回转身走进房去拾起了伞，把它张开，小心地放在地板上。

“这又有什么办法呢？”觉慧在门口看着他做这一切，带笑地说，“我的性情永远是这样。可笑你催我快，结果反而是你耽搁时间。”

“你总是嘴硬，我说不过你！”觉民笑了笑，就往前走了。觉慧依旧带笑地跟着他的哥哥走。他的脑海里现出来一个少女的影子，但是马上又消失了，因为他走进了上房，在他的眼前又换了新的景象。

围着一张方桌坐了六个人，上面坐着他的继母周氏和姑母张太太，左边坐着张家的琴表姐和嫂嫂李瑞珏，下面坐着大哥觉新和妹妹淑华，右边的两个位子空着。他和觉民向姑母行了礼，又招呼了琴，便在那两个空位子上坐下。女佣张嫂连忙盛了两碗饭来。

“你们今天怎么回来得这样晏？要不是姑妈来玩，我们早吃过饭了，”周氏端着碗温和地说。

一九一八年四月。

CPSIA information can be obtained at www.ICGtesting.com
Printed in the USA
BVOW07s0030261214

380862BV00001B/39/P